Practical
Fire and Arson
Investigation

ELSEVIER SERIES IN
**PRACTICAL ASPECTS OF CRIMINAL
AND FORENSIC INVESTIGATIONS**

VERNON J. GEBERTH, BBA, MPS, FBINA *Series Editor*

**Practical Homicide Investigation: Tactics, Procedures, and Forensic
Techniques, Second Edition**
Vernon J. Geberth

**The Counter-Terrorism Handbook: Tactics, Procedures,
and Techniques**
Frank Bolz, Jr., Kenneth J. Dudonis, and David P. Schulz

Forensic Pathology
Dominick J. Di Maio and Vincent J. M. Di Maio

Interpretation of Bloodstain Evidence at Crime Scenes
William G. Eckert and Stewart H. James

Tire Imprint Evidence
Peter McDonald

Practical Drug Enforcement: Procedures and Administration
Michael D. Lyman

**Practical Aspects of Rape Investigation: A
Multidisciplinary Approach**
Robert R. Hazelwood and Ann Wolbert Burgess

**The Sexual Exploitation of Children: A Practical Guide to
Assessment, Investigation, and Intervention**
Seth L. Goldstein

**Gunshot Wounds: Practical Aspects of Firearms, Ballistics, and
Forensic Techniques**
Vincent J. M. Di Maio

Friction Ridge Skin: Comparison and Identification of Fingerprints
James F. Cowger

Footwear Impression Evidence
William J. Bodziak

Practical Fire and Arson Investigation
John J. O'Connor

Practical Fire and Arson Investigation

JOHN J. O'CONNOR
Lieutenant
New York City Police Department

Elsevier
New York • Amsterdam • London

Elsevier Science Publishing Co., Inc.
655 Avenue of the Americas, New York, New York 10010

Distributors outside the United States and Canada:
Elsevier Science Publishers B.V.
P.O. Box 211, 1000 AE Amsterdam, The Netherlands

© 1987 by Elsevier Science Publishing Company, Inc.

Library of Congress Cataloging in Publication Data

O'Connor, John J.
    Practical fire and arson investigation.

    (Elsevier series in practical aspects of criminal
and forensic investigations)
    Includes indexes.
    1. Arson investigation—United States. 2. Fire
investigation—United States. 3. Arson—United States.
4. Fires—United States. I. Title. II. Series.
HV8079.A7027 1987   363.2'5   86-16777
ISBN 0-444-00874-8

Cover photograph courtesy of Sean Grennan.

Current printing (last digit)
10 9 8 7 6 5

Manufactured in the United States of America

*This book is dedicated to
those investigators who seek the truth
in ashes.*

To Ruth, Brian, Shawn, and Liam

Contents

Foreword

Fire is an enormously powerful tool that has played an extremely important role in making human civilization possible. Like any powerful tool, however, fire can be—when used with malice—a devastating weapon. Its potential as a weapon was evidenced during the 1970s in this country, when arson was said to be epidemic.

This was a turbulent period for America, as many individuals who were bent on crime adopted fire as their favorite weapon. Urban centers across our land suffered huge losses in housing stock, and scores of neighborhoods were lost forever.

While theoreticians sought to understand the forces behind the problem, federal, state, and local governments mounted aggressive campaigns to strengthen our first line of defense—fire and arson investigation.

The art of determining the cause of a fire and of capturing the person(s) responsible is complicated by the fact that the crime of arson actually encompasses several crimes (murder, assault, criminal mischief, fraud, extortion, coercion, etc.). Thus, we expect the investigator not only to determine whether a crime was committed, but also to discern what crime the offender actually intended (notwithstanding the charge of arson).

The job of the fire/arson investigator is multifaceted and requires a sound working knowledge of such areas as building construction, chemistry (the nature of fuels), physics (behavior of fire), electricity (as a heat source), the law, motives, the human body's reaction to fire, and psychological disorders that are believed to be associated with fire-setting behavior. Also, the investigator must be adept at interviewing, interrogation, surveillance, evidence handling, and courtroom testimony, as well as many other skills required of the criminal investigator.

Because fire/arson investigation encompasses a diverse set of subject matter, a book that logically incorporates such information into one central theme, as this book does, is an invaluable reference tool.

This book does more than accomplish that task; it also offers a practical guide. In view of the fact that practitioners are asked to assimilate a great deal of knowledge in a short period of time, it is unreasonable to expect that they be able to apply this newfound knowledge without some practical guidance. I am confident that this book will fill the void.

ANGELO PISANI
Deputy Director, Parking Violations Bureau
Formerly Coordinator, Arson Strike Force
City of New York

Preface

In the five or six minutes that it takes the average reader to thumb through this text, at least ten intentional fires will be set.

The investigative specialists (public and private) who will be called to these ten fire scenes are operating in a unique field. Their experience, technical knowledge, and ability to collect and evaluate complex information enable them to determine the truth where others perceive only confusion and chaos.

Tens of thousands of fire scenes will be investigated this year. These investigations will not only strain already limited resources but will, unfortunately, lead to relatively few arrests and even fewer criminal convictions. America's insurance industry will grudgingly process millions of dollars in unwarranted insurance settlements.

This year alone, arson will dramatically impact the livelihood and well-being of millions of Americans. More importantly, well over 1,000 people will die and ten times that number will be injured or badly disfigured.

The purpose of *Practical Fire and Arson Investigation* is to provide practical information for the novice fire investigation student, as well as a ready reference for the tenured veteran.

This text is based upon the author's experience both as a fire fighter and as a fire investigator. It represents a systematic (nuts and bolts) approach to the multifaceted and highly technical field of fire investigation.

Many excellent texts have been written on the subjects of fire and arson investigation by highly respected experts in the field. This text was not written to supersede these earlier works but rather to complement them and, it is hoped, provide a distinctive approach to a subject that is still imbued with misinterpretation.

Every fire scene is different and represents a long list of investigative considerations. Every fire investigator has had the experience of standing knee-deep in ash and debris, not knowing what he'll find, but just hoping that he'll recognize "it" when he sees "it." If this text, in any way, aids in that recognition, then my efforts have been worthwhile.

JOHN J. O'CONNOR

Acknowledgments

I would like to thank the following people for their time, suggestions, and support. Without their encouragement and considerable contributions this work would not have been a reality. I want to apologize in advance to anyone I may have inadvertently overlooked.

Richard J. Abbott, Director, Fire Science Institute, John Jay College of Criminal Justice; Thomas Brown, Rockland Country B.C.I.; Inspector Robert Burke, N.Y.P.D.; Joseph Butler, Chief Arson Investigator, Westchester County District Attorney's Office; Detective Donald Calderone, N.Y.P.D.; S.A. Kevin Carroll, Criminal Division, I.R.S.; Supervisory Fire Marshall Bernard Casey, N.Y.F.D.; Lt. Louis DelNevo, N.Y.P.D.; James Domorod, Safety Engineer, University of Delaware; Professor Edward Donovan, Pennsylvania State University; Arthur D. Dresdner, Private Consultant; Detective Harold Dugan, retired, N.Y.P.D.; Sgt. Edward Flanagan, retired, N.Y.P.D.; Fire Marshal Donald Forster, N.Y.F.D.; Detective Kenneth Dudonis, retired, N.Y.P.D. Bomb Squad; Dr. Arthur Goldman, D.M.D., President, American Academy of Forensic Science; Lt. Vernon Geberth, Commanding Officer, Bronx Detective Task Force; Detective Sean Grennan, retired, N.Y.P.D.; Lt. Barbara Gore, N.Y.P.D.; Sgt. Michael Gorman, N.Y.P.D.; Detective Thomas Hyland, N.Y.P.D.; Inspector Robert J. Houlihan, retired, N.Y.P.D.; Investigator Arthur Handing, I.C.P.I.; Dr. Donald Hoffman, Senior Chemist (Toxicology), New York City Medical Examiner's Office; Detective Kenneth Kleinlein, N.Y.P.D.; Fire Marshal Gene Loughran, N.Y.F.D.; Fire Marshal Jonathan LeBow, N.Y.F.D.; Kenneth Lang, New York Property Insurance Underwriting Association; Detective James Mohan, retired, N.Y.P.D.; Lt. John Madigan, N.Y.P.D.; Elizabeth Morse, N.Y.P.D.; Assistant Chief Michael McNulty, retired, N.Y.P.D.; Mohammed Nagi, Chief Investigator, Brooklyn Union Gas Company; Sgt. William O'Connor, retired, N.Y.P.D.; Deputy Chief Fire Marshal Joseph O'Dowd, retired, N.Y.F.D.; Deputy Chief Louis G. Rainford, Jr., Brooklyn Detective Commander; Chief Fire Marshal John Regan, N.Y.F.D.; Supervising Fire Marshal Francis Russo, N.Y.F.D.; Dr. Robert Shaler, Chief of Serology, New York City Medical Examiner's Office; Sgt. John Skelly, N.Y.P.D.; David Redsicker, Vice President, Peter Vallas Associates; staff of the New York Fire Academy; staff of the New York City Mayor's Arson Strike Force; Lt. Thomas Sullivan, Commanding Officer, Rockland County B.C.I.; Sgt. Elmer Toro, Terrorist Task Force, N.Y.P.D.; Barbara L. Thompson, N.Y.P.D.; Ex-Chief Frederick Viohl, Dept. 26, Rockland County; Detective Robert Volpe, retired, N.Y.P.D.; Captain Anthony Vastola, N.Y.P.D.; Honorable Benjamin Ward, Police Commissioner, N.Y.P.D.; Professor William Walsh, Pennsylvania State University; Lt. Michael Yanda, N.Y.P.D.

A very special word of thanks to Assistant District Attorney Naomi Werne, author, and the Commissioner and Staff at the Division of Criminal Justice Services, New York State, for permission to reprint "New York State Law Governing Arson"; and to Vernon Geberth, Dr. Arthur Goldman, and Michael Gnat for their very special assistance.

Practical
Fire and Arson
Investigation

Arson: The American Experience

1

Arson has been identified and quantified as the fastest growing crime in America today. The rate of arson has increased well over 300% during the past ten years. National statistics show that, when measured on a cost-per-incident basis, arson is the most expensive crime committed. The average loss per incident for arson is about ten times that for robbery. Some overall statistics for U.S. arson are given in Table 1.1.

The response to the problem of arson, when examined nationally, has been, at best, haphazard. Few cases lead to arrests, and less than 20% of arrests end in conviction. This haphazardness is not difficult to accept and understand when you examine the various segments of society and the environment of the official agencies involved in the suppression and investigation of the problem.

Fire Service

Approximately 85% of the fire protection in America is provided by volunteer fire departments. Like their paid counterparts, these individuals are specifically trained and equipped to suppress fire, not to investigate its causes. The dedication and personal bravery of the fire service, whether paid or volunteer, go without question. Members of the fire service risk their lives daily to save lives and property in blazes, the causes of which may never be determined. Many fire fighters sacrifice their lives in this endeavor. Nationwide, 106 fire fighters died in the line of duty and over 100,000 were injured during 1983 (NFPA 1984).

Table 1.1 Selected U.S. Arson Statistics, 1982–1983

Property classification	1982			1983		
	Number of offenses	Percent distribution	Average damage	Number of offenses	Percent change from 1982	Percent cleared by arrest
Total	86,681	100.0	$9,731	84,700	−2.29	18.8
Total structure	49,671	57.3	15,270	51,690	+4.06	21.7
Single-occupancy residential	21,261	24.5	11,415	24,371	+14.63	19.4
Other residential	8,392	9.7	8,871	8,064	−5.71	25.5
Storage	5,388	6.2	14,039	5,154	−4.34	18.5
Industrial/ manufacturing	897	1.0	54,599	825	−8.03	15.5
Other commercial	6,586	7.6	33,459	6,223	−5.51	18.3
Community/ public	4,829	5.6	15,533	4,750	−1.64	37.1
Other structure	2,318	2.7	9,205	2,303	−0.65	19.6
Total mobile	21,151	24.4	3,734	19,724	−6.75	11.3
Motor vehicles	19,340	22.3	2,643	17,992	−6.97	10.8
Other mobile	1,811	2.1	15,388	1,732	−4.36	16.6
Other	15,859	18.3	381	13,286	−15.22	18.3

Based on data from U.S. Dept. of Justice (1982, 1983).

Police Service

The law enforcement community has not been spared from the menace of arson and fire in general. A police officer is very often the first official representative at the scene of a fire. This is true because of the usual mode of operation, patrol. A police officer may be the first person to realize that there is a problem. Many officers, after first notifying the appropriate fire department, have risked their lives while trying to save others, again in fires that may receive little or no follow-up.

Most fire departments and most of the over 40,000 police agencies nationwide are too small and fiscally restricted to provide the people and equipment necessary to specialize in and conduct detailed follow-up investigations in the field of fire investigation. Many state fire marshal offices are so understaffed and inadequately financed that they too must be very selective in the type and number of fires that they investigate.

Volunteer and paid fire fighters have traditionally been investigative generalists avoiding detailed fire investigations because of a lack of appropriate training. As a result, many fires that warrant scrutiny are either totally ignored or investigated too late to have any legal bearing. This combination of factors has resulted in the misclassification of

Figure 1.1 Fire fighters risk their lives daily. Unfortunately, very few of these fire scenes will receive an adequate investigative follow-up. In some cases, the cause of the fire will never be determined.

perhaps as many as half of all the fires occurring yearly and the inappropriate payment of millions of dollars in insurance proceeds.

Public Awareness

Americans are becoming distinctly aware of the far-reaching consequences of arson, in large measure because of the success of arson awareness programs. In recent years federal, state, and local governments, the insurance industry, and the mass media have disseminated substantial amounts of information regarding the crime of arson specifically and the causes of fire in general. The best indication that these messages and warnings are being taken seriously is the tremendous growth in the manufacture and sale (in the millions) of smoke and/or flame detectors. Community groups have formed throughout the nation in an effort to curtail the seemingly unchecked spread of arson in their respective neighborhoods. The public is outraged and demanding swift action.

One type of official response to these demands has been the creation of arson task forces at all levels of government. The task force approach represents a broad-based reaction to the fact that "arson is no longer a crime against property, but a crime against each and every citizen and a brazen attack on the entire economy of our country" (Dodson 1980, p. 20).

Model Arson Task Force

A model arson task force would incorporate the intelligence-gathering networks of each separate investigative agency into one cohesive, co-ordinated, and goal-directed entity. This would provide for a more comprehensive attack upon a selected number of subjects (e.g., suspects, leads) and avoid unnecessary duplication of effort. It would also utilize assigned personnel and available resources more efficiently. The sharing of investigative specialties (fire, police, etc.) and experience in a spirit of free-flowing communication would broaden the investigative capabilities of each investigator.

Role of the Fire Investigator

The fire investigator is a specialist operating in a unique field—an individual with the commensurate field experience and technical training necessary to collect and evaluate factual information and identify criminal activity in situations where others perceive only confusion and chaos.

The primary role of a fire investigator, as of any criminal investigator, is to determine the truth. In seeking the truth, the investigator must complete a postfire examination of the structure or vehicle that is the subject of a suspicious fire and determine the cause and origin of the fire. Interviews must be conducted, evidence collected, and comprehensive reports of all findings prepared. To complete these tasks, the fire investigator must know and understand the rules governing proper crime scene techniques, the significance of interviewing strategies, and the technical requirements of fire science.

If, during the initial stages of inquiry, actions evincing criminal conduct or evidence of criminality are uncovered, the fire investigator must automatically shift to his secondary role: to identify and move against those responsible. A fire investigator who has reason to believe that arson was committed is morally and professionally obligated to develop the case to its fullest extent.

Managing the Fire Investigation

Arson and its related offenses are universally viewed as being among the most serious crimes that an individual can commit. As such, they warrant the most diligent and unfaltering of investigations. To ensure

Figure 1.2 A fire investigator must be prepared to cope with any eventuality at the fire scene. Mobile investigative units, like the one pictured here, permit the ready availability of equipment and supplies. These highly visible units may also serve as a deterrent. A homeowner or small businessman may think twice about "selling his premises to an insurance company," if he believes that a highly specialized and equipped investigative unit is likely to respond to the fire scene and may uncover his culpability.

that every possible avenue is adequately explored and documented, an assigned investigator should follow an investigative checklist. A ranking officer assigned to supervise a fire investigation unit must continuously monitor, coordinate, and direct the cases under investigation by subordinate personnel. The field investigator conducts the actual investigation while the supervisor, utilizing personal experience and expertise, monitors investigative actions and provides administrative follow-up. This type of system is employed by the overwhelming majority of fire investigation units nationally.

Case Management

In order to optimize the use of limited resources (personnel and equipment), many agencies throughout the nation have developed case management systems. There is a distinction between urban and rural settings in their use of case management systems. This is due primarily to the difference in the volume of cases involved. Certain rural areas of the nation may refer every arson case to a case management system to ensure that every classified arson is adequately investigated. In an urban area with a high volume of cases to be investigated, the case management system is used to determine which of the cases will be given priority.

In some urban jurisdictions, for example, those cases of fire occurring in abandoned buildings are quickly closed: the fire scene is examined and the case accurately classified, but there is no follow-up investigation unless additional information is forthcoming. Even when such follow-up is conducted, no further action is taken unless the additional information provides specific data that may lead to a quick arrest in the case. The only action that might be taken would be to notify the appropriate city or state agency to order or request the demolition of the abandoned structure. Under normal circumstances, a fire intentionally set in an abandoned building and causing a death or other serious injury, or extending to and causing damage to an occupied building, is referred to the case management system.

Every case involving death or other serious injury is usually assigned to case management. However, for cases involving only property loss, some agencies use total dollar loss as the primary factor in designating a case for additional follow-up. For example, in Seattle, Washington, every fire causing at least $1000 in damage is thoroughly investigated.

Investigative Checklist

There are three main reasons to use an investigative checklist:

1. To ensure that every pertinent fact about the case has been identified.
2. To identify those cases to be assigned to case management.
3. To serve as a supervisory tool in evaluating an individual investigator's performance and in the assignment of additional cases based on case load.

An investigative checklist should include the following types of data:

identity of the assigned investigator;

victim information;

suspect/defendant information;

detailed information relating to the incident, including time, address, identity of the fire chief, first fire fighter and police officer at scene, and so on;

classification of the offense (e.g., arson [occupied, abandoned, etc.], arson/homicide);

detailed information relating to the investigative procedures and steps taken (e.g., photos, sketches, canvass);

identification of physical evidence and follow-up procedures (e.g., results of laboratory analysis);

identification relating to the prosecution of the case (e.g., grand jury, assigned prosecutor); and

witness information.

Crime Analysis

An integral part of the case management system is the maintenance of pertinent and statistical data relating to the incidence of arson and related offenses occurring within the area for which the fire investigation unit is responsible.

The design of the crime analysis system depends on the length of time to be considered and the volume of cases occurring within that specified period. The types of data to be extrapolated from the related reports would include the following:

chronologic listing of incidents;

date and time;

classification, including whether

residential or commercial, occupied or abandoned, forest or brush;

point of origin (where the fire started—e.g., room, basement, attic, floor);

type of accelerant used or suspected, if any;

classification of damage; and

death or other injury.

References and Selected Readings

Braun, Kenneth J., and Ford, Robert E., "Organizing an Arson Task Force," *FBI Law Enforcement Bulletin*, 50(3), March 1981.

DeLuca, Tim (Battalion Chief, Los Angeles City Fire Department), "Los Angeles Arson Suppression Task Force," *Arson: Resource Exchange Bulletin*, Federal Emergency Management Agency, U.S. Fire Administration, July 1980.

Dodson, H. C. (Fire Marshals' Association of North America), "Is Arson Legislation Adequate/Inadequate?" *Arson: Resource Exchange Bulletin*, Federal Emergency Management Agency, U.S. Fire Administration, July 1980.

National Fire Protection Administration (NFPA), "Fire Loss in the United States during 1983," *Fire Journal*, September 1984.

Sanders, Robert E., "National Response Teams: ATF's Coordinated Effort in Arson Investigations," *FBI Law Enforcement Bulletin*, 50(12), December 1981.

U.S. Department of Justice, *Uniform Crime Reports: Crime in the United States, 1982* (also, . . . *1983*), U.S. Government Printing Office, Washington, D.C., 1983 (also, 1984).

Weisman, Herman M. (ed.), *Arson Resource Directory*, Arson Resource Center Office of Planning and Education, U.S. Fire Administration, Washington, D.C., March 1980.

Wood, William (SAC Explosives Branch, ATF), "The Bureau of Alcohol, Tobacco, and Firearms Arson Program," *Arson: Resource Exchange Bulletin*, Federal Emergency Management Agency, U.S. Fire Administration, October 1980.

Arson Motives and Pathology

2

Some people mistakenly believe that the poor, the elderly, and the mentally ill have "cornered the market in fire." These same people believe that these groups suffer from some strange compulsion to burn themselves out of house and home. It would serve the arsonists in our society well to have us believe this nonsense.

The fact of the matter is that many supposedly respectable people are making tremendous sums of money as arson brokers and would-be "torches." If we were to examine the backgrounds of the people who have been arrested and convicted for arson, we would readily see that they represent a complete cross section of American society. In fact, our sample would cut across the entire fabric of social respectability. During the past decade, we have seen people from every walk of life sentenced to prison terms after being convicted for this, the fastest-growing crime in America. Those convicted for arson have included public officials, law enforcement and fire service personnel, lawyers, doctors, accountants, teachers, and insurance and real estate brokers, as well as organized crime operatives, drug addicts, and the poor, the elderly, and the mentally ill.

It has been said that:

> There is a cause and effect for everything people do, or fail to do. Although the individual may be otherwise normal, the act of destructive firesetting is not normal (Bromley et al., undated, §4.1, p. 1).

By those who are *not* "otherwise normal," we mean those suffering from some form of mental illness. Such *pathological* motives are discussed in the section on Psychological Compulsion. Most arsonists,

Figure 2.1 South Bronx. The motives for arson are as diverse as are the walks of life from which the fire setters derive. These motives include profit (fraud), revenge, vandalism, excitement, crime concealment, and psychological compulsion.

however, are nonpathological; nevertheless, each does have some motive:

> Motive is some inner drive or impulse that causes a person to do something or act in a certain way. Basically, it is the cause, reason, or incentive that induces or prompts specific behavior. In a legal context, motive explains "why" the offender committed his unlawful act, e.g., murder, rape, or arson.
>
> Though motive, unlike intent (willfulness), is not an essential element in criminal prosecution, it often lends support to it. Motive, for instance, frequently plays a crucial role in determining the cause of a fire, as well as the identity of the person or persons responsible for setting it (Rider 1980).

The motives for arson are as diverse as the walks of life from which arsonists derive. These motives include but are not limited to profit (fraud), revenge, vandalism, excitement, crime concealment, and the aforementioned psychological compulsion. Each of the major motives for arson is described and discussed in the remainder of the chapter.

Arson for Profit

Arson for profit is responsible for approximately half of all the fire-related property damage in America. It is probably the primary motive for the nearly 25% yearly increase in the rate of arson. The business of arson for profit has traditionally been one of high economic gain and low risk. Nationally, only 9% of all arson cases are cleared by arrest, and only 2% result in convictions. Insurance companies have historically paid billions of dollars on fire claims even though many of these cases were still under active investigation by one or several investigative agencies. As for the risk, an arsonist in America has less than one chance in ten of being arrested, and an even smaller chance of being convicted.

The economic gain to be derived from an arson-for-profit scheme can be either direct or indirect. A homeowner who destroys his or her home for the insurance proceeds gains directly when the insurance company settles the claim. A security guard who starts and extinguishes a fire in a warehouse where he is employed gains indirectly when rewarded for quick action in saving the warehouse.

Insurance Fraud

Insurance fraud is probably the most common target in an arson-for-profit scheme. The expression "sell it to the insurance company" has become the call to arms for anyone who wishes to but cannot dispose of a defective automobile, a neglected residence, or an unprofitable business. Insurance fraud has also been referred to as "the modern way to refinance."

One such scheme, which is most evident in our urban areas, involves the purchase of old, economically unsound, abandoned, and dilapidated buildings in economically depressed areas. These purchases are made with the smallest investment of funds possible. Over the course of the next several months or years, the property is sold and resold, back and forth, among a small group of investors. In this way, at least on paper, the value of the holdings increases. The building is then insured at the inflated "paper" value.

Another example is the situation of a person who purchases a new or used automobile and either cannot make additional loan payments and fears the loss of the initial investment or finds that the automobile is unreliable and cannot get satisfaction from the dealer. The purchaser in such a position may seriously consider "selling the car to the insurance company"; in 1983 alone, there were almost 18,000 automobile arsons in the United States (U.S. Dept. Justice, 1984).

A third and all too common example of insurance fraud is what is referred to as the *redecoration fire*. A homeowner who wants to renovate his or her kitchen but cannot afford the $10,000 cost quoted by a subcontractor conveniently arranges a kitchen fire. Thus, the insurance settlement pays for the renovation.

Figure 2.2 The expression "sell it to the insurance company" has become the call to arms for someone who views fire as a shortcut to disposing of a defective or unreliable automobile. (Photo courtesy of D. Redsicker.)

Welfare Fraud

The following rules are displayed in every social service (welfare) office in the City of New York:

> *Moving expenses:* Clients may move whenever they wish. However, moving expenses will be provided only if the move is necessary and if it is determined that the fees (i.e., moving expenses, security deposit, broker's fee, rent in advance) cannot be avoided. Moving expenses will not be provided more than once in two years unless the following conditions exist:
>   A. The move is the result of a fire or a disaster. . . .

Although a disaster is impossible to arrange, a fire is not, and a large proportion of America's inner-city arson has been the direct result of welfare fraud fires.

In a typical welfare fire, the welfare recipient is either dissatisfied with his current living conditions or in need of cash. On his own, he locates a new apartment in a more desirable area. Then, usually under cover of darkness, he moves all of his belongings (furniture, clothing, pet, etc.) to the new apartment. The next step is to replace some of the removed items with run-down furniture and clothing purchased at a second-hand store or junk yard. Soon after this is done, he sets a fire. After applying to the local department of social services, he will receive funds to replace all of his belongings that were supposedly lost. In addition, his moving expenses will be covered and he will receive a finder's fee for having found a new apartment without departmental assistance.

It should be noted that some supposed welfare fires are actually insurance fraud fires disguised by the building owner to draw attention away from the nonresident owner and instead to the resident welfare recipients. In some cases, the building owner encourages arson by arranging to have the services in the building (e.g., heat, hot water) rendered inoperable (usually citing economic considerations). A resident of the building, after exhausting whatever administrative recourse is available, may then see fire as the only way to escape these horrendous conditions. Such a fire is correctly labeled a welfare fraud fire, but the conditions that precipitated it are rarely examined.

Business-Related Fraud

Eliminating Competition

One example of arson for business-related (-motivated) fraud is the setting of a fire to limit or eliminate competition. Say that a person owns a well-established business, one that has been operating in a particular neighborhood for many years. A new store, selling the same items, opens around the corner and, in time, cuts into the older store's business. After a series of price wars, the established store's owner determines that it is time to use alternative means to reduce or eliminate the competition. The simplest way is to burn them out.

In one actual case, the owner of a large piece of real estate offered to buy out the owner of a five-and-ten-cent store, one of his tenants. The property owner wanted to tear down the five-and-ten and build a parking lot and restaurant, which would service a nearby state-operated betting parlor. However, the owner of the five-and-ten refused to sell his lease. The property owner was eventually arrested and convicted for a fire that destroyed an entire block of stores.

Organized Crime

Organized crime groups in America have been and are well entrenched in the "arson-for-hire" business. The sequence of events in a typical organized crime operation, referred to as a *bankruptcy scam*, clearly highlights the magnitude of their involvement.

A person owns a successful business with an excellent credit rating. His only vice is betting on horse races or playing at the gaming tables. As the result of gambling losses, involvement with a loan shark, or extortion, he involuntarily and begrudgingly accepts a new partner: an organized crime member or associate who may have purchased the

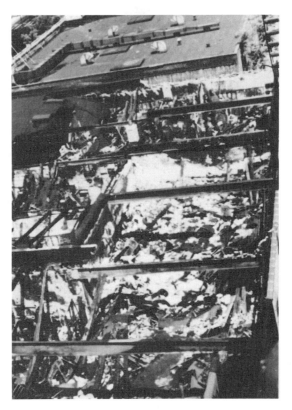

Figure 2.3 Eleven independently owned businesses were destroyed by this fire, which burned out an entire city block. The investigation of such massive scenes is arduous and costly. Insurance companies will often cooperate and assist by supplying or funding the type of heavy equipment that is required to adequately dig out the scene.

store owner's contract from a local loan shark. At the direction of his new partner, the store owner purchases, to the extent of the store's credit, large volumes of items that may easily be fenced. When these items are delivered, they are simply reloaded onto another truck and resold (at a fraction of their original cost) to the general public via a network of reliable fences. Since the business is now in debt to the extent of its credit, the bills that come due in 90 or 120 days cannot be paid, and the organized crime partner arranges for the business to file for bankruptcy. While the bankruptcy proceedings are pending, the store conveniently burns to the ground. The fire, which was part of a package deal, was intended to:

destroy the business's books and records,

destroy the merchandise that was supposedly available for sale, and provide the basis for an insurance claim.

The partners then split the insurance settlement and the revenue from the fenced goods, according to a preconceived plan. The creditors, following the bankruptcy settlement, receive, at best, ten cents on a dollar.

Organized crime factions also use arson (and murder) to intimidate witnesses, to eliminate other criminal factions, and as a form of discipline to maintain order within their own ranks.

Demolition and Rehabilitation Scams

Another real estate scam in which the participants gain indirectly is the situation in which a speculator purchases a large parcel of land that is dotted with old, abandoned buildings. The buildings are in such a state of disrepair that the land is more valuable without them than with them. The reason for the difference in value is that anyone who might consider buying and building on the property must add on the cost of the demolition of the old structures. The landowner has a similar problem. The costs involved in having the building(s) torn down and carted away may be prohibitive, and a fire may be seen as the owner's only alternative. If the fire does its work, the speculator will save on the cost of demolition and the property will be more appealing to a prospective buyer.

A second and related scheme in this area involves the demolition companies themselves. Take, for example, the case in which bids are being accepted for the demolition of a ten-story building. Each demolition company (depending on the city) must add to its costs an allowance for *dumping fees*: charges for each truckload of debris dumped at a city-owned landfill. If, after winning the contract, a company realizes that its original bid was too low, it conveniently has one or more fires in the building to be demolished and blames the fire on local juveniles or vandals. The more the building burns, the less there is to be trucked away; therefore, fewer dumping fees have to be paid. In this way, the demolition company either breaks even or makes a profit.

A third scheme, referred to as the *rehabilitation scam*, involves the rehabilitation of real property under the guise of a redevelopment project. The insurance industry and federal lending agencies, such as the Small Business Administration (SBA), are usually the targets of this type of scheme.

An individual purchases, at a nominal cost, an abandoned or nearly abandoned building in an area of the city that has been designated for redevelopment. The purchaser then announces his or her intention to rehabilitate the old building and to make it habitable once again. The old building, the builder's "good intentions," and the political climate are all used as collateral and as an inducement to secure the largest SBA loan possible. So, for example, for an investment of only $2000 or $3000 and a show of good faith, this speculator may have as much as several hundred thousand dollars of working capital. The next step in this scam is to amass receipts for materials that were never purchased and for work that was never done. The builder may rehabilitate one apartment out of 20 in a five-story walk-up apartment building. A telephone may be installed and the utilities may be operational in that one apartment. A friend or family member is identified to authorities as a tenant, and the apartment is furnished. The building is now occupied (telephone and utility bills, rent receipts) and qualifies for insurance. Some time after the building is insured, there is a fire. An insurance claim is filed, and there are ample bills and receipts to account for the SBA loan.

There have been numerous reasons given by practitioners of arson for profit in business-related frauds (after conviction) to explain their use of fire. Among these reasons are the following:

relocation when otherwise unable to break a lease or sell the old location,

dissolution of the business,

ridding the business of obsolete or unsalable merchandise,

completion of a seasonal business,

imminent business failure (business going bad),

upgrading of equipment,

labor or union problems, and

employees who are afraid to come to work (crime in the area).

Building Strippers

Others who profit indirectly from arson include a small group of people referred to as *building strippers*. A building stripper or junk dealer is an individual who strips abandoned buildings of bathroom fixtures, copper tubing, and anything else of value to be sold as junk. Most building strippers realize that there is a much easier way to expose the items that they are interested in taking. Now, instead of spending hours cutting through sheetrock and plaster walls, they simply start several carefully planned fires, and the responding fire units do the work for them. In suppressing the fires, the fire personnel punch or cut holes in the floors and walls, inadvertently saving the building strippers hours of work. This is in addition to the damage caused by the fire itself. As soon as the fire department has left the scene, the strippers remove the only items left of any value. In New York City, building stripping is a summonsable offense for which a small fine can be imposed. Building strippers are rarely brought to task for the crime of arson or for the unnecessary risk their fires pose to the fire personnel who ultimately respond.

Commercial Fire Checklist

Good information is vital to the successful conclusion of an arson case. Many times a person will answer questions early in an investigation to avoid the aura of suspicion.

The investigation of an arson-for-profit scheme is very similar to many other white-collar-crime investigations. If a motive is to be discovered and documented for court presentation, the criminal investigator must have the assistance of an investigative accountant. A comprehensive physical examination is usually enough to confirm the fact that the crime of arson was committed. The "paper case," which develops from an analysis of the business's books and records, usually identifies the motive and connects the defendant to the commission of the crime.

The following is a typical line of inquiry that an investigator would follow when investigating a suspicious supermarket fire. A similar program would be required when investigating suspicious fires in most commercial establishments (Lindsey, unpublished).

Start gathering information as soon as possible after the fire.

What is the relationship among the owners of the store?

Names and addresses of suppliers (meat, groceries, beer, etc.).

Did the owners of the store reduce their supplies before the fire?

What is the dollar volume of business that the store does per week on meats? (An estimate of total volume can be developed.)

What are the owner's gross earnings per week and the percent of markup?

Does the owner have any financial interest in other stores nearby?

Check storerooms and shelves for merchandise, beer, and meat that is the most expensive.

Check with suppliers as to whether bills are overdue or checks for merchandise are bouncing.

How much money does the owner owe suppliers?

What is the name of the owner's insurance company and what is the extent of coverage? Check with the insurance agent.

Has the owner applied to the Small Business Administration or any such lending agency for a loan?

Is the store protected by an alarm (burglar or fire)? If so, what time is it turned on daily? Was it on or off at the time of the fire? Was it circumvented?

Was the sprinkler system working?

Ask to see business records and tax returns.

What flammable liquids are kept in the store (charcoal and lighter fluids, spray cleaners, etc.)? Where are they kept?

Are flammable liquids used to clean the floors or areas of the store? What types and when were they used last?

"It is certainly possible to prove the arson fraud scheme without positive evidence linking the subject to the fire scene," according to Special Agent Robert E. Walsh of the Criminal Investigations Division, Federal Bureau of Investigation (Walsh 1979). "Investigators often are required to initiate arson investigations involving fires in buildings that were torched several months previously and have since been razed." Walsh also suggests that "investigators must review available information and reports to establish the identities of fires that have been included in this scheme." Such information sources include "police/fire department records, local newspapers, State Fire Marshals, insurance representatives, and informants." Walsh notes that

while reviewing potential inner-city arson files, the following clues will indicate positive circumstantial evidence that the fire was set for an insurance fraud:

1. presence of incendiary material,
2. multiple origins of fire (arson must be a total loss to be profitable),
3. location of the fire in a building (look for fires near the roof, because many insurance adjustors will declare a fire a total loss once the roof is destroyed),
4. suspicious hours (no witnesses),
5. holiday fires,
6. vacant building,
7. renovation of building,
8. recent departure of occupants,
9. removal of objects (woodwork, plumbing, etc.),
10. property for sale,
11. previous fire,
12. building overinsured,
13. habitual claimants,

14. fires occurring shortly before policy expiration,
15. fires where insurance has recently been obtained, and
16. recent sale of building.

Agent Walsh further suggests:

After compiling a list of possible inner-city arson fires, the investigator may be able to develop positive circumstantial evidence of fraud from available records and demonstrate the property investor's involvement by showing conflicting information, deception, and false statements. . . . It may be much easier to solve an arson fraud than it would be to prove a straight arson case (Walsh 1979).

Revenge and Prejudice

Arson motivated by revenge, spite, and jealousy accounts for a very high percentage of the total number of intentional fires occurring in the United States. Those who commit such arson include "jilted lovers, feuding neighbors, disgruntled employees, quarreling spouses, persons getting even after being cheated or abused, and persons motivated by racial or religious hostility" (Boudreau et al. 1977, p. 19).

A fire that destroyed a Hispanic social club and killed 25 partygoers in October 1976 in the Bronx, New York City, was motivated by revenge. The jilted boyfriend of one of the victims apparently started the fire because his girlfriend would not leave the party to talk to him.

From an investigative standpoint, once the revenge motive has been identified, the number of people to be investigated can be narrowed tremendously because of the connection between the subject(s) and the target of the arson.

Fires motivated by racial, religious, or similar biases are investigated in the same manner as those motivated by revenge. Most local newspapers are laden with articles describing in detail the burning of a group home for the retarded, a house of worship, or the home of a black family in an all-white neighborhood. The investigator must realize that constitutional as well as criminal statutes may have been violated in a racially or religiously motivated fire.

Vanity

This category of arson motive is also referred to as the *hero syndrome*. A night watchman or security guard who feels that he is being ignored may start a fire and then save the entire plant. This "heroic" act may draw attention to the splendid job he is doing and warrant a raise in pay, a bonus, or a reward. Vanity fires have been started by volunteer fire fighters who happened to live in quiet residential areas where there were few calls for service, to gain the attention of their family and neighbors and the respect of fellow fire fighters for being the first to respond to the firehouse or scene. According to FBI Special Agent Anthony O. Rider, vanity arsonists, although few in number, have "the propensity for serious destructiveness" (Rider 1980, p. 12).

Fire Buff Arson

A special case of the vanity-motivated fire setter worth mentioning here is that of the fire "buff"—a person who enthusiastically attends fires, perhaps to associate with and assist fire-fighting personnel. The term *buff*, in fact, most probably derives from the buff overcoats worn by volunteer fire fighters in early-nineteenth-century New York City. Says Agent Rider:

> The fire "buff," like the police "buff," is an enthusiastic "hanger-on." He generally represents a frustrated would-be fireman or would-be policeman. Although many buffs are civic-minded and constructive in their associations with the police and fire service, others are characteristically immature, inadequate, and underachievers. The fire buff who sets fires is seeking attention and attempting in a pathological way to win praise and social recognition for his alertness and heroism in reporting fires and giving assistance in fighting them (Rider 1980).

Juvenile Fire Setters and Vandalism

In 1982, over 60% of New York State's reported incendiary fires were due to the actions of juveniles. The nationwide figure is over 50%. In some cases, the motive is certainly profit. Juveniles may be hired as incendiaries or "torches" by people who are unable to contact a professional torch or who are afraid to start the fire themselves. A juvenile hired to set a fire will generally work for much less than an experienced or professional torch. It is because of their lack of experience and their reliance upon whatever supplies are available (e.g., gasoline) that these young incendiaries are likely to be trapped and die in any fire they might set.

A motive for juvenile fire setters is not always apparent:

> Vandalism is a common cause ascribed to fires set by juveniles who seem to burn property merely to relieve boredom or as a general protest against authority. Many school fires as well as fires in abandoned autos, vacant buildings, and trash receptacles are believed to be caused by this type of arsonist (Boudreau et al. 1977).

Fire setting has been recognized as behavior that is learned, and at a very early age (Redsicker, unpublished). Children as young as two

Figure 2.4 The foundation is all that remains of this recently completed high ranch. Juveniles, either for a thrill or just on a dare, burnt the new home to the ground. David Redsicker, a faculty member at the New York State Fire Academy who has conducted a great deal of research on juvenile fire setters, recently concluded that in 1982 juvenile fire setters were responsible for over 60% of New York State's incendiary fires and for over 50% of the incendiary fires reported nationwide. (Photo courtesy of T. Brown.)

years old have started fires, destroying property and lives. An increasing number are revenge-motivated or have what is known in the profession as the "cry-for-help" syndrome. These young people are often the victims of neglect and abuse. Attempts to reach these children are being made through juvenile fire setter programs across the country. These programs are an innovative approach, not only to recognize juvenile fire setters, but, more importantly, to identify the underlying problems that surface as fire-setting behavior.

Crime Concealment

Escaped prisoners and armed robbers will often burn their (stolen) escape vehicles at the time that they are abandoned. They do this to destroy fingerprints or other evidence that law enforcement officers might use to connect them to the vehicle and, therefore, to the scene of the escape or robbery. Torched getaway cars are only one example of arson for crime concealment:

Figure 2.5 An employee identified this desk as the central repository for all the business records for a company that had burned to the ground over a long holiday weekend. Although gasoline had been poured throughout the structure, the desk was not destroyed as planned. The business books and records had been moved before the fire.

Criminals sometimes set fires to obliterate the evidence of burglaries, larcenies, and murders. The fire may destroy any evidence that a crime was committed, destroy the evidence connecting the perpetrator to the crime, or, in the case of murder, make it impossible to identify the victim. Persons may set fires to destroy records that contain evidence of embezzlement, forgery, or fraud. Arson has also been used as a means of diverting attention while the perpetrator burglarized another building, and as a means of covering attempted escapes from jails, prisons, and state hospitals (Boudreau et al. 1977).

Evidence that might indicate arson for crime concealment includes the recovery of burglar's tools (e.g., crowbar, lock picks) from the fire scene, or personal property strewn about a room that exhibits little or no fire damage. A detailed follow-up investigation is required if:

business or personal records were left out (or file drawers left open) and exposed to fire; or

valuable personal items or expensive office equipment or stock are found to be missing after a close examination of debris (and presumed to have been stolen before the fire started).

A fire set to conceal a burglary several years ago in Westchester County caused the death of more than 20 people who were attending a dance several doors away from the scene of the burglary.

Psychological Compulsion

As we have seen, there are elements of many cases of arson that might best be described as psychological: vanity, prejudice, revenge, and, perhaps, even a desire to "beat the system." Developing a psychological profile of an arsonist during an investigation

> can be an invaluable aid to the investigator. It assists him in focusing his investigation, identifying potential suspects, and developing appropriate techniques and strategies for interviewing the various types of fire setters (Rider 1980, p. 2).

This kind of psychological understanding is crucial in cases for which there would seem to be no motive or, at least, none that is as readily comprehensible as those we have already examined. Such "motiveless" fire setting may be attributable to *psychological compulsion*.

In order to understand the role of psychological compulsion as it relates to fire setting, it is first necessary to examine the types of affective disorders that may lead to psychopathic behavior or criminal conduct.

Mania and Depression

Mania and depression are two behavioral extremes that are generally viewed as psychoneurotic or psychotic disorders. *Mania* is marked by mood elevation, physical and mental hyperactivity, and disorganized behavior. *Depression* may involve lethargy, lack of concentration, and sadness or dejection. Cycles of alternating mania and depression in an individual are termed *manic-depressiveness*.

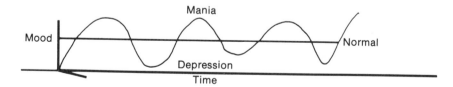

Depression is a factor in some arson/homicide cases. As abhorrent as the idea may be to a rational person, the fact is that people do commit suicide by fire. Suicide by fire is rare in Western culture, but common in Japan and the most common form of suicide in Bangkok, Thailand.

A person in the depths of depression has one overriding concern: "How to die?" (See also Chapter 7, Investigating Fatal Fires.)

Pyromania

The *pyromaniac* (not clinically a manic) is a person who has an inordinate or ungovernable enthusiasm for starting fires—"an individual who lacks a conscious motivation for his fire setting" (Rider 1980). Some writers have argued the point that "pyros" set fires to gain some sort of sexual gratification (Battle and Weston 1975, p. 98). Whether or not this is true, it would seem that the overwhelming majority set fires to gain *some* type of sensual pleasure.

Pyromaniacs set fires impulsively; they do not plan their fires. Rather than carry flammables or combustibles to use as fuels in setting fires, they simply ignite whatever combustibles are close by when they have the urge to start a fire. There is generally no connection among the targets of a pyromaniac's fires other than that they may occur along a common route or path followed daily, for example, to a bus stop, to work, or to a local store.

A single pyromaniac may cause large amounts of damage and start numerous fires before a pattern or common thread is identified by an investigator. Once the pattern becomes significant, the investigator should recommend and coordinate an extensive surveillance operation in the area.

Schizophrenia

Schizophrenia is the most serious of the affective disorders. It is generally characterized by disintegration of personality (inappropriate affect, disorderly thought and behavior) and withdrawal into self-centered subjective mental activity (autism). Of the four general types of schizophrenic personality (paranoid, simple, hebephrenic, and catatonic), the paranoid schizophrenic seems to be the most likely to be an arsonist.

There is a tendency on the part of the paranoid schizophrenic toward excessive and irrational suspiciousness. Everything is perceived from a defensive standpoint. The paranoid schizophrenic fire setter, because of this bizarre or perverted sense of reality and defensive posture, may use fire and fire setting as a weapon against whatever is perceived as a threat.

Profile of the Pathological Arsonist

Rider (1980) found that, although there is no such thing as a "typical" pathological fire setter, the following cluster characteristics are common among them:

1. less than 25 years old,
2. reared in distressing and pathological environments,
3. father absent from home,
4. domineering mother,
5. academic retardation,
6. slightly below-average intelligence,
7. emotional and psychological disturbance,
8. social and sexual maladjustment,
9. unmarried,
10. psychological inadequacy and insecurity, and
11. cowardice.

The pathological fire setter may be "motivated by a multiplicity of factors" and spurred on by a "precipitating stressful situation or experience" (Rider 1980).

Mass Civil Disturbance (Riot)

The massive civil disturbance that rocked Miami, Florida, beginning in May 1980 was reminiscent of our country's turbulent past. News reporters and photographers documented the all-too-familiar clouds of smoke billowing from fire-ravaged sections of the city.

The problems that plagued the authorities in Miami (arson, looting, sporadic shootings, mass arrests) were the same as those faced by the officials of New York City and many other cities during the 1960s. The words "riot" and "arson" often seem to be inextricably linked. The indiscriminate burning of businesses, homes, and automobiles during a riot, though a *consequence* of the civil disorder, is not *motivated* by it. People in a mob may commit acts that they would never do as individuals (*mob mentality*). Clearly, however, a riot may incite those already motivated for arson and provide chaos within which to escape.

Terrorism

In his *Minimanual of the Urban Guerrilla*, the Brazilian theoretician of urban guerrilla warfare Carlos Marighella defined terrorism as "an action, usually involving the placement of a bomb or fire explosion of great destructive power, which is capable of effecting irreparable loss against the enemy" (Marighella 1970, p. 32). One of the weapons in the terrorist's arsenal is fire. This is often overlooked; media attention has traditionally focused on terrorist bombings and kidnapping incidents.

Because the primary goal of terrorists is often publicity, their violence is directed mainly against civilian targets. For example, the FALN (Fuerzas Armadas de Liberación Nacional Puertorriqueña—Armed Forces of Puerto Rican National Liberation) claimed responsibility for the extensive use of incendiary devices against department stores in New York City. A number of these devices were secreted in the merchandise on shelves and clothing racks.

Terrorists have also used arson as a diversionary tactic, and their associates have used the proceeds of insurance fraud (arson) to finance covert operations and to purchase weapons and equipment. In one series of cases, insurance settlements from fires that occurred in New York City were being used to further the goals of terrorists in the Middle East.

Today's investigator must be aware of the current trends and tactics of the urban guerrilla and maintain a liaison with local intelligence units.

References and Selected Readings

Battle, Brendan P., and Weston, Paul B., *Arson: A Handbook of Detection and Investigation*, Arco Publishing, New York, 1975.

Boudreau, John F., et al., *Arson and Arson Investigation: Survey and Assessment*, U.S. Government Printing Office, Washington, D.C., 1977.

Bromly, James, et al., *Cause and Origin Determination*, Office of Fire Prevention and Control, Department of State, State of New York, undated.

Fitch, R. D., and Porter, E. A., *Accidental or Incendiary*, Charles C. Thomas Publishing, Springfield, Illinois, 1968.

Lindsey, Arlene (Former Assistant DA, Bronx, New York), "Commercial Fire Check List," unpublished course material, Arson Investigation Course, NYC Police Academy.

Marighella, Carlos, *Minimanual of the Urban Guerrilla*, New World Liberation Front (underground U.S. publisher), 1970.

Redsicker, David (New York State Fire Academy), unpublished research.

Rider, Anthony O. (FBI Special Agent), "The Firesetter, a Psychological Profile," *Law Enforcement Bulletin*, June–August 1980.

U.S. Department of Justice, *Uniform Crime Reports: Crime in the United States, 1983*, U.S. Government Printing Office, Washington, D.C., 1984.

Walsh, Robert E. (FBI Special Agent), "Inner-City Arson," *Law Enforcement Bulletin*, October 1979.

Building Construction: Fire Problems and Precautions

3

To evaluate any structural fire effectively, an investigator must have a basic understanding of building construction techniques. A working knowledge of commonly used materials and their effect on and reaction to fire spread is essential. Under normal conditions (e.g., no accelerants or explosives) the rate of burning and the intensity and path of a fire are directly affected by a building's construction and the types of materials used.

Personal safety is of the utmost importance to any investigator. Before entering a fire-damaged structure, an investigator must be able to evaluate its stability. The potential for internal collapse poses the greatest danger.

Classification of Building Construction

There are five nationally recognized types of building construction, though various state and local governments have further narrowed these classifications to meet their particular conditions:

1. fire-restrictive,
2. noncombustible or limited-combustible,
3. ordinary construction,
4. heavy timber, and
5. wood frame.

The New York City Fire Department (NYCFD), for example, uses the following building construction class designations:

fireproof,
fire-protected,

Figure 3.1 The intensity of this gasoline-fed fire was evident in the annealing and twisting of an 80-foot steel I beam.

nonfireproof,

wood construction,

metal or fire-retardant wood, and

heavy timber.

The correspondence of these systems is shown in Table 3.1.

Fire-restrictive/fireproof: High-rise housing projects are probably the best example of this type of construction. The structural members are of noncombustible or limited-combustible materials.

Noncombustible/limited-combustible/fire-protected: The structural members are also of noncombustible or limited-combustible material, but with a faster burn time than for class 1. This type or class of construction is very rarely found.

Ordinary construction/nonfireproof: Row or town houses (brick veneer and wood joisted) are an example of this type of construction. These multiple-family, five- and six-story walk-ups are probably

Table 3.1 Building Construction Classifications

National classification	NYCFD class	Fire resistance
Fire-restrictive	1	4 hr
Non/limited-combustible	2	3 hr
Ordinary construction	3	1 hr
Heavy timber	6	1–2 hr
Wood frame	4–5	Metal/wood: no fire resistance Fire-retardant wood: ≤1 hr

the most common type encountered in the urban centers through-out the nation. The overwhelming majority of New York City's 850,000 buildings are classified as nonfireproof.

Heavy timber: This type of construction is probably more common in the New England area than anywhere else in the nation. Col-umns, beams, and girders are heavy timber, floors are wood, and there are no concealed spaces in roof construction.

Wood frame/wood–metal–fire-retardant wood: This type of con-struction is most commonly used in residential and some rural commercial construction. Wood and metal offer no fire resistance. Fire-retardant wood may have a 1–2-hr fire resistance.

Building Components

Walls and Partitions

Masonry, plaster, and drywall construction provide resistance to fire attack, whereas the use of wood studs, wood paneling, and plywood products can greatly increase a fire's intensity and actually add to the fire load. Paint and other commonly used finishes may burn rapidly and facilitate the lateral movement of fire. Electrical wiring, telephone lines, plumbing lines, and other service equipment may be concealed within walls and may provide unprotected openings through which fire may travel unobstructed. A fire that originates in or burns into a wall area can burn unnoticed for some time. If unobstructed by fire-breaks (*cats*), the fire could very well travel vertically for some distance in the chimneylike space between studs. Under heavy fire conditions, an investigator may expect a wall to collapse in an average of 28 minutes.

Figure 3.2 Fire fighters and fire investigators respond thousands of times each year to single-occupancy wood frame structures like the one pictured here. (Photo courtesy of S. Grennan.)

Floor and Ceiling Assemblies

Regardless of the type or class of construction, hung ceilings and the like provide for the rapid, unobstructed lateral movement of fire in the concealed space between the ceiling and the floor above. This space serves as a horizontal chimney. Many of the materials commonly used for ceiling assemblies are combustible. The vapors released from the ceiling assemblies are very often toxic. The associated intense, high burning has a tendency to facilitate a burn-through to the attic, roof, or living space above. The secondary burning that can result from an internal collapse may obliterate the point of origin and hamper physical examination. Older buildings that have been rehabilitated or remodeled numerous times over several years may have as many as two or more separate hung ceilings in any given room.

On the other hand, collapsing ceiling materials and the associated loose ash may *assist* the investigation by both smothering the original source of the fire and insulating the point of origin from further damage. Under heavy fire conditions, an investigator can expect a floor to collapse in approximately 15 minutes, on average.

Attics and Cocklofts

Fully attached row or town houses built prior to World War II were, for economic reasons, constructed with a common roof. Although some of these common roofs were as long as an entire city block, no provision was made for dividing parapets. Construction materials in attics and *cocklofts* (small garrets) are generally combustible, and fires that advance to a common cockloft are most often responsible for the extension of fire to adjoining buildings. Torches and "fire-for-hire" rings, aware of this vulnerability, will often select the cockloft or concealed ceiling space as the point of origin. The total loss of a roof, especially on commercial properties, usually results in a very favorable insurance settlement.

Many roofing materials (shingles, tar paper, etc.) are a blend of petroleum by-products and, therefore, combustible. The associated melting can facilitate the spread of fire.

Air and Light Shafts

Many older buildings were constructed with vertical air and light shafts. These are most obvious in row-type houses where the air/light shaft was intended to provide air and sunlight in the kitchen. Fully attached row houses could, understandably, only have windows on the front and rear of the building. To provide side windows and cross ventilation, vertical shafts were required.

These shafts act like a chimney during a fire, enhancing the vertical spread. Secondary fire can occur above the original point of origin. In these cases, the fire typically extends into the common cockloft and this extension facilitates the lateral movement of the fire.

Structural Loads

"Dead," "live," "impact," and "fire loads" are terms describing specific circumstances that can have a direct impact on how completed structures perform during a fire.

Dead load: the total weight of the building plus the total weight of all permanent or built-in equipment.

Live load: the total weight of those items added to the building, including all furnishings, stock and storage, and occupants.

Fire-fighting operations can greatly increase the live load. Consider the added weight of fire fighters in turnout gear and the total weight of the water added to the structure to suppress the fire. (One gallon of water weighs approximately $8\frac{1}{3}$ pounds.) Water can accumulate in pools or be absorbed into stock and furnishings and, in some areas, this total live load may exceed the maximum floor tolerance.

Impact load: the load that is brought to bear in a short period of time. This can result from the added weight caused by the collapse of internal structural elements and explosions.

Fire load: the total number of British thermal units (Btu) that might evolve during a fire, and the rate at which heat will evolve.

For example, consider the total potential for Btu production that might evolve from the total involvement of a five-story, brick and wood-joisted structure (type 3, ordinary construction). One could easily consider this type of structure as a lumber yard surrounded by brick walls. The best estimates available indicate that at least $12\frac{1}{2}$ tons of wood are introduced into the brick enclosure during construction. One pound of wood, if completely burned, produces 8000 Btu. A quick mathematical calculation clearly illustrates that the total potential for Btu production is astronomical.

High-Rise Construction

High-rise construction in the United States had its origins in the late nineteenth century. At that time, any building that extended above the reach of the tallest aerial ladder available was considered to be a high rise. During the intervening 90 years, three generations of high-rise construction have evolved.

First Generation

First-generation high-rise buildings appeared in the 1890s. They had panel wall exteriors usually constructed of masonry or brick. The interiors consisted of all-wood floors supported by cast-iron or unpro-

Figure 3.3 A view of a typical inner-city housing complex.

tected steel columns. The furnishings and interior surfaces were made almost entirely from wood. The primary design problems for buildings constructed during this time were the obvious danger of floor collapse and the number of unprotected vertical openings on vertical shafts. A typical first-generation high-rise building ranged from 10 to 15 stories. The Flatiron Building in New York City is a good example of a first-generation high rise.

Second Generation

The 1920s saw the emergence of second-generation high-rise construction. The Empire State and Chrysler Buildings in New York City are perfect examples of this type of construction. Buildings constructed during this period had panel-wall exteriors constructed of brick or masonry. There was very limited use of combustible materials. The interior of the buildings consisted of poured concrete or masonry floors supported by protected steel beams. The steel superstructure was protected by enclosing it in a masonry sheath. All internal walls and partitions were constructed of masonry, which provided for compartmentation; a fire occurring in a given area would be virtually restricted to that area. Vertical shafts were enclosed, and the danger from internal collapse was virtually nonexistent. The primary design flaws of the first generation had been corrected.

Third Generation

Modern technology and economic considerations pushed high-rise construction into its third generation in the early 1960s. The availability of and need for lighter and lighter materials, staggering construction costs, modern architectural breakthroughs, and spiraling property values in the urban centers combined to produce structures that allowed the population to work and live in the clouds.

The typical exterior of a third-generation high rise has curtain walls constructed almost exclusively from lightweight steel and glass. The New York City Fire Department describes this generation of high-rise buildings as semicombustible rather than fire-resistant, because of the large amounts of synthetics and combustible furnishings that are used. These items burn hotter and produce more toxic by-products than do ordinary combustibles.

Structural Fire Precautions

Modern fire codes and construction standards address the substantive issues regarding structural fire precautions, both for new construction and for rehabilitation of old buildings. These code standard changes have evolved slowly over the years; if followed, they create reasonably safe working and living environments.

It is important for the investigator to scrutinize available information (e.g., from the Department of Buildings) to determine the year in which a building under investigation was constructed. The authorized building codes in effect at the time may very well explain and account for the type of fire extension and damage observed at the scene.

Two code requirements, the dividing parapet and the fire door, have been responsible for the limitation of fire damage or fire extension in many cases.

Dividing Parapet

A *dividing parapet*, parapet, firewall, or *party wall* is a wall designed to prevent the extension of fire. They are usually constructed of masonry or other fire-resistant material. The evolution of the dividing parapet is a perfect example of the development of fire safety standards.

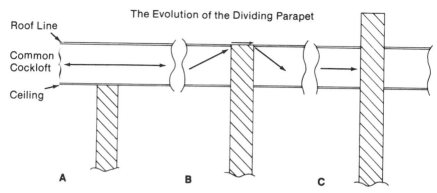

Figure 3.4 The evolution of the dividing parapet. (A) From 1916 to 1930, the party wall extended vertically through the building, but ended at the uppermost ceiling. Cockloft acted like a horizontal chimney. (B) The party wall (1930–1940) extended through the attic or cockloft, but ended at the underside of the roof. Cockloft was subdivided, but fire was still able to extend laterally over common roof. (C) After 1940 the party wall was extended through the roof, thus subdividing the cockloft and common roof.

From 1916 to 1930, the party wall extended vertically through the building but ended at the top of the uppermost ceiling; it did not protrude into the cockloft or attic space. This type of construction was directly responsible for the loss of entire city blocks due to the rapid extension of fire within the secluded space provided. From 1930 to 1940, the party wall was extended through the attic or cockloft space and ended at the underside of the roof. The common cockloft was successfully subdivided, but the fire was still able to extend over the wall and spread to adjoining buildings via the common roof. After 1940, the party wall was extended through the roof, thus subdividing the common roof and cockloft. In the late 1970s, federal funds were selectively made available to extend party walls through the roofs of row houses that were originally constructed with common cocklofts in the 1920s and 1930s.

Fire Door

A *fire door* is usually constructed of metal and is designed to prevent the spread of fire through doorways or other wall openings. Fire doors are constructed to meet a variety of different standards, which are governed by the type of occupancy and the potential fire hazards. Glazed doors are available with and without wired glass.

A fire door may be equipped with a spring-loaded or electromagnetic closing device, or with heat-sensitive fuses that, when activated, trigger the fire door to close. An arsonist will often intentionally bypass these safeguards in order to achieve the desired result.

Fire Extension and Accepted Architectural Designs

The universally recognized characteristic of a fireproof or fire-restrictive (class 1) construction is that the building will restrict a fire to one floor or other limited area (in the absence of an explosion or other unusual condition). Financial considerations, construction shortcuts, and the introduction of lightweight building materials have detracted from this recognized standard. Civil litigation and long-term court cases have stalled the institution of newly written building and fire codes. Some enterprising real estate holders have delayed much-needed change by carefully utilizing the judicial system. In the interim, older, less expensive building codes are applied to new construction.

Design Problems

Lightweight Floor Construction

"Q" deck flooring, which is a combination of 2–3 inches of floated or slab concrete supported by corrugated steel sheets, offers substantially less fire resistance than the older 6- or 8-inch poured concrete floors. Much more heat is transferred via conduction through the newer floor design. It is less than half the weight of the conventional poured floor, which permits the use of lighter structural steel. This is a major factor in modern construction, since the height of a building is affected by its total dead weight.

Open Floor Design

The open floor design reduces and, in some cases, virtually negates compartmentation. Commercial office buildings are constructed with each floor exhibiting a huge expanse of undivided space; portable, quickly assembled partitions are used to separate hallways and offices. An official from the New York City Fire Department stated,[*] "The life safety hazard in these buildings is increased by the omission of features which can confine fires to a single space long enough to permit evacuation. Large open floor areas in some high-rise buildings, when

---

[*] During a lecture at the Victor Collingmore Institute (Advanced Training for New York City Fire Marshals), offered in conjunction with the John Jay College of Criminal Justice, City University of New York, March 9, 1981.

ınvolved in fire, are beyond the control of manual fire-fighting operations."

Central Core Design

The central core design is characterized by all utilities, elevator shafts, stairwells, air conditioning ducts, and electrical, plumbing, and telephone lines being located and passing vertically up through each floor in the central core of the building. Little fire-fighting strategy is permitted, since all fire-fighting operation must operate from the central core. Fire fighters could conceivably find themselves surrounded by fire.

Curtain Wall Construction

A curtain wall is a prefabricated (non-load-bearing) exterior wall made of panels that are supported by the structural frame of the building. The method of attachment and the details of construction between the curtain wall and the floor slab are crucial; there is usually a space between the end of the floor slab and the curtain wall. This space acts as a vent for the vertical spread of fire. The old philosophy that a building itself, by its design and construction, should aid in the control of a fire, is not employed today.

Atrium

In ancient times, an atrium was the main room in a Roman home, with a large open area extending to the roof. Today the term *atrium* is used to describe a large open area extending overhead from the lobby at least several stories and possibly to the roof. A ventilation unit or skylight designed to operate automatically and vent the atrium is located at its zenith. Living and working areas are located on corridors that front on the open area. The fire hazards associated with this type of construction are numerous. If a fire were to start on one of the lower floors, the heat, smoke, and toxic gases produced could conceivably collect at the top of the atrium faster than the vents could dispose of them. The gas and smoke would then bank down and be forced by the accompanying increase in air pressure through the various hallways and into the living and working areas, thus trapping the occupants in those areas. If the fire were to extend into the lobby or entrance area and sufficient fuel were present, it could, being unobstructed, quickly rise several stories.

Construction and Materials Problems

Plenums

In an effort to save the expense and labor associated with the installation of additional ductwork, many builders are commonly using the concealed space between the ceiling and the underside of the floor as a plenum. Spent air from the living and working areas is routinely vented via the ceiling plenum, which serves as an air shaft to carry the spent air to the building's central core. This concealed, unobstructed space is equivalent to a common cockloft located on each floor. A fire with its associated smoke, heat, and toxic gases extending into this space could easily travel great distances unnoticed. The electrical wiring and other similar materials ordinarily contained in this space would most certainly exacerbate any fire and greatly increase the types and amounts of toxic gas produced.

If the ceiling plenums vent into the central core, from which fire-fighting operations will be conducted, then a life-threatening situation awaits responding fire fighters.

Central Air Conditioning Systems

The ductwork of a central air conditioning system acts like a chimney for any fire or smoke that might find its way into the system. Many commercial and residential high-rise buildings are equipped with several very large (multiton) air conditioning units that service multiple floors. Any fire problem that might contaminate that system would, therefore, affect large areas of the building.

The ducts in such a system should be equipped with smoke detectors and dampers that would warn both building security personnel and occupants, automatically cordon off the contaminated areas, and shut down the affected system. The protection provided by such smoke detectors and dampers, once installed, is directly related to the maintenance and testing schedules applied.

Elevators and Elevator Shafts

Elevators should never be used to evacuate a building in the event of a fire; an elevator shaft serves as a very effective chimney. Moreover, in older buildings, an elevator's electronic call button may react to the heat on the fire floor, holding it there. People attempting to use this elevator during the emergency may thus find themselves stopping on the fire floor and trapped as the doors open.

Most jurisdictions now require that the central elevator panel, usually located in the lobby, be equipped with an override device that, when activated, automatically causes all the building's elevators to return immediately to the lobby.

Elimination of the Fire Tower

A *fire tower* is a stairway enclosed in a separate structure that has its own exterior walls. It is connected to the primary building by balconies located on each floor. A person using the fire tower is required to exit the primary building via a fire door, cross the connecting balcony, and enter the fire tower via a second fire door. Since it is a completely separate structure, people fleeing a fire in the primary building would be safe within the fire tower.

In new construction, fire towers have been replaced by interior enclosed stairways. The emergency stairwells above the fire floor may be rapidly contaminated by smoke and other hazardous by-products when occupants on the fire floor evacuate that floor. A stairwell, like an elevator shaft, acts as a chimney. Heat and smoke entering the interior, enclosed stairway at the fire floor quickly rise, trapping those above. The egress doors to the enclosed stairways are fire rated and permit access from only one side. Occupants on upper floors (above the fire floor) attempting to exit via the enclosed stairway could conceivably find themselves trapped in that stairway.

Consider the following scenario: You are working or living on the 32nd floor of a modern high-rise building. A serious fire breaks out on the fifth floor. The occupants of the fifth floor exit safely via the interior stairway but, in so doing, inadvertently jam the fire door to the stairway in an open position. Heat, smoke, and toxic gases produced by the fire enter and contaminate the stairway. You receive an urgent call from a security officer who advises you to evacuate the building immediately. You and the other occupants of your floor, who received the same frantic call, run to the interior stairway and begin to walk down the stairs. The fire door on the 32nd floor closes and locks behind you. By the time you reach the 25th-floor landing, you realize that your exit is blocked by the smoke and heat below. Since all of the fire doors leading to each floor are locked, your only way out of the stairway is to proceed up to the roof. You are now faced with two serious questions. First, is the roof door open or locked? You know for a fact that maintenance people often lock that door without considering the consequences. Second, can you even get to the roof before you are overcome by the smoke and carbon monoxide that are rapidly spreading up the stairway?

Plastic Furnishings

Over the past several decades plastics and related products have invaded and changed our entire way of life. Polyvinyl chloride (PVC), polyurethane, polystyrene, and other synthetics are commonly used, and virtually every phase of construction has been affected. Electrical wiring, insulation, furniture, and a wide range of other products are wholly made of or encased in plastic.

Once ignited, plastics and the other related synthetics tend to burn with much more intensity than do other ordinary combustibles. The by-products of their combustion almost always include toxic gases.

Fire-Detection, -Alarm, and -Suppression Systems

A fire, in its earliest stages, presents a minimal risk to human life and is easily controlled. The earlier in its development a fire can be detected, the better the chances for escape, survival, and suppression with limited extension.

More people are killed in fires in the United States than in any other nation in the world. The overwhelming majority of those who are killed are asleep at the time of the fire. Deaths result from the inhalation of the gaseous products of combustion: carbon monoxide and other toxic gases. Relatively few people die from exposure to flame. Thousands of lives could be saved every year if smoke detectors were installed and properly maintained in the home and workplace.

Fire-Detection Systems

The primary purpose of a fire-detection system is to discover a fire when it is in its earliest phase and respond by activating an alarm. There are two basic classifications of fire detectors: smoke detectors and heat detectors.

Smoke Detectors

Smoke detectors are designed to react to the products of combustion. The environment surrounding the point of origin of a fire contains particles of unburned fuel (carbon), toxic and nontoxic gases, and electrically charged atoms called *ions*. A smoke detector will respond either to the visible products of combustion (smoke) or to the invisible (chemical) changes in the atmosphere. There are two common types of smoke detectors: the ionization type and the photoelectric type.

Ionization Detector. An ionization detector uses a radioactive source (usually americium-241) to transform the air inside it into a conductor of electrical current (Chapman 1977). The radioactive source emits alpha particles, which ionize the air within the detector. A minute electrical current flows through the ionized air, which serves as a sampling chamber. Any visible or invisible products of combustion

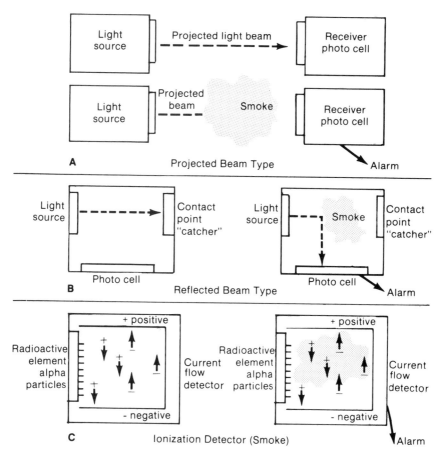

Figure 3.5 Different types of photoelectric smoke detectors: (A) projected beam type; (B) reflected beam type; (C) ionization detector (smoke).

entering this chamber interrupt the current flow, which, in turn, activates the alarm.

Photoelectric Detector. A photoelectric smoke detector may consist of a projected light beam to cover large areas, or a reflected light beam or spot-type detector to cover small areas. In the *projected beam* detector, a beam of light is projected from a light source to a receiving unit equipped with a photoelectric cell, which constantly monitors the intensity of the light beam. Smoke from a fire blocks or diminishes the amount of light striking the photoelectric cell, thereby interrupting the current flow. The *reflected (spot-type) beam* detector is a single unit containing a light source (projected across a narrow chamber), a light "catcher" or contact point, and a photoelectric cell positioned at a right angle to the light source. Smoke entering the chamber obstructs the directed light beam, reflecting light from the light source onto the photoelectric cell, thereby completing the circuit.

An example of a specialized smoke detector is the *air duct detector*. This is designed to mount on or within an air duct system and continuously sample the air moving within the duct pipe to detect both visible smoke particles and invisible by-products of combustion. A duct detector is usually equipped with a specially designed ionization, photoelectric, or other smoke sensor.

Heat Detectors

There are two types of basic heat (thermal) detectors: the rate-of-rise detector and the fixed-temperature detector.

The *rate-of-rise detector* is calibrated so that a rapid increase in room temperature will cause the detector to react and activate. This type of heat detector allows for a gradual or natural increase in room temperature due to the sun's rays, the normal operation of machinery, or the activation of the building's heating plant. It cannot differentiate between these natural increases in temperature and a slow-developing fire. The detector normally is calibrated to allow temperatures within a certain range, but automatically activates when the permitted maximum temperature is surpassed.

The *fixed-temperature detector* is preset to activate at a given temperature. The detection unit may come from the manufacturer with a fixed temperature rating but be equipped with a calibration screw, allowing an installer or contractor to reset the unit to avoid unnecessary or unwanted false alarms.

There are several different types of internal components in standard heat detectors. The two most common heat-sensitive components are:

1. the *thermocouple*, which converts heat energy into a small electrical current; and
2. fusible plastic or bimetallic strips, which react to heat and either open or close a circuit.

A somewhat more unusual form of fixed-temperature heat detector is the *thermal plastic wire*. Such a wire consists of two or four metallic conductors (*actuators*) individually insulated in a special heat-sensitive plastic sheath. The insulated conductors are twisted around each other (braided) and encased in an outer plastic shell. When subjected to high temperatures, the heat-sensitive plastic layer of insulation yields and permits the conductors (which carry a minute monitoring current) to come into contact with each other. The resultant short circuit activates the alarm.

Heat and light energy radiate away from their source (the flame) in the form of electromagnetic waves, and *heat and flame detectors* have been designed to monitor the radiation of these waves. Because it would be impractical for such a system to respond to the *visible light* range of radiation without responding to any illumination source, these sophisticated detectors are equipped with electric cells sensitive to either ultraviolet (UV) or infrared (IR or heat) rays. Their activation causes the alarm to sound.

Water-Flow Detectors

One final type of detector worth mentioning is the *water-flow detector*, which reacts to the flow of water within a sprinkler system. Although generally designed to allow for sudden changes in water pressure within the system, the detector cannot differentiate between water flow due to a system malfunction (a crack or rupture in the piping, breakage due to age, poor maintenance, or improper installation) and that prompted by a fire.

Selecting a Fire Detector

The following criteria are usually considered in the selection of the most appropriate fire detector:

  type of structure and type of occupancy;

  estimated fire load;

  cost, considering budget allocations;

  unique considerations (e.g., high heat sources, alarm delay factors, high hazard storage); and

  local fire code requirements.

Fire Alarm Systems and Components

The size, complexity, and cost of fire alarm installation in any particular building vary with the types of occupancy and the number of zones or subunits to be protected.

All segments of a fire detection/alarm system are connected to a central unit called the *control panel*. The control panel is hard-wired to an AC source with a DC (battery) backup. A modern control panel is almost exclusively divided into a series of computerized modules

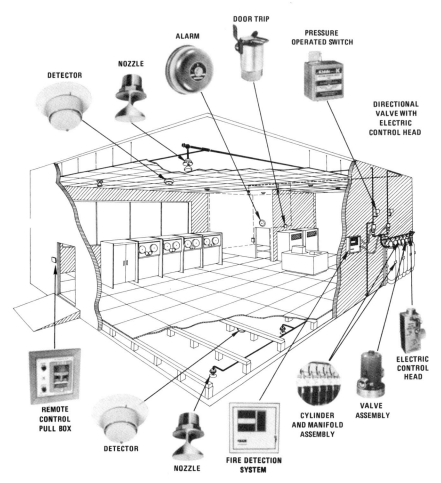

DOOR TRIP

ALARM

PRESSURE
OPERATED SWITCH

NOZZLE

DETECTOR

DIRECTIONAL
VALVE WITH
ELECTRIC
CONTROL HEAD

ELECTRIC
CONTROL
HEAD

VALVE
ASSEMBLY

REMOTE
CONTROL
PULL BOX

CYLINDER
AND MANIFOLD
ASSEMBLY

DETECTOR

NOZZLE

FIRE DETECTION
SYSTEM

Figure 3.6 Electronic data processing and tape storage rooms—Kidde remote local and automatic operated Halon 1301 fire extinguishing system. (Photo courtesy of Walter Kidde, Division of Kidde, Inc., Wake Forest, N.C.)

that are designed to monitor an incredible number of separate unrelated functions including the following:

operation of a wide variety of different smoke, heat, and light detectors and manual stations (*pull boxes*);

activation of alarms, both audible (horn, bell, gong, sirens) and visible (flashing, strobe, and emergency lights);

release of fire suppressants (water, halon, carbon dioxide, dry chemical or high-expansion foam); and

Figure 3.7 World's largest electrically driven Hi-Ex Foam system protects Lockheed Aircraft Company's L-1011 test hangar at Palmdale, California. (Photo courtesy of Walter Kidde, Division of Kidde, Inc., Wake Forest, N.C.)

notification, via a *central station alarm company*, of the local fire and police departments.

The *initiating circuit* connects the individual fire (security) detectors to the central control and annunciator panels. A *receiving element* converts the activation of a fire detector into an electric, pneumatic, or otherwise-generated audible or visible alarm.

Fire-Suppression Systems

Many structures, because of either insurance requirements or local fire codes, are equipped with sprinkler systems. Sprinklers and other such systems are designed to extinguish a fire during the incipient phase by:

direct wetting or cooling,

cooling the ambient atmosphere,

cooling any exposed elements, or

reducing the available oxygen.

An investigator must be able to examine and evaluate whatever fire suppression system might be in place in a fire-damaged structure. The investigator should interview the officers and fire fighters from the "first-in" fire department company or unit to determine the suppression system's operation and effectiveness during the fire.

Sprinkler Systems

There are four common types of sprinkler systems. Many variations of these systems exist.

1. *Wet pipe:* In a wet-pipe system, the supply pipes to the sprinkler heads contain water at all times. Thus the system is always charged. Approximately 75% of all the sprinkler systems in the United States are wet-pipe systems.
2. *Dry pipe:* The dry-pipe system is generally used in areas where excessive cold and the resultant danger of freezing are a problem. In this type of system, the supply pipe contains compressed air and not water. When activated, the sprinkler heads open, the compressed air escapes, and a dry-pipe valve opens to allow water to flow through the system.
3. *Preaction:* This type of system may be used in areas that are subject to extensive water damage. Water is supplied to the system by a valve that operates independently from the sprinkler heads, activated either by human action or, more commonly, by a predesigned automatic fire alarm or detection device.
4. *Deluge:* This type of system is commonly used in areas where immediate cooling is required because of extremely hazardous conditions. The sprinkler heads in the area to be protected (e.g., liquid propane storage) are open at all times. The release of water to those heads is activated by a fire-detection system.

Many variations of these sprinkler systems may be encountered; however, the combination of dry pipe and preaction is not widely used.

Specialized Suppression Systems

Certain types of occupancy require, and local jurisdictions may mandate, the installation of specialized suppression systems. In these cases, ordinary sprinkler systems could prove to be inappropriate in terms of both cost and effectiveness. Some flammable and hazardous materials require the use of specific extinguishing agents. The owner of a multimillion dollar computer operation would certainly cringe at the mere thought of water spraying over so much valuable electronic equipment. Specialized extinguishing systems include:

halogenated extinguishing agents (including Halon 1202, Halon 1211, Halon 1301, and Halon 2402);

high-expansion foam systems;

dry chemical systems (including sodium bicarbonate, potassium bicarbonate, and potassium chloride); and

carbon dioxide systems.

Neutralizing Fire-Protection Systems

Any security or fire-protection (detection, alarm, or suppression) system currently available can be circumvented or defeated. A person or group with the proper multifaceted technical expertise, given the required time, could neutralize even state-of-the-art equipment. It is possible for an arsonist (with the technical expertise) to circumvent the electrical security and fire-protection devices in a modern computer center, empty ("blow") both the primary and backup Halon 1301 cylinders, and start a fire, the investigation of which would defy all but the most experienced investigators. Arson rings with this type of expertise do exist and are active in the field.

Acoustical tile   special tile for walls and ceilings, made of mineral, wood, vegetable fibers, cork, or metal, whose purpose is to control sound volume while providing cover

Air duct   pipe that carries warm/cold air to rooms and back to furnace/air conditioning system

Ampere   unit for measuring the rate of flow of electricity (current)

Apron   paved area such as the junction of a driveway with the street or with a garage entrance

Backfill   gravel or earth replaced in the space around a building wall after foundations are in place

Baluster   upright support of a balustrade rail

Balustrade   row of balusters, topped by a rail, edging a balcony or a staircase

Baseboard   board along the floor against walls and partitions to hide gaps

Batting   insulation in the form of a blanket (as fiberglass) rather than loose filling

Batten   small thin strip covering joints between wider boards on exterior building surfaces

Beam   one of the principal horizontal wood or steel members of a building

Bearing wall   wall that supports a floor or roof of a building

Bibcock   water faucet to which a hose may be attached; also called a *bib*, *hose bib*, or *sill cock*

Bleeding   piece of wood or other material used to form a triangle and stiffen some part of a structure

Braced framing   construction technique using posts and cross bracing for greater rigidity

Brick veneer   brick used as the outer surface of a framed wall

Bridging   small wood or metal pieces placed diagonally between floor joists

Building paper   heavy paper used in walls or roofs to dampproof

Built-up roof   roofing material applied in sealed, waterproof layers where there is only a slight slope to the roof, to increase the pitch

Butt joint   end-to-end joining of two pieces of wood or molding

BX cable   electrical cable wrapped in rubber with a flexible steel outer covering

Cantilever   projecting beam or joist, not supported at one end, used to support an extension of a structure

Carriage   member that supports the steps or treads of a stair

Casement   window sash that opens on hinges at the vertical edge

Casing   door and window framing

Cavity wall   hollow wall formed by firmly linked masonry walls, providing an insulating air space between them

Chair rail   wooden molding on a wall around a room at the level of a chair back

Chamfer   pared-off or angled edge, as on molding; also called a *bevel*

Chase   groove in a masonry wall or through a floor to accommodate pipes or ducts

Chimney breast   horizontal projection (usually inside a building) of a chimney from the wall in which it is built

Chimney cap   concrete capping around the top of chimney bricks and around the chimney at each floor to protect the masonry from the elements

Circuit breaker   safety device that opens (breaks) an electric circuit automatically when it becomes overloaded

Cistern   tank to catch and store rain water

Clapboard   long thin board, thicker on one edge, overlapped and nailed on for exterior siding

Collar beam   horizontal beam fastened above the lower ends of rafters to add rigidity

Coping   tile or brick used to cap or cover the top of a masonry wall, usually with a slope

Corbel   architectural member projecting from within a wall and supporting a weight, as under the overhanging part of a roof

Cove lighting   concealed light sources behind a cornice or horizontal recess that direct the light onto a reflecting ceiling

Crawl space   shallow, unfinished space beneath the first floor of a house that has no basement (or in the attic, immediately under the roof), used for visual inspection and access to pipes and ducts

Cripples   cut-off framing members above and below windows

Door buck   rough frame of a door

Dormer   projecting frame of a recess in a sloping roof

Double glazing   use of an insulating window pane formed of two thicknesses of glass with a sealed air space between them

Double-hung windows   windows with an upper and lower sash, each supported by cords and weights

Downspout   spout or pipe to carry rainwater down from a roof or gutters

Downspout leader   pipe for conducting rainwater from the roof to a cistern or to the ground by way of a downspout

Downspout strap   piece of metal that secures the downspout to the eaves or wall of a building

Drip   projecting part of a cornice that sheds rainwater

Dry wall   wall surface of plasterboard or material other than plaster

Eaves   extension of a roof beyond house walls

Efflorescence   white powder that forms on the surface of brick

Effluent   treated sewage, as from a septic tank

Fascia   flat horizontal member that covers the joint between the top of a wall and the eaves

Fill-type insulation   loose insulation material that is applied by hand or blown into wall spaces mechanically

Flashing   noncorrosive metal used around angles or junctions in roofs and exterior walls to prevent leaks

Floor joists   framing pieces that rest on outer foundation walls and interior beams or girders

Flue   passageway in a chimney for conveying smoke, gases, or fumes to the outside air

Footing   concrete base on which a foundation sits

Foundation   substructure of a building, usually of masonry or concrete and below ground level

Framing   rough lumber of a house—joists, studs, rafters, and beams

Furring   thin wood or metal applied to a wall to level the surfaces for lathing, boarding, or plastering, to create an insulating air space, and to dampproof the wall

Fuse   short plug in an electric panel box that opens (breaks) an electrical circuit when it becomes overloaded

Gable   triangular part of a wall under the inverted V of the roofline

Gambrel roof   roof with two pitches—steeper on its lower slope and flatter toward the ridge—designed to provide more space on upper floors

Girder   main member in a framed floor supporting the joists that carry the flooring boards; it carries the weight of a floor or partition

Glazing   fitting glass into windows or doors

Grade line   line on which the ground rests against the foundation wall

Green lumber   lumber that has been inadequately dried and tends to warp or "bleed" resin

Grounds   pieces of wood embedded in plaster of walls to which skirtings are attached; also wood pieces used to stop the plaster work around doors and windows

Gusset   brace or bracket used to strengthen an angle in framework

Gutter   channel at the eaves for conveying away rainwater

Hardwood   close-grained wood from broad-leaved trees such as oak or maple

Headers   double wood pieces supporting joists in a floor, or double wood members placed on edge over windows and doors to transfer the roof and floor weight to the studs

Heel   end of a rafter that rests on the wall plate

Hip   external angle formed by the juncture of two slopes of a roof

Hip roof   roof that slants upward on three or four sides

Jalousie   window with movable, horizontal glass slats (louvers) angled to admit ventilation and keep out rain; also used for outside shutters of wood constructed in this way

Jamb   upright surface that lines an opening for a door or window

Joist   small rectangular sectional member arranged parallel from wall to wall in a building, or resting on beams or girders, to support a floor on the laths or furring strips of a ceiling

Kiln-dried lumber   lumber that is artificially dried; superior to most lumber that is air-dried

King post   central post of a triangular truss

Lag screws   large, heavy screws, used where great strength is required, as in heavy framing or when attaching ironwork to wood; also called *coach screws*

Lally column   trademark for a cylindrical steel tube filled with concrete and used to support girders or other floor beams

Lath   one of a number of thin narrow strips of wood nailed to rafters, ceiling joists, wall studs, and so on to make a groundwork or key for slates, tiles, or plastering

Leaching bed   tiles in the trenches carrying treated wastes from septic tanks

Ledger   piece of wood attached to a beam to support joists

Lintel   horizontal piece over a door or window that supports walls above the opening

Load-bearing wall   strong wall capable of supporting weight

Louver   opening with horizontal slats to permit passage of air but exclude rain or sun or provide privacy

Masonry   walls built by a mason, using brick, stone, tile, or similar materials

Molding   strip of decorative material having a plane or curved narrow surface prepared for ornamental application; often used to hide gaps at wall junctions

Moisture barrier   treated paper or metal that retards or bars water vapor, used to keep moisture from passing into walls or floors

Mullion   slender vertical framing that divides the panes of windows (or units of screens)

Newel upright posts (or the upright formed by the inner or smaller ends of steps) about which steps of a circular staircase wind; the principal post at the foot or at a landing of a straight staircase

Nosing rounded edge of a stair tread

Parget rough coat of mortar applied over a masonry wall as protection or finish; may also serve as a base for an asphaltic waterproofing compound below grade

Pilaster projection of the foundation wall used to support a floor girder or stiffen the wall

Pitch angle of slope of a roof

Plasterboard gypsum board, used instead of plaster; see *Dry wall*

Plates pieces of wood placed on wall surfaces as fastening devices; the bottom member of the wall is the *sole plate* and the top member is the *rafter plate*

Plenum dead space that is used for running phone lines, as an electrical conduit, and as a distribution area for heating or cooling systems; generally between a false ceiling and the actual ceiling

Pointing treatment of joints in masonry by filling with mortar to improve appearance or protect against weather

Post-and-beam construction wall construction in which beams are supported by heavy posts rather than many smaller studs

Prefabrication construction of components such as walls, trusses, or doors before delivery to the building site

Rabbet groove cut in a board to receive another board

Radiant heating electrical coils or hot water or steam pipes embedded in floors, ceilings, or walls to heat rooms

Rafter one of a series of structural roof members spanning from an exterior wall to a center ridge beam or ridge board

Reinforced concrete concrete strengthened with wire or metal bars

Ridge pole thick longitudinal plank to which the ridge rafters of a roof are attached

Riser upright piece of a stair step, from tread to tread

Roof sheathing sheets, usually of plywood, that are nailed to the top edges of trusses or rafters to tie the roof together and support the roofing material

Sandwich panel panel with plastic, paper, or other material enclosed between two layers of a different material

Sash movable part of a window, the frame in which panes of glass are set in a window or door

Scotia concave molding

Scuttle hole small opening either to the attic, to the crawl space, or to the plumbing pipes

Seepage pit sewage disposal system composed of a septic tank and a connected cesspool

Septic tank   sewage settling tank in which part of the sewage is converted into gas and sludge before the remaining waste is discharged by gravity into an underground leaching bed

Shake   log-split shingle

Sheathing   first covering of boards or material on the outside wall or roof prior to installation of the finished siding or roof covering; see *Wall sheathing*

Shim   thin tapered piece of wood used for leveling or tightening a stair or other building element

Shingle   piece of wood, asbestos, or other material used in an overlapping outer covering on walls or roofs

Shiplap   boards with rabbeted, overlapping edges

Siding   boards of special design nailed horizontally to vertical studs with or without intervening sheathing to form the exposed surface of outside walls of framed buildings

Sill plate   lowest member of the house framing resting on top of the foundation wall; also called the *mud sill*

Skirting   narrow board around the margin of a floor; baseboards

Slab   concrete floor placed directly on earth or a gravel base and usually about four inches thick

Sleeper   wood laid over concrete floor to which the finished wood floor is nailed or glued

Soffit   visible underside of structural members such as staircases, cornices, beams, and eaves

Softwood   easily worked wood; wood from a cone-bearing tree

Soil stack   vertical plumbing pipe for wastewater

Stringer   long, horizontal member that connects uprights in a frame or supports a floor or the like; one of the enclosed sides of a stair supporting the treads and risers

Stud   in wall framing, a vertical member to which horizontal pieces are nailed; studs are spaced either 16 or 24 inches apart

Subfloor   usually, plywood sheets that are nailed directly to the floor joists and that receive the finished flooring

Sump   pit in the basement in which water collects to be pumped out with a sump pump

Swale   wide shallow depression in the ground to form a channel for storm water drainage

Tie   wood member that binds a pair of principal rafters at the bottom

Tile field   open-joint drain tiles laid to distribute septic tank effluent over an absorption area or to provide subsoil drainage in wet areas

Toenail   drive nails at an angle into corners or other joints

Tongue-and-groove   carpentry joint in which the jutting edge of one board fits into the grooved end of a similar board

Trap   bend in a water pipe to hold water so gases will not escape from the plumbing system into the house

Tread   horizontal part of a stair step

Truss   combination of structural members usually arranged in triangular units to form a rigid framework for spanning between load-bearing walls

Valley   depression at the meeting point of two roof slopes

Vapor barrier   material such as paper, metal, or paint used to prevent vapor from passing from rooms into the outside walls

Venetian window   window with one large fixed central pane and smaller panes at each side

Vent pipe   pipe that allows gas to escape from plumbing systems

Verge   edge of tiles, slates, or shingles projecting over the gable of a roof

Wainscoting   lower three or four feet of an interior wall when lined with paneling, tile, or other material different from the rest of the wall

Wall sheathing   sheets of plywood, gypsum board, or other material nailed to the outside face of studs as a base for exterior siding

Weather stripping   metal, wood, plastic, or other material installed around door and window openings to prevent air infiltration

Weep hole   small hole in a wall that permits water to drain off

References and Selected Readings

Brannigan, Francis L., *Building Construction for the Fire Service*, National Fire Protection Association, Boston, Mass., 1971.

Brannigan, Francis L., et al., *Fire Investigation Handbook*, National Book Store Handbook No. 134, U.S. Government Printing Office, 1980.

Carroll, John R., *Physical and Technical Aspects of Fire/Arson Investigations*, Charles C. Thomas Publishing, Springfield, Illinois, 1979.

Chapman, E., "Smoke Detectors for the Home," *WNYF* (*With New York Firefighters*), Issue 3, New York City Fire Department, 1977.

French, Harvey M., *The Anatomy of Arson*, Arco Publishing, New York, 1979.

Huron, Benjamin S., *Elements of Arson Investigation*, Reuben H. Donnelley Corp., New York, 1963.

Kirk, Paul L., *Fire Investigation*, John Wiley and Sons, New York, 1969.

McKinnon, Gordon P., *Fire Protection Handbook* (14th ed.), National Fire Protection Association, Boston, Mass., 1979.

Underdown, George W., *Practical Fire Precaution* (2nd ed.), Bower Press, Westmeal, Farmborough, Hants., England, 1979.

Chemistry and Behavior of Fire

4

The phenomenon of fire has fascinated humanity since the beginning of time. Our ancestors deified it; we still respect it. Its value as a weapon of war and as a tool of devastation has long been recognized.

Fire is a series of chemical reactions. It is often defined as the visible, active phase of combustion. *Combustion* is a chemical process accompanied by the evolution of heat and light. More accurately, it is the rapid oxidation of a fuel so as to produce flame (burning gases), heat, and light. The most common form of combustion, and that to which we address our attention, is due to *oxidation*. This occurs when an atom, the fundamental particle of an element, combines (i.e., forms a chemical bond) with an atom of oxygen. Though there are other types of combustion supported by other gases, such as nitrous oxide (laughing gas), the overwhelming majority of fires are oxygen-related.

Components of Fire

Traditionally, fire has been portrayed as having three components: heat, oxygen, and fuel. This triad was illustrated by the *fire triangle*, which symbolized, in the most basic terms, a chemical relationship that would have required hours to explain. We now realize, however, that the fire triangle falls short of integrating all the components involved in producing flaming combustion. Today, the fire triangle is technically used to explain *glowing combustion*, which occurs when a fuel mass glows without flaming. This is referred to as a *solid-to-gas* reaction (fuel being a solid, and the oxidizing agent a gas).

The additional component needed to explain flaming combustion is a *chemical chain reaction*. Such a reaction yields energy or products

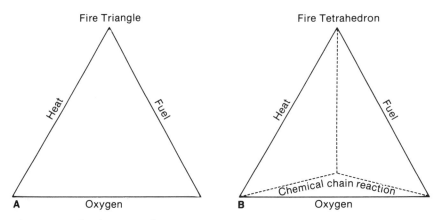

Figure 4.1 The fire triangle.

that cause further reactions of the same kind, and this is self-sustaining. To show the interrelation of all four components, a more sophisticated geometric figure than a triangle is needed; the three-dimensional, four-faceted tetrahedron is the most appropriate and commonly used.

In *flaming combustion*, fuel and the oxidizing agent are both in the gaseous state; hence this is referred to as a *gas-to-gas reaction*.

Heat

A fire/arson investigator must be able to understand and recognize how heat is produced and transferred and how it applies to the fire's ignition and development. *Heat* is the energy possessed by a material or substance due to molecular activity. Heat should not be confused with *temperature*, which is the measurement of the relative amount of heat energy contained within a given substance. Temperature is an *intensity* measurement, with units in *degrees* on either the Celsius (centigrade), Fahrenheit, or Kelvin scale. *Heat* is a measurement of *quantity* and is given in British thermal units (Btu). One Btu is the amount of heat required to raise one pound of water one degree Fahrenheit (1°F):

1 Btu heats 1 lb of water 1°F,

1 gallon of water weighs 8.33 lb,

8.33 Btu heat 1 gallon of water 1°F, and

833 Btu heat 1 gallon water 100°F.

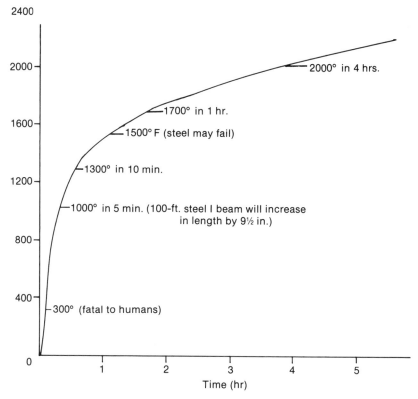

Figure 4.2 Standard time–temperature curve.

Heat Production

There are five ways to produce heat:

1. *Chemical.* As we have already seen, chemically produced heat is the result of rapid oxidation. The speed of the oxidative reaction is an important factor; rust is also the product of oxidation, but of very slow oxidation.

2. *Mechanical.* Mechanical heat is the product of friction. Our ancestors would rub sticks together to generate enough heat to start a fire. Internal metal components of machinery can overheat, due to lubricant breakdown or to ball-bearing failure, and cause ignition of available combustibles.

3. *Electrical.* Electrical heat is the product of arcing, shorting, or other electrical malfunction. Poor wire connections, too much resistance, a loose ground, and too much current flowing through an improperly gauged wire are other sources of electrical heat.

4. *Compressed gas.* When a gas is compressed, its molecular activity is greatly increased. Consider the operation of a diesel engine. The gaseous fuel is compressed within the cylinder, increasing its molecular activity. The heat generated by this activity eventually reaches the ignition temperature of the fuel itself. The resulting contained explosion forces the piston back to the bottom edge of the cylinder, and the process repeats over and over again. The drive train converts the energy produced into a mechanical action that causes the vehicle to move.

5. *Nuclear.* Nuclear energy is the product of the carefully controlled splitting or fusing of atomic particles (fission or fusion, respectively). The tremendous heat energy that results is used to produce steam to turn steam turbines.

When more heat is produced than is lost (transferred), there is a *positive heat balance.* When more heat is lost than is produced, there is a *negative heat balance.*

Heat Transfer

There are only three ways to transfer heat: conduction, convection, and radiation.

Conduction.   This refers to the transfer of heat via molecular activity within a material or medium, usually a solid. If you touch a hot stove, the pain you feel is a direct result of conducted heat passing from the stove directly to the hand that is in contact with it. Direct contact is the underlying factor in heat transferred through conduction.

The amount of heat that any item may conduct is a function of that particular item's *thermal conductivity*, represented as K. The K value of copper is 0.92, wood is 0.0005, and aluminum is 0.50. The thermal conductivity of any substance relates directly to its ability to conduct electricity as well as heat. The formula for determining the amount of heat that is passing through an object or material is:

$$H = K \frac{A(t^2 - t^1)}{L} T,$$

where

H is the amount of heat flowing through the object (in Btu);

L is the length of the body (in feet);

T is the time interval of the flow (in hours);

K is the thermal conductivity;

t^2 is the measured temperature (in °F) at the hot end of the object;

t^1 is the measured temperature (in °F) at the cold end of the object; and

A is the cross-sectional area of the object tested (in square feet).

In a structural fire, superheated pipes, steel girders, and other structural members such as walls and floors may conduct sufficient heat to initiate fires in other areas of the structure.

Convection. Heat transfer by convection is chiefly responsible for the spread of fire in structures. Convection entails the transfer of heat via a circulating medium, usually air or a liquid. The superheated gases that evolve from a fire are lighter than air and consequently rise. As they travel through and collect in the upper reaches of the structure, they can and do initiate additional damage. In large fires or *BLEVES* (Boiling Liquid Evaporation Explosions), the high fireball that accompanies the incident is referred to as a *fire storm* and is an example of convected heat.

Radiation. Radiated heat moves in waves and rays much like sunlight or x-rays. Radiated heat (energy) travels at the same speed as does visible light: 186,000 miles per second. It is primarily responsible for the exposure hazards that develop and exist during a fire. The heat waves travel in a direct or straight line from their source until they strike an object. The heat that collects on the surface of the object or building in the path of the heat waves is subsequently absorbed (into its mass) through conduction.

Oxygen and Oxidation

For combustion (specifically oxidation) to occur, a combustible fuel and an oxidizing agent (oxygen) must come together. The air we breathe is 21% oxygen. If the oxygen level drops below 15%, a fire may be extinguished in time or literally smothered due to a lack of oxygen. This is an example of an *oxygen-regulated* fire. Conversely, a fire that develops in an oxygen-rich environment would evolve and burn at a rate that accelerates directly in relation to the oxygen supply. This type of fire is considered to be a *fuel-regulated* fire.

Certain unusual fuels, due to their chemical composition, do not adhere to this basic rule. For example, pyroxylin plastics (e.g., cellulose nitrate, which is used in lacquer coatings and adhesives) contain enough oxygen in their chemical composition to maintain decomposition (smoldering) or even partial combustion in the absence of ad-

Figure 4.3 The owner of this building made the mistake of storing mattresses too close to a gas hot-water heater in the basement. Radiated heat from the unprotected burner entrance was absorbed by the mattresses, which eventually ignited.

ditional oxygen in the air. Other such exceptions include sodium nitrate and potassium chlorate.

Let us examine a very basic oxidation reaction. Hydrogen (H) and oxygen (O) are two basic atoms. In their natural state, they are diatomic; that is, they exist in molecules composed of two atoms, H_2 and O_2, respectively. When we oxidize hydrogen by combining it with oxygen, we form two molecules of water (H_2O) and heat. The following chemical equation describes the reaction:

$$2H_2 + O_2 = 2H_2O + \text{heat.}$$

This equation illustrates a very basic *exothermic* (heat-producing) reaction. An *endothermic* reaction, conversely, is one that requires or absorbs heat.

If we oxidize an atom of carbon (C), another common element, but one that is *monatomic* (occurs in one-atom molecules), we find that carbon dioxide (CO_2) and heat are produced. This reaction is shown in the following chemical equation:

$$C + O_2 = CO_2 + \text{heat.}$$

However, if we restrict the supply of oxygen or double the available carbon, we find that carbon monoxide rather than carbon dioxide is produced:

$$2C + O_2 = 2CO + heat.$$

This third equation is an important one. The production of carbon monoxide is very common at most fire scenes. Carbon monoxide asphyxiation is the primary cause of death in fatal fires. Carbon monoxide is also a fuel with an ignition temperature of 1128°F, and is believed to be the likely cause of most *backdrafts* or smoke explosions.

Fuel and Its Physical States

Fuel is matter, and matter exists in the three physical states: gas, liquid, and solid. Solids melt to become liquids, and these may vaporize to become gases. The state of a substance is, therefore, an accepted characteristic of that substance unless the conditions of temperature and pressure are specified. Ordinary conditions are a temperature of 65°–70°F and a pressure of 14.7 pounds per square inch.

The basic rule, unusual conditions and circumstances notwithstanding, is that at sufficiently high temperatures all fuels can be converted to gases. Gasoline as a liquid does not burn; it is the vapors rising from the liquid fuel that burn. Likewise, wood, the most common solid fuel, is not flammable, but gives off flammable resin vapors. Although these burn, the structure of the wood itself decomposes, yielding other flammable vapors.

Each of the physical states exhibits different physical and chemical properties that directly affect a fuel's combustibility.

Gas

Gaseous fuels are those in which molecules are in rapid movement and random motion. They have no definite shape or volume and assume the shape and volume of their container. Other properties include: compressibility, expandability, permeability, and diffusion.

Compressibility and expandability refer to the potential for changes in volume. A gas will spread and eventually equalize its distribution (pressure) throughout a fixed room or container. Its volume is directly related to two other factors, pressure and temperature. The nature of this interrelation is as follows:

$$PV = KT,$$

where P is pressure, V is volume, T is temperature, and K is a proportionality constant.

An increase (decrease) in the *temperature* will cause a proportional increase (decrease) in the volume if the pressure is constant, or in the pressure if the volume is constant.

An increase (decrease) in the *pressure* will cause a proportional decrease (increase) in the volume if the temperature is constant, or increase (decrease) in the temperature if the volume is constant.

An increase (decrease) in *temperature* will proportionally increase (decrease) the pressure if the volume is fixed, or the volume if the pressure is constant.

Diffusion is the uniform distribution, seemingly in contradiction to the laws of gravity, of molecules of one substance through those of another. The rate at which a gas diffuses is inversely proportional to the square root of its density (Graham's Law). *Permeability* means simply that other substances may pass through or permeate a gas.

How well a gas diffuses in air depends on its *vapor density* or density relative to air. The nearer this is to the vapor density of air (which has a value of 1.0), the greater the ability of the gas to mix with air. The vapor densities of several gas fuels are as follows:

methane = 0.6 (lighter than air),

ethane = 1.0 (same as air), and

propane = 2.5 (heavier than air).

When a gas fuel (or vapor from a liquid fuel) diffuses sufficiently into air, the mixture may ignite or explode. The percentage of gas-to-air at which this occurs is the lower limit of that gas's *flammable (explosive) range*. The upper limit is the percentage at which the mixture is too concentrated to ignite (that is, there is too little oxygen; for natural gas, this range is 5%–15%).

Liquid

Liquids, like gases, assume the shape of their containers and may diffuse. Unlike gases, they have a definite volume (though they may be compressed slightly).

Liquids exhibit a free surface and, if left to stand uncovered, will evaporate. *Evaporation* occurs when individual molecules of the liquid escape as gas into the surrounding atmosphere. Any increase in temperature will cause an increase in the rate of evaporation and, consequently, an increase in the vapor pressure. The temperature at which a liquid turns into a gas by producing continuous vapor bubbles is called its *boiling point*. At this temperature, the vapor pressure is equal to normal atmospheric pressure (14.7 pounds per square inch).

Because a liquid's boiling point evinces its readiness to vaporize, it is one measure of the volatility of a liquid fuel. A low boiling point means high volatility and an increased risk of fire. Other indicators include flash point and fire point.

Flash Point. Temperature at which a liquid gives off sufficient vapor (gas) to form an ignitable mixture (that is, a mixture within the explosive range) (see section on Gas). For gasoline, this is $-50°F$; for kerosene, $100°F$.

Fire Point. Temperature at which a liquid produces vapors that will *sustain* combustion. This is several degrees higher than the flash point. For example, the fire point of gasoline is $495°F$; for kerosene, $110°F$.

The National Fire Protection Association (NFPA) define a *flammable liquid* as one whose flash point is below $140°F$. A liquid with a flash point of $140°F$ or higher is a *combustible liquid*. (The temperature used to distinguish flammable from combustible liquids is defined as $100°F$ by the National Fire Academy and as $80°F$ by the U.S. Department of Transportation.)

Solid

Solids have a definite shape and volume. A solid fuel's combustibility is directly affected by the size and configuration of its mass. Finely divided, powdered fuels differ from bulky or large-dimension solid fuels with respect to combustibility because of the obvious difference in their masses; the larger the mass of the solid fuel, the greater the potential loss due to conduction. Imagine a lit match placed against the side of a section of telephone pole. The match burns out long before there is any sign of ignition on the pole because:

1. some of the heat generated by the match is being lost to its surroundings through convection and radiation; and
2. the surface temperature, at the point of contact, is dissipated due to the transfer of heat by conduction evenly throughout the mass of the pole.

The temperature at which a solid turns into a liquid is called its *melting point*.

A solid (other than an explosive) that is likely to ignite due to friction is called a *flammable solid*.

Pyrolyzable and Nonpyrolyzable Solids

Pyrolysis is the chemical decomposition of matter through the action of heat. This decomposition may take place in the absence of oxygen, and the vapors released may include both combustible and noncombustible gases.

Pyrolyzable solid fuels include many of the ordinarily accepted solid combustibles: wood, paper, and so on. The vapors released via their chemical decomposition support flaming combustion. This exemplifies a gas-to-gas reaction: the vapors released mix with oxygen in the air to produce a flame.

Nonpyrolyzable solid fuels are difficult to ignite. A common example is charcoal. The liquid charcoal lighter that people commonly use to start their barbecue is necessary to raise the temperature sufficiently so that the surface fuel will interact directly with the oxygen in the air. Chemical decomposition does not occur because there are no pyrolyzable elements present. No vapors are released. The glowing combustion that results is an example of a gas-to-solid reaction.

Pyrolysis of Wood

Wood, the most commonly encountered fuel, is composed of many tubular fiber units, or *cells*, cemented together. The walls of these cells are made of *cellulose*. The chemical decomposition of cellulose in the presence of open flame is represented by the following formula:

$$C_6H_{10}O_5 + 6O_2 = 5H_2O + 6CO_2 + heat.$$

This equation represents an ideal oxidation reaction. In reality, however, the burning of a wood frame structure would most likely be fuel-regulated; that is, the rate of burning and the amount of readily available wood fuel would exceed the available air supply. This condition would lead to the evolution of huge amounts of carbon monoxide.

The first portion of the equation represents an endothermic (heat-absorbing) reaction. This changes to exothermic (heat-producing) as the chemical action (fire) becomes self-sustaining.

Number 2 common lumber, which is the most common building material used in ordinary construction, has an ignition temperature of approximately 660°F. It will ordinarily burn at the rate of 1 inch in 45 minutes at 1400°F. However, when exposed to a temperature of 250°F for an extended period of time (e.g., due to the improper installation of a wood or coal stove), a condition known as *pyrophoric carbon* (carbonized wood) occurs. The continuous baking of the wood causes pyrolysis, resulting in the carbonization of the lumber. At first, the surface of the wood darkens and then begins to char; eventually the carbonized portion becomes deeper and deeper. Carbonized wood is ordinarily rich in oxygen and ignites at the same temperature at which it forms.

Hydrocarbons

Hydrocarbons are chemical compounds that contain only carbon and hydrogen. They include gases (e.g., methane), liquids (e.g., benzene), and solids (e.g., naphthalene). As fuels, they tend to burn much hotter than other compounds. Organic compounds containing carbon, hydrogen, and oxygen are called *carbohydrates*. Hydrocarbons are either saturated or unsaturated.

In a *saturated hydrocarbon*, all of the available carbon atoms contain the maximum number of hydrogen atoms. Saturated hydrocarbons do not have a tendency for spontaneous combustion. Examples include:

$$
\text{methane} \quad CH_4 \qquad
\begin{array}{c}
H \\
| \\
H\!-\!C\!-\!H \\
| \\
H
\end{array}
$$

$$
\text{butane} \quad C_4H_{10} \qquad
\begin{array}{c}
H \quad H \quad H \quad H \\
| \quad\ | \quad\ | \quad\ | \\
H\!-\!C\!-\!C\!-\!C\!-\!C\!-\!H \\
| \quad\ | \quad\ | \quad\ | \\
H \quad H \quad H \quad H
\end{array}
$$

In an *unsaturated hydrocarbon*, not all of the available carbon atoms contain the maximum number of hydrogen atoms; some are bonded to other carbon atoms. Such a compound can accommodate additional hydrogen atoms by breaking those carbon-carbon bonds. Therefore, unsaturated hydrocarbons have a tendency for spontaneous combustion. Examples include:

benzene C_6H_6

$$
\text{acetylene} \quad C_2H_2 \qquad H\!-\!C\!\equiv\!C\!-\!H
$$

Hydrocarbons having an open-chain structure, such as methane, butane, and acetylene, are called *aliphatic*. Those containing at least one benzene-like ring, such as benzene itself or naphthalene, are called *aromatic*.

Petroleum fractions are the usable by-products created from the re-fining of crude oil. These include gasoline, kerosene, and naphthalene. All of the products of fractional distillation are hydrocarbons. As a group, they probably represent the most commonly used accelerants. They will not ignite spontaneously.

Chemical Chain Reaction

As mentioned earlier, until recently it seemed clear that: combustion = oxidizing agent (O_2) + combustible material (fuel) + ignition source (heat). In the past decade, however, it became evident that some unknown factor played a direct role in the combustion process. For years, experts in the field were at a loss in trying to explain the reason that dry chemical (powder) extinguishers were so effective in the suppression of fire. We have come to realize that such extinguishers, as well as those that use chlorinated hydrocarbon gases (Halon) or several other extinguishing agents, suppress fire, either by interfering with the transfer of energy or by combining with radicals generated by the combustion process. In so doing, they prevent the *chemical chain reaction* necessary to produce self-sustaining combustion. This chain reaction is a complex series of events that must be continuously and precisely reproduced in order to maintain self-sustained flaming combustion. Among the events required are these two:

1. The oxidation reaction produces sufficient heat to maintain continued oxidation.
2. The fuel mass must be broken down into simpler compounds and liberated (vaporized) from the mass itself; in turn, these unburned vapors must combine with available oxygen and be continuously drawn up into the flame.

Other Terms Relating to the Chemistry of Fire

Heat of combustion: The amount of heat that a fuel will release during a complete oxidation reaction. It is measured in Btu per pound of fuel. The heat output may vary depending on the specific composition of the fuel. Examples are shown below:

Type of Fuel	Btu Released
Paper, wood	6000–7000
Coal	12,000–13,000
Common liquid accelerants	16,000–21,000
Flammable gases	20,000–22,000

Ignition temperature: Temperature at which a flammable material will ignite, whether it be a gas, liquid, or solid; for example:

gas	acetylene	571°F
liquid	turpentine	488°F
solid	magnesium	1200°F

Note that due to the variation in the grades and octane of gasoline, its ignition temperature may vary from 495°F to 850°F. Two important kinds of ignition temperature are the following:

Autoignition temperature: Temperature to which a material must be heated in order for it to burst into flame, free of an ignition source such as a spark or match.

Autogenous ignition temperature: The lowest temperature at which an oxidation reaction can self-sustain itself to either flaming or glowing ignition; that is, the point at which the reaction changes from endothermic to exothermic.

Q^{10} *value.* Value assigned to the rate of chemical reaction (e.g., fire), which doubles with every 10°C or 18°F increase in the temperature.

Specific gravity. The weight of a substance compared with an equal volume of water (thus, water = 1.0). Most flammable liquids have a specific gravity less than that of water. Gasoline's specific gravity is 0.70 so it will float on water. That of carbon disulfide is 1.3, so it will sink in water. (Compare vapor density for gases.)

Spontaneous ignition. This occurs if the inherent characteristics of the materials involved cause an exothermic (heat-producing) chemical reaction to proceed without any exposure to external sources of spark or abnormal heat. For example, a rug soaked in linseed oil, if tightly packed and insulated, may ignite spontaneously. A substance that ignites spontaneously in air at normal temperatures (65°–70°F) is called *pyrophoric.*

Behavior of Fire

The way that a fire develops is affected by many factors. At first, it is most affected by the initial fuel supply; obviously sufficient oxygen is readily available in the surrounding air. Fire evolves and spreads to other combustibles following a natural path of least resistance. It extends up and away from its point of origin, leaving behind distinctive patterns common to all fires. The color of the smoke and flame produced by a fire is also distinctive and depends on the type of fuel and the temperature at which it is burning.

As a fire continues to grow, environmental factors become increasingly important in influencing its ultimate extent. Of particular importance is the amount of oxygen present to sustain combustion in the immediate fire area. Other such factors include fuel supply and composition, structural design and construction (see Chapter 3), and fire suppression.

Eventually, unable to sustain any one of the four components necessary for its continued existence, a fire is extinguished.

Classification of Fire

Fires may be classified according to the type of material (fuel) that is burning. There are four classifications of fire by fuel:

A. ordinary combustibles or materials that produce an ash or glowing embers or coals (e.g., wood, paper, cloth, rubber),

B. flammable or combustible liquids (e.g., gasoline, kerosene, alcohol, fuel oil),

C. energized electrical equipment (*note:* class C fires revert to class A or B when the equipment is no longer energized), and

D. combustible metals, (e.g., magnesium, titanium).

Structural fires are generally classified by extent of damage:

those that are extinguished quickly and cause little damage,

those that, although extinguished, cause extensive damage to a limited area of the building, and

those that cause almost complete or total structural destruction.

Phases of Fire

As a fire progresses, it normally passes through four phases: incipient, emergent smoldering, free burning, and oxygen-regulated smoldering. Many factors can directly or indirectly alter the rate and intensity of a fire's evolution.

No two fires are exactly the same. They vary in many ways from incident to incident.

Incipient

This earliest phase of fire may or may not occur unnoticed. The degree to which this event is observable depends almost entirely upon the magnitude and source of ignition and the type of fuel involved. This phase may last anywhere from a fraction of a second to several hours or days, again depending upon fuel and ignition source. The incipient phase for a liquid accelerant in the presence of an open flame is obviously much shorter than that of a prolonged exothermic reaction, such as in spontaneous combustion.

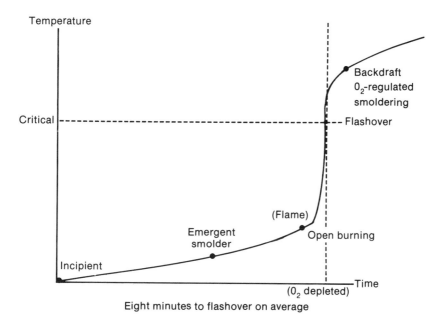

Figure 4.4 Phases of fire.

The products of combustion in this phase may be so minuscule as to be detected only by an ionization detector. The minute changes in atmospheric chemistry in the room or area of the fire's origin may arise without human detection. Some heat energy will be generated, but the temperature of the room or its surroundings will not be affected.

Emergent Smoldering

During this phase, the products of combustion become increasingly more pronounced. There is no meaningful change in the oxygen content of the air. Water vapor, carbon dioxide, carbon monoxide, and other gases, including minute traces of unburnt fuel, may rapidly reach the level of olfactory detection. The open flames that may occur in the later stages of this phase may approach a temperature of 1000°F. The room and surrounding temperature may be only slightly increased.

It should be noted that some fires, such as a smoldering mattress fire, may pass directly from this second phase to oxygen-regulated smoldering (phase 4). The smoldering mattress may reduce the oxygen level in the room of origin sufficiently to cause self-extinguishment, leaving everything in the room covered with a thick blanket of soot, with no open flame (free-burning phase 3) ever being produced (Fire/Arson Training Committee, 1981).

Figure 4.5 The photograph illustrates a condition called "baked effect." There is a demarcation line visible between affected and unaffected areas. Wood and painted surfaces appear baked and covered with heavy soot deposits, and there is a graduation in the depth of charring. (Photo courtesy D. Redsicker.)

Free Burning

During this phase of the fire, the rate and intensity of open burning increases geometrically. The intensity of the fire doubles with each 18°F (10°C) increase in temperature (see Q^{10}). Heat, rapidly evolving from the original point of the fire, is convected and collects in the uppermost areas of the structure or room. Additional heat is transferred through the action of conduction and radiation. The convected (superheated) gases themselves become a source of radiated heat, radiating heat energy downward onto all the available surface areas directly below them. This heat is absorbed by conduction into the mass of those items whose surfaces are struck, causing surface pyrolysis (*baked effect*). When the temperature reaches the ignition temperature of these items, a *flashover* occurs; flames instantly "flashover" the entire area. The average fire reaches flashover in eight minutes.

One condition that signals the imminent threat of a flashover is that referred to as "fairies flying." This occurs when small pockets of flammable gases ignite, and may be spotted by fire fighters within the fire building.

The lack of normal fire spread due to a flashover can exacerbate the search for the point of origin. In fact, the scene may appear as if an accelerant were used, so careful analysis is necessary.

Oxygen-Regulated Smoldering

If the room or area of the fire's origin is adequately airtight, thereby limiting the amount of oxygen-rich air being drawn into that area, then the open burning that occurs in free-burning phase 3 will deplete the available oxygen. The gradual cessation of oxygen supply causes flaming combustion to end, replacing it to a large extent by glowing combustion. The room becomes completely filled with dense smoke and gases, which are forced from all cracks under pressure. The fire continues to smolder and the room to fill with smoke and gases at a temperature of well over 1000°F. Such intense heat evaporates the lighter fuel fractions, such as hydrogen and methane, from the combustible material in the room. The resultant superheated mixture of gases needs only a fresh supply of oxygen to resume free burning at an explosive rate (Fire/Arson Training Committee, 1981). This type of explosive burning is referred to as a *backdraft* or *smoke explosion*. A backdraft may result if someone opens a "hot door." This is why fire fighters are trained to touch a door with their bare hands and feel its temperature before opening it. Venting, the controlled removal of smoke, heat, and gases from a building, may also produce a backdraft by displacing venting combustion products with oxygen-rich air.

One of the superheated gases produced by fire is carbon monoxide. As mentioned in the section on Oxygen and Oxidation, carbon monoxide results from the oxidation of carbon in an oxygen-depleted atmosphere. This odorless, colorless gas collects and mixes with air (oxygen) to within its explosive or flammable limits: 12.5%–74% of the atmosphere by volume. Carbon monoxide is highly flammable and has an ignition temperature of 1128°F. When ignition occurs, the entire cloud of smoke within the area or room literally explodes or bursts into flames. The unburnt particles of fuel, which color the smoke, also burn at the same time.

Rate of Burn

Oxygen plays a key role in regulating the rate at which most materials burn. With an unlimited oxygen supply, the rate of burn increases, more heat is produced, and the fuel is consumed more completely.

The area of origin of a slow-burning, smoldering fire generally will show:

uniform ceiling and wall damage, down to a line three or more feet below the ceiling;

a baked appearance on painted or wooden surfaces and a graduation in the depth of charring; and

smoke stains around windows, doors and eaves and on window glass.

Figure 4.6

The area of origin of a fast-burning, intense fire will generally show:

severe overhead damage;

definite burn patterns on walls;

severe charring on exposed wood surfaces;

distinct line between charred and uncharred areas of boards near the point of origin; and

sharp line between burned and unburned areas around windows and doors, and crazed (finely cracked) window glass, broken in irregular rectangular pieces (see Glass in Chapter 5).

Structural Fire Spread

Fire spread involves the extension of fire from one point to another. Naturally, the transfer of heat plays a large role in this extension. As we have already seen, superheated girders, pipes, and even walls and floors may initiate fires in other areas of a structure by *conduction*. In addition, superheated gases spread structural fires by both upward *convection* (the predominant means of transfer) and downward *radiation* (as in the case of a flashover; see section on Free Burning). However, heat transfer is not the only force at work in the spread of fire. *Air movement* (wind, drafts, venting) can encourage convection to new fuel areas, and can deliver additional oxygen to sustain old fires and

A

B

Figure 4.7 (A) The heavy rolling char (alligatoring on the staircase) and the clean soot-free (white) spot on the walls adjacent to the stairs identified this area as one of five separate points of origin in this major commercial fire. Gasoline had been poured on the concrete floor and ignited. The rolling blisters were caused by the rapid intense movement (extension) of heat and flame. The wall surface was so hot that soot was unable to adhere. (B) An investigator holds one of the surviving heavily (deeply) charred stairs from the staircase.

promote new ones. Internal structural collapse may also contribute to spread, as when burning material falls through to lower floors, starting fires there.

Direction and Rate of Spread

Flame and superheated gases are lighter than air and, therefore, rise. In doing so, they preheat any fuel or combustible material located above the point of origin. Once heated sufficiently, this ignites, greatly increasing the volume and upward progression of flame and heated gases. Thus, upward burning occurs at a very rapid rate; estimated at some 96 ft/sec (approximately 65.5 mph) (A. Dresner, personal communication).

Downward or lateral (sideways) burning, on the other hand, moves slowly and occurs when:

the fuel source above the point of origin is depleted;

an unusual draft condition forces the fire to progress in this unnatural direction; or

a highly flammable fuel (perhaps an accelerant) is present and runs

Figure 4.8 (A) Indication of a rapidly burning fire: a sharp line of demarcation separates the charred and unburned areas of the wood. (B) Indication of a slow-burning fire: a gradual change from charred area of wood to unburned wood. (Sketch prepared by D. Redsicker, New York State Fire Academy.)

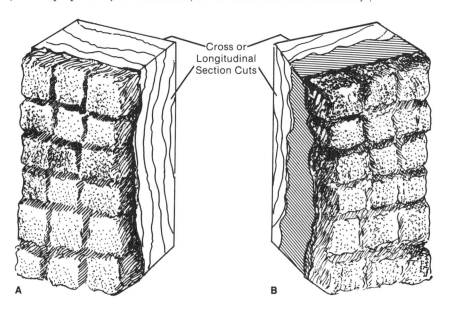

Cross or
Longitudinal
Section Cuts

A   B

below the point of ignition and, when ignited, carries the fire downward.

Chimney Effect

Since there is a natural tendency for flame and heated gases to rise, any structural element that enhances this upward movement serves as a natural chimney. Such an enhancement is called the "chimney effect" (see Building Components in Chapter 3). Because they intensify the fire's upward movement, these areas are often deeply charred and exhibit flame and burn damage many times in excess of that at the point of origin.

In one case, for example, a young man spilled gasoline on the front door to his apartment as the result of a domestic quarrel (his wife had locked him out). Although the original point of ignition was small, the fire quickly extended to a nearby staircase. The staircase acted as a natural chimney and the fire took off. The staircase and the top two floors of the five-story walkup were almost totally destroyed. The damage at the point of origin was minor in comparison.

Types of configuration that act as a chimney during a fire include

Figure 4.9 The spiral staircase enhanced the upward movement of flame and heated gases. The opening for the staircase served as a natural chimney. This condition is called the "chimney effect."

staircases and stairwells, elevator shafts, laundry chutes, dumbwaiters, concealed spaces within walls, and any other unprotected vertical openings (including those created by internal collapse).

The rapid movement and vigorous burning that occur when a fire extends into a cockloft or other concealed ceiling space is akin to the chimney effect. Cocklofts and similar structures should be seen as horizontal chimneys (see Building Components in Chapter 3).

Burn Patterns

As flame and superheated gases pass upward through a structure, they leave behind distinctive patterns. The most common pattern associated with this upward movement is the "V" pattern, the apex (pointed end) of the V representing the point of ignition. The formation of the V pattern is a natural phenomenon. As the flame and heated gases rise, they typically spread laterally as the atmosphere in the room or confined space attempts to equalize the temperature and pressure. This pattern is most evident when the point of ignition is located against a wall or other partition. When the point of ignition is located at the center of a room, away from a wall, a circular burn pattern results directly above, on the ceiling.

The breadth or width of the V (also called the *funnel pattern*) is affected by (and, hence, indicative of) the buildup, progression, speed, and intensity of the fire. An intense, rapidly moving fire produces a narrow V pattern, whereas a slow, less intense fire produces a wide V pattern.

Rapid Movement-Slow Movement

The upward movement of flame and gases can be affected and altered by many factors. Among the most common are the following:

a draft or crosswind from an open window, door, or skylight;

an available, secondary fuel source in close proximity to the original point of ignition;

a highly combustible fuel at the point of origin (e.g., large pool of liquid accelerant, when ignited, causes the apex of V to be at least as wide as the pool); and

environmental considerations, such as class and type of construction, and other conditions that might impede or block the upward progression of the products of combustion.

Table 4.1 Smoke and Flame Colors for Certain Fuels

Smoke color	Flame color	Fuel
Gray to brown	Red to yellow	Wood/paper/cloth
Black	Red to white	Gasoline
White to gray	Yellow to white	Benzine
Black to brown	Yellow to white	Turpentine
Black	Dark red to orange-yellow	Kerosene
Black	Blue white to white	Naphtha

Note: Overall the lighter the color of the flame, the higher the temperature. The significance of the color of smoke and flames in a fire should be considered with the time at which they were observed.

Smoke and Flame Color

The color of smoke and flame associated with a particular fire can indicate the type of combustible material or fuel that is burning (Table 4.1). The color of the flames can also indicate the approximate temperature of the fire (Table 4.2). The colors observed in the early stages of a fire could be indicative of burning accelerants. However, in the later stages of a fire, little significance can be assigned to color of smoke and flame because many petroleum-based building materials and contents become involved.

Fire Suppression

Combustion ends when one of the four faces of the fire tetrahedron (fuel, oxygen, heat, chemical chain reaction) is removed.

Fuel: Combustion ends either when the fuel is consumed (as in the case of ordinary combustibles) or when the source of fuel is removed (as in the case of methane or natural gas).

Oxygen: Combustion ends once the oxygen level drops below that required to maintain it (normally 15%). The foams used in certain fire-

Table 4.2 Flame Colors and Temperature Ranges

Flame color	Temperature	Flame color	Temperature
Light red	900–1000	Salmon	1600–1700
Dark red	1000–1100	Orange	1700–1800
Dark cherry	1100–1200	Lemon	1800–1900
Medium cherry	1200–1300	Light yellow	1900–2100
Light cherry	1300–1400	White	2150–2250
Bright red	1400–1500	Bright white	2500 and over

Note: Overall the lighter the color of the flame, the higher the temperature. The significance of the color of smoke and flames in a fire should be considered with the time at which they were observed.

suppression operations extinguish (smother) the fire by cutting off the oxygen supply. Remember that oxygen is not a fuel, and neither burns nor explodes. It merely supports oxidative combustion.

Heat: Water (H_2O) is the most commonly used extinguishing agent. It is used because of its great heat-absorbing ability. This cools the surface temperature of the burning fuel to a point below its ignition temperature.

Chemical chain reaction: When the oxidation reaction is chemically inhibited, the fire is extinguished. Certain extinguishing agents (Halon, carbon tetrachloride, potassium bicarbonate, etc.) combine with the radicals freed during the process of combustion to form new molecules. This chemical action prevents transfer of heat energy, and the fire is extinguished.

References and Selected Readings

Bates, Edward B., *Elements of Fire and Arson Investigation*, Davis, Philadelphia, 1975 (revised 1977).

Battle, Brendan P., and Weston, Paul B., *Arson: A Handbook of Detection and Investigation*, 5th ed., Arco, New York, 1960.

Bradley, John H., *Flame and Combustion Phenomena*, Barnes and Noble, New York, 1969.

Browning, B. L. (ed.), *The Chemistry of Wood*, Wiley-Interscience, New York, 1963.

Bush, Loren S., and McLaughlin, James, *Introduction to Fire Science*, Glencoe Press, Beverly Hills, Calif., 1970.

Carroll, John R., *Physical and Technical Aspects of Fire/Arson Investigations*, Thomas Publishing, Springfield, Ill., 1979.

Carter, Robert E., *Arson Investigation*, Glencoe Press, Beverly Hills, Calif., 1978.

Fire/Arson Training Committee, New York State Division of Criminal Justice Services, Bureau of Municipal Police, Fire/Arson Course Material, Module 1, Lesson 2, 1981.

Fitch, R. D., and Porter, E. A., *Accidental or Incendiary?* Thomas Publishing, Springfield, Ill., 1968.

French, Harvey M., *The Anatomy of Arson*, Arco, New York, 1979.

Heidl, James H., *Hazardous Materials Handbook*, Glencoe Press, Beverly Hills, Calif., 1972.

Huron, Benjamin S., *Elements of Arson Investigation*, Reuben H. Donnelley Corp., New York, 1963.

Ingle, Harry, *The Chemistry of Fire and Fire Prevention*, Spon and Chamberlain, New York, 1900.

Kennedy, John, *Fire and Arson Investigation*, Investigations Institute, Chicago, Ill., 1962.

Kirk, Paul L., *Fire Investigation.* Wiley, New York, 1969.

Lewis, B., and Von Elve, G., *Combustion, Flames and Explosions of Gases*, 2nd ed., Academic Press, New York, 1961.

McKinnon, Gordon P., *Fire Protection Handbook*, 14th ed. National Fire Protection Association, Boston, Mass., 1976.

O'Hanlon, Joseph, *Scientific Fire Fighting*, Hubert A. Howson, New York, 1968.

Phillipps and McFadden, *Investigating the Fireground*, Prentice-Hall, Englewood Cliffs, N.J., 1982.

Roblee, C. L., and McKechnie, A. J., *The Investigation of Fires*, Prentice-Hall, Englewood Cliffs, N.J., 1981.

Determining Cause and Origin

5

The primary reason for conducting a postfire examination of the fire scene is to determine the cause and origin of the fire. The factual determination of cause and origin is the principal area of expertise that separates the arson investigator from other investigative specialists.

The *point of origin* of a fire is simply the location where the fire began—the place of beginning. The term *area of origin* is sometimes used when fire originates over a large tract or space or when the exact point of origin cannot be located. Multiple points of origin are said to exist when a fire has more than one place of beginning or when several separate fires are burning in the same structure at the same time.

The *cause* of a fire usually can be determined from a detailed inspection of the charred debris, combustibles, devices, and residues located at the point of (or within the area of) origin. Theoretically, the cause of a fire can be categorized into one of four classifications:

1. *providential:* act of God (e.g., lightning);
2. *accidental:* unintentional and explainable;
3. *undetermined:* cause unknown, unable to be identified; and
4. *incendiary:* intentionally set.

With regard to criminal prosecution, only two of these classifications are relevant: accidental and incendiary.

Physical Examination of the Fire Scene

In order to improve the chance of success, an investigator must approach the investigation of the fire in a systematic way. The physical examination of a structural fire involves a series of increasingly focused

Figure 5.1 An all-too-common sight to the experienced fire investigator: the charred interior of a building under investigation. (Photo courtesy of S. Grennan.)

analyses: first the exterior, then the interior, the room of origin, and the point of origin, and finally the determination of cause.

The reconstruction and examination of the fire scene can be seriously impeded by the indiscriminate or haphazard handling of the routine fire-fighting operation known as the *overhaul*. This involves the inspection of and, when necessary, the movement or reshuffling of debris in an effort to locate or discover concealed sparks, embers, or flame that might rekindle the fire. In the case of a suspicious fire, the overhaul process should be *minimized*. If circumstances permit, the room of origin should not be overhauled before an investigator is present on the scene and can supervise the operation. Otherwise, evidence could conceivably be destroyed or buried. An objective estimate should be completed for each area overhauled to determine whether the debris encountered is normal for that area, and whether items consistent with a normal life-style are missing. The presence of items foreign to the environment is to be viewed with suspicion.

Figure 5.2 In "exclusive opportunity" cases, all entrances and exits (doors, windows, etc.) must be examined. Did responding fire fighters force entry? Is the damage due to natural or firematic venting or is it possible that someone else (burglar, etc.) forcibly entered the building and intentionally started a fire to conceal another crime? (Photo courtesy of S. Grennan.)

Exterior Examination

The exterior examination begins with the interviewing of those fire department officers, fire fighters, and police officers who were first at the scene. As the first-in company, they may have made observations relevant to the nature and origin of the fire. The initial interviews should cover the following types of information:

1. Were any people or vehicles observed in the vicinity of the fire?
2. If so, could their conduct or actions be interpreted as suspicious? That is, were they:
   a. fighting or arguing?
   b. too eager to help or provide information?
   c. attempting to obstruct fire-fighting operations?
   d. observed fleeing the scene?
   e. observed at other fire scenes?
   f. dressed in a manner suggesting obvious haste (relative to time of day/night or season)?

If suspicions were raised, record accurate descriptions, license plate numbers, and so on.

3. Was the structure fully involved?
   a. Was the fire consistent with the types of combustibles readily available?
   b. Was it consistent with the class and type of construction?
   c. Were flames visible?
   d. What side of building was involved?
   e. Was there fire through the roof?
   f. Had flames extended through windows? If so, which windows?
   g. What color were the smoke and flames?
   h. Were the flames quietly lapping up the side of the structure or were they roaring violently?

4. Were the doors and windows open or closed?
   a. Were they locked or nailed shut?
   b. Were shades open or closed, or windows painted to obscure view?
   c. Were entrances blocked (e.g., by storage, rubbish)?
   d. Was forced entry made and, if so, by whom?

5. What was the approximate *reflex time* (time elapsed between alarm and first water = *response time* + *setup time*)?

6. Were any unusual odors noticed?

7. Were hydrants, standpipes, and sprinkler systems operational?
   a. Were hydrants blocked, hidden, or rendered inoperable?
   b. Were caps missing or cross-threaded?
   c. Were fire detection or other safety systems circumvented or rendered inoperable?

After completing the initial interviews, the investigator should examine and evaluate the fire damage observed on the structure's exterior. If possible, walk around the structure. Note the damage around windows and doors, under the soffit, and around vents or other exterior openings. Where is the area of greatest exterior damage? Does it appear that the fire originated outside the building and extended into the structure? Is a "V" pattern visible on the exterior shell of the structure? Where is the lowest point of exterior burning? Examine any containers or items observed on the ground around the structure, and photograph the exterior of the building.

Except in rare cases where the fire is positively identified as having originated outside the structure and extended into it (e.g., from burning rubbish), the cause and origin of a fire cannot be determined and should not be assumed only upon the basis of the exterior examination. This is generally an internal area or room of the structure that, while exhibiting little fire damage relative to the rest of the interior, adjoins the external point of greatest damage. The extreme point of the fire's extension may be an appropriate location to begin the interior examination.

Interior Examination

With the exterior examination completed, the investigation shifts to the interior of the structure. To the extent that the conditions permit, the investigator should attempt to complete a detailed survey of the structure interior, wearing full turnout gear or its equivalent at all times.

Remember, a fire-damaged building is a dangerous place in which to work, and an investigator must evaluate its stability before entering. Floors, walls, staircases, and similar structures may be in danger of collapse, and temporary supports may have to be put in place. Heavy equipment may be needed to excavate a building that has already collapsed. Structural members of steel or, in older buildings, cast iron may be twisted and distorted or may have cracked. Steel I beams that expanded during the heat of the fire may have punched holes in the face, rear, or sides of the building, and portions of the building may have sagged due to the failure of the steel superstructure.

Attempt to reconstruct mentally what happened during the fire. All observations made during this survey should be recorded, including answers to the following:

1. Does the fire spread appear natural?
2. Was the extension of fire natural?
3. Was the intensity of the fire natural?

Figure 5.3 "Exclusive opportunity" cases are difficult to prosecute. One element that must be documented is that the responding fire fighters made a forcible entry. The investigator should photograph the forcible-entry damage and identify the fire fighters who made the entry.

Figure 5.4 The investigator must be aware of and explain any holes in the roof of the structure. Are they the result of burn-through or of venting by fire fighters, or precut by an arsonist? The photograph shows an interior view of a hole cut in the roof by fire fighters (venting). This firemanic procedure allows smoke and the other by-products of combustion to escape, and greatly reduces the danger of a backdraft.

4. Were the furnishings, clothing, appliances, and so on normal for the type of occupancy?
5. Were personal items removed before the fire? Was there any substitution of contents (for instance, cheap or used in place of expensive)?
6. Was there fire in unusual locations (under staircase, in closets and attics, in desk drawers or file cabinets)?
7. Were the body of fire and the path of heat travel consistent with the type of construction and contents?
8. Is your approximation of the burn time consistent with the combustibility characteristics of the types of material (fuel) involved?
9. Are there any holes in the floors or walls? If so, are they a natural consequence of the fire or a possible indication that an accelerant was used? (An arsonist will sometimes punch holes in walls to allow for better cross ventilation and to facilitate the lateral movement of fire.)
10. Are there any holes in the roof? Are they the result of natural burn-through from the fire or of venting during the fire-fighting oper-

ations? Are they residual damage from a prior fire, or were they precut by an arsonist to accommodate the use of a liquid accelerant?

11. Are there any unusual puddle-like burn patterns to indicate that a liquid accelerant may have been used?

Room and Points of Origin

By observing the burn patterns and tracing back the order in which they were formed, the investigator gradually migrates to the area of the most severe damage. This is usually the area where the fire burned the longest (except when flammable liquids were involved). A fire generally burns longest at or near its point of origin because oxygen is sufficiently available there during the early stages of the fire (Bromley et al., undated p. 2-2). Therefore, the room with the greatest damage is most apt to be the room of origin. Locating this room is very significant because it contains the point or area of the fire's origin* as well as clues to its cause.

Many different factors and criteria are commonly used to isolate the point(s) of origin within the room of origin. These are discussed in the section on Fire Language, which follows. If the investigator locates several distinct (unconnected) points of origin, each must be carefully examined. The crime scene, photographs, sketches, and notes should clearly indicate that the multiple points of origin were not the result of normal fire travel, flashover, or burning material having been moved during suppression, overhaul, or salvage operations. *Falldown fires* (burning material falling to the floor) or explosions can also give the appearance of multiple points of origin (Bromley et al., undated, p. 2-9).

The discovery of multiple points of origin is prima facie evidence that the fire was of incendiary origin, since the existence of such a condition is highly improbable and virtually impossible under normal conditions.

Fire Language

From the interior examination to the determination of the fire's point of origin and cause depends upon the ability of the fire/arson investigator to detect and characterize the visible remains of the fire. These disclose information about the fire, including the path of spread, temperatures reached, and fuels involved. The physical signs and sub-

---

* Note that if there are highly combustible materials in a room adjacent to the point of origin, that room will exhibit the heaviest damage when the fire reaches it, and it might be mistaken for the room of origin.

stances that reveal, by implication, how a fire developed are referred to as "fire language." To be effective, a fire/arson investigator must be able to read this technical language. Examples of fire language include depth of char, low points of burning, heat indicators, chromium discolorations, and various features of glass.

Depth of Char

Char is the carbonization of a fuel by the action of heat or burning. The term is generally applied to the combustible residue remaining after the pyrolysis of wood. The depth of char refers to the total depth of the charred material. Its value is obtained by measuring the distance from the surface of the original dimensional wood (lumber) to the boundary of the carbonized fraction and comparing this with the unburned matter that remains.

From an investigative standpoint, the depth of char indicates the length of time that a wooden structural member was exposed to flame. Ordinarily, a section of exposed dimensional lumber ignites at about 660°F and chars at the rate of 1 inch in 45 minutes at 1400°F. The depth of char is usually the deepest where the fire burned the longest (excluding the use of accelerants) and, thus, can be used to identify the point of origin.

In some cases, a careful and diligent examination of the observable char patterns may, by their very nature, suggest the possible use of an accelerant. Commonly used liquid accelerants may burn at temperatures far in excess of 1400°F and, accordingly, radically increase charring. Deep "alligatoring" (large rolling blisters) on an exposed wooden surface ordinarily indicates an intense, rapidly moving body of flame. This condition may be associated with the use of an accelerant.

Low Points of Burning

As mentioned earlier (see Burn Patterns in Chapter 4), the most common pattern associated with the upward movement of flame and heat is the "V" pattern, the apex (pointed end) of which represents the point of origin. All low points of origin must, therefore, be examined carefully. The lowest point of burning within the apparent room of origin is usually the point of origin.

The point of origin may be concealed. As a fire progresses upward, damaged items (such as sheetrock, plaster from walls and ceilings, paintings, and wall ornaments) tend to fall or collapse and cover the point of origin. Thus, it is incumbent upon the investigator to sift carefully through the debris, layer by layer. The lowest layer displaying

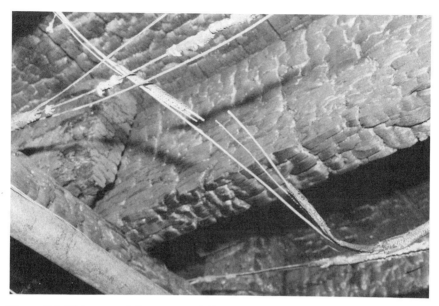

Figure 5.5 This type of char pattern (alligatoring or large rolling blisters), which ordinarily appears in floor joists or rafters above the point of origin, is consistent with uniform fire spread. Any structural members above the point of origin (accidental or incendiary) will routinely be exposed to extreme temperatures and flame for extended periods of time.

fire damage would necessarily identify the lowest point of burning and the point of origin.

The lowest point of burning can also be identified by carefully examining the undersides of household items (such as TV sets, appliances, furniture, and shelves) for burn damage. The presence of burn damage on the underside of any particular item may indicate that the fire started below that point; its absence would indicate the reverse.

Spalling

Spalling is a condition ordinarily associated with masonry and cement (concrete) building materials. It may appear as a distinctive discoloration of brick or concrete and, in some cases, the surface of these building materials may be pitted and rough. This is because an intense fire may cause the moisture within the brick or masonry element to convert to steam. As they expand, these steam pockets may burst through the surface of the cement or brick floor or wall, leaving the surface pitted or pock-marked.

Figure 5.6 During the physical examination the investigator must recognize those patterns associated with the upward movement of flame and heat. Notice the broad "V" pattern extending from the pile of clothing and debris.

Figure 5.7 Here the burnt clothing and debris have been cleared, revealing the apex of the "V" pattern. The apex of the pattern proved to be the lowest point of burning and the point of origin. A liquid accelerant had been used.

Figure 5.8 It took hours of digging for investigators to uncover the accelerant pattern (spalling) on the cement floor of this nearly completed home. Several teenagers, apparently for a thrill, poured gasoline on the floor beneath a staircase. (Photo courtesy of T. Brown.)

Table 5.1 Fusing Temperatures of Some Materials

Material	Temperature (°F)	Material	Temperature (°F)
Solder	361	Iron	2802
Tin	449	Nickel	2651
Lead	618	Stainless steel	2462–2822
Aluminum	1220	Steel	2552–2882
Copper	1980	Platinum	3224
Cast iron	2000–2800	Chromium	3407

Although this condition may be associated with the use of an accelerant, the discovery of spalling does not in itself indicate that the fire was incendiary. Other common combustibles that burn with great intensity can also cause this condition. It may even be the result of a ruptured gas line.

Heat Indicators

Heat indicators are those pieces of fused or molten metal (and/or glass) that serve to suggest both the path of fire spread and the location of highest temperatures. The most severe heat damage is usually found (use of accelerants excluded) at or near the point of origin.

On finding a piece or section of fused material, the investigator must do two things:

1. attempt to identify the composition of the material, and
2. determine its fusing temperature.

This done, the investigator must then endeavor to determine the source of the temperature range so indicated. The fusing temperatures of some materials are shown in Table 5.1.

Heat Discoloration of Chromium

Many household appliances and fixtures (toasters, ashtrays, light fixtures, etc.) are plated with chromium to prevent corrosion. Chromium has a tendency to discolor when exposed to intense temperatures, and this discoloration can serve as a heat indicator (Table 5.2). Many of the high-temperature colors may not remain after the chromed object cools. However, a distinctive rainbow of color may persist, suggesting intense temperatures.

Glass as an Indicator

Glass items, such as mirrors, window panes, and so on, are also affected by heat buildup, smoke, and flame. Heat damage (fusing) and smoke staining on glass items tend to occur in direct relation to:

Table 5.2 Chromium Discoloration

Color	Temperature (°F)	Color	Temperature (°F)
Yellow	450–500	Bright red	1400–1500
Purple–brown	550–575	Salmon	1600–1700
Blue	600–875	Lemon	1800–1900
Light red	900–1000	White	2000–2400
Dark red	1100–1300	Sparkling white	2400+

the heat buildup,

the intensity of the fire,

the speed of fire spread, and

proximity to the fire.

A detailed inspection of glass items can afford a reasonably precise determination of the items' location with regard to the fire's point of origin. The following is a classification by structure of common kinds of glass (Redsicker, personal communication):

1. *Single-phase glasses* are made up of the vitreous silica family. Among these are *fused quartz*, with a melting temperature of 3133°F (1723°C). This material softens at 2876°F (1580°C). Another member of this family is *fused silica*, used in some wood stove windows. This material softens at 2732°F (1500°C).

2. *Soda lime glasses* contain a mixture of alkali and alkaline earths to make them more durable and easier to produce. This family of glasses accounts for nearly 90% of all glass produced. Such glass is used for container window glass, pressed- and blown-ware, and lighting products where exceptional chemical durability and heat resistance are not required. Its melting temperature is 1005°F (695°C).

3. *Borosilicate glasses* are made by replacing the alkali with boric acid, producing a lower expansion glass. These glasses are harder, more durable, and capable of withstanding higher temperatures. They can be found in oven-ware, laboratory equipment, glass piping, and seal-beam headlights. Their melting temperature is 1190°F (780°C).

4. *Aluminosilicate glasses* are made by using alumina. These glasses are harder than soda lime and borosilicate glasses and are found in airplane windows, frangible containers, and stovetop uses. Their melting temperature is 1670°F (910°C).

5. *Lead glasses* contain lead oxide and, sometimes, lead silicate and melt easily. These glasses are used for commercial radiation windows, fluorescent lamp envelopes, and television picture tubes. Low-melting solder glasses and frit for decorating enamels (used to decorate table-

ware, etc.) are based upon these low melting lead glasses. Their melting temperature is 785°F (380°C).

The porcelain on a kitchen sink is not actually porcelain, but a vitreous glaze with a melting temperature in the range 1652°–3092°F (900°–1700°C). Vitreous glazes are bonded to metals at temperatures above 797°F (425°C), with aluminum bonding at a lower temperature than iron and steel.

Smoke-Stained and Checkered Glass

An increase in the temperature (heat energy) of a glass item causes a proportional increase in that item's molecular activity. The hotter the item, the greater the molecular activity on its surface. Increased molecular activity on a surface inhibits the amount of soot (smoke staining) that will occur. An item heavily stained by smoke and soot was, therefore, cooler than one that exhibits a light buildup of soot. A heavy soot buildup on a glass surface suggests that the item was remote from the point of origin of the fire. However, a light soot buildup in a location suggests that the item may be at or near the point of origin.

Checkering of glass refers to the half-moon shapes that are sometimes observed on the surface of glass items. These half-moon shapes result after droplets of water (usually from the fire-fighting operation) land on a heated glass surface. They are significant in that they usually indicate that the glass was in place or intact (e.g., in the window, door, or picture frame) when the source of the water was applied. The presence or absence of a pane of glass in a window or door may be very significant if the fire is declared incendiary and the issue of exclusive opportunity becomes manifest.

Crazed and Fractured Glass

Crazing refers to the cracking of glass into smaller segments or subdivisions in an irregular pattern. The extent to which a glass item (e.g., window pane) will crack or craze is related to the type of glass involved, the thickness of the glass, the temperature range to which it was exposed, and its distance from the point of origin.

Crazing into small segments or pieces suggests that the item was subjected to a rapid and intense heat buildup. It also suggests that the item may be located at or close to the point of origin. On the other hand, a glass item that exhibits a larger crazing pattern implies that it may have been located in an area some distance away from the point of origin.

An investigator can determine whether a particular pane of glass

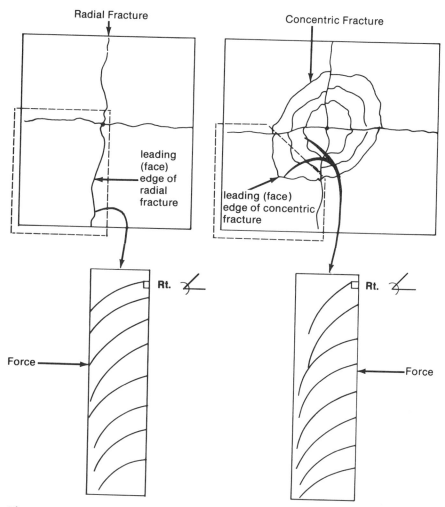

Figure 5.9 Types of glass fractures: radial and concentric fractures.

was *fractured* as the result of pressure applied from the interior or exterior of the structure. When pressure is applied to glass, radial and concentric fractures result. *Radial fractures* start from the point of impact and carry to the perimeter of the pane. *Concentric fractures* form around the point of impact and create a spiderweb appearance. The labeling and removal of glass fragments are simple procedures. A criminologist or laboratory expert may be required to testify at trial regarding the analysis of the glass fragments. The steps in these procedures are as follows:

1. Carefully label (either inside or outside) a fragment of glass still attached to the window/door frame.
2. Remove the glass fragment and identify the type of fracture (radial/concentric). Carefully examine the edge of the fracture (leading edge).
3. Look at the trails of the stress fractures that result from the crackling along the glass's lattice structure.
4. In a *radial* fracture, there is a right angle between the *striations* (fracture lines) and the *face away from* that side of the pane on which the original pressure was applied. In a *concentric* fracture there will be a right angle between the striations and the *same face* of the pane that received the pressure.

Light Bulbs

When found intact, a deformed or distended incandescent light bulb can be a valuable aid to the fire investigator. The glass envelope surrounding the filament (conductor) in an incandescent bulb will soften at approximately 900°F and distend in the direction of the heat source, which may also be the point of origin. Unfortunately, few light bulbs survive either the fire itself or the suppression efforts. Those that do

Figure 5.10 The identification of the lowest point of burning is very significant. One phenomenon that serves to protect the lowest point of burning is the fact that as fire extends upward, items such as wall and ceiling materials, paintings, and wall ornaments that are damaged tend to fall or collapse and may cover the low point of burning.

Figure 5.11 It is incumbent upon the investigator to sift carefully through the debris, layer by layer. This technique is called "layer checking."

survive are almost exclusively in ceiling fixtures. Fluorescent bulbs do not react in the same way and are even less likely to survive than incandescent bulbs.

The investigation of the cause of the fire includes the identification of both the source of ignition (heat source) and the initial ignited material (fuel). The floor at the point of origin must be carefully cleaned, checking through the debris layer by layer. In some cases, the investigator is required to dig through several inches of loose ash, which serves as a thermal insulator and may protect the point of origin.

Throughout the entire process, the investigator must be vigilant for signs of criminality. If a crime has been committed, he or she must act accordingly to build a viable case. For example, during the examination at the point of origin, the investigator may uncover certain devices, burn patterns, or other conditions that indicate that the fire was intentionally set. Nevertheless, the investigator must still endeavor to eliminate every possible accidental cause for the fire. All fires are presumed to be accidental until absolute proof to the contrary is uncovered. (Elimination of Accidental Causes is discussed at length in Chapter 6.)

Evidence of Incendiarism

Throughout this chapter, we have already mentioned many kinds of evidence that might indicate the incendiary nature of a fire. The following list recapitulates:

1. suspicious behavior of individuals observed at the fire scene;
2. signs of forced entry unrelated to fire-fighting operations;
3. precut holes in floors, walls, or roof;
4. sabotaged fire detection or water delivery systems (e.g., hydrants, sprinklers);
5. multiple points of origin; and
6. abnormalities (inconsistencies with construction materials and contents) with regard to:
   a. rate of spread,
   b. direction of spread (e.g., unusual locations of fire, burn patterns),
   c. extent of spread, and
   d. intensity of fire (i.e., temperature, as indicated by smoke and flame color, depth of char, burn time, spalling, etc.).

Time-Delayed Ignition Devices

In an incendiary fire, the source of ignition may be direct or time-delayed (indirect). *Direct ignition* involves the direct application of an ignition source (e.g., match) to a combustible fuel. The fuel used may range from a crumpled newspaper to a liquid accelerant. Many novice "torches," who know nothing about the combustibility of different types of fuel, are seriously injured or killed when they become trapped in their own fires. However, the use of a time-delayed ignition device allows the arsonist to leave the scene safely *before* ignition occurs. Some of these devices are very crude and somewhat unpredictable. Others are very sophisticated and permit the arsonist sufficient time to set up and develop seemingly flawless alibis. The following devices are commonly used.

Electric timers: An electric timer, which can be purchased almost anywhere for well under $10, can delay ignition for anywhere from a few minutes to almost 24 hours. It is used in conjunction with an ignition source (e.g., soldering iron, heating element), which is simply placed in a combustible fuel (e.g., sawdust) or a flammable liquid (e.g., gasoline).

Cigarette matches: A lit cigarette can serve as a 10 to 12 minute fuse when used in combination with a book of matches. The lit cigarette is simply tucked into a closed book of matches, and the device placed close to a combustible material.

Candles: A candle with a 7/8-inch diameter (2 11/16-inch circumference) will burn 1 inch in 57 minutes in a draft-free environment. A 6-inch candle with the same diameter and circumference provides almost 6 hours of burn time before ignition of an adjoining combustible.

Chemicals: Certain terrorist groups have been very successful in the

Figure 5.12 The hot plate pictured above was used in conjunction with a 24-hour timer and a gallon jug of gasoline by an arsonist determined to destroy his business. Portions of the molten plastic jug can be seen fused to the hot plate.

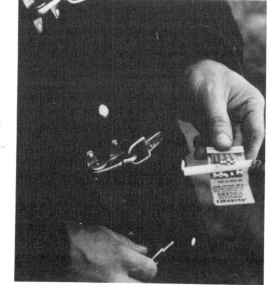

Figure 5.13 A cigarette was placed in a book of matches to serve as a crude time-delay device.

use of chemical igniters. One of these has been the combination of potassium chlorate, powdered sugar, and sulphuric acid.

Countless other devices (including common light bulbs) have also been used, limited only by the imagination of the arsonist.

During the examination of the fire scene, the investigator must be able to recognize the remains of a time-delayed device. He or she must also be aware of the fact that more than one device may have been secreted in various areas of the structure.

Accelerants and Related Burn Patterns

An *accelerant* is any substance that is used to accelerate (and sometimes direct) the spread of a fire. The most commonly used liquid accelerants include gasoline, lighter fluid, kerosene, and turpentine.

A *plant*, sometimes referred to as a *booster*, is either a pool of liquid accelerant or a pile of combustibles (oily rags, newspaper, painting supplies, etc.) that is used by an arsonist to enhance the quality of fire in a selected location. An accelerant-soaked mattress or couch could serve the same purpose. A plant is intended to boost the progress of a fire by producing a large body of fire.

A *trailer*, sometimes referred to as a *streamer*, is an arrangement or configuration of flammable or combustible materials that is intended to carry fire from one location to another (or from one plant to another). Commonly used trailers include gasoline-soaked towels tied end-to-end, liquid accelerant splashed across the floor, lengths of safety fuse, or accelerant-soaked newspaper.

When used, a liquid accelerant is generally accompanied by distinctive burn patterns, as well as unnatural fire spread and intensity. A typical burn pattern resulting from the use of a liquid accelerant is called *puddling*. This burn pattern is distinctive and should not be confused with other irregular patterns that might result from drapes or clothing burning on a floor. When spilled on a tongue-and-groove (hardwood) floor, liquid accelerant is drawn down between the individual floorboards. Once ignited, the accelerant burns up through the spaces between the floorboards. In the case of a tiled floor, the accelerant seeps down between the individual tiles and, once ignited, causes the edges of the surrounding tiles to curl.

In addition, since only the vapors burn, the pool of liquid accelerant itself serves as an insulating barrier between the burning vapors above and the floor below. As the pool of liquid burns from its upper surface down and inward from its perimeter, it leaves a burn pattern that is deeper at the perimeter of the pool than toward its center.

When the liquid accelerant is spilled on a concrete floor and ignited, *spalling* may result (see discussion earlier in this chapter). The heat

Figure 5.14 An accelerant pour pattern (trailer) on carpeting. (Photo courtesy of T. Brown.)

from the burning accelerant causes trapped moisture within the concrete slab to turn to steam. The resultant steam pressure causes the surface of the slab to pop, leaving behind a very uneven (pitted) skin.

Accelerant splatter may occur in several different ways. It is usually identified by the presence of highly distinctive finger-like patterns. It may be found under the following circumstances:

1. *Accompanying the puddle effect*—When liquid accelerant seeps down through the floor, it may contact and run down the face of the floor joists.
2. *Below the exterior of a window*—When fire extends through a window, it naturally laps up the face of the structure above the window. The existence of an unusual finger-like pattern *below* a window may suggest that a Molotov cocktail thrown by an arsonist shattered against the window and that its flammable contents ran down the exterior wall before igniting.
3. *Around holes cut in interior walls for introducing accelerant—*

Figure 5.15 A typical burn pattern resulting from the use of liquid accelerants is called "puddling." This type of pattern is distinctive enough so that it should not be confused with other irregular patterns, which might result when drapes or other cloth items burn on the floor.

While cutting such holes, the arsonist, in haste, may have inadvertently spilled excess accelerant down the face of the wall in the area of the hole. This liquid, in addition to running down the face of the wall, may have seeped in behind the wall molding at floor level.

Summary

To determine a fire's cause and origin, an investigator is required to draw on knowledge of fire chemistry and behavior, building construction, and accidental and incendiary causes of fire, as well as the full

Figure 5.16 Puddling patterns viewed from the floor below the point of origin. A liquid accelerant will seep down between floor sections and be absorbed by the supporting joists. Notice the "finger-like" patterns (accelerant splatter) on the sides of the joists, while the leading edge of the joists is untouched.

A   B

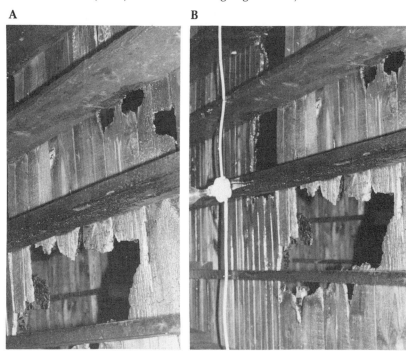

Figure 5.17 Molotov cocktails are still popular devices with amateur arsonists. An investigator should be aware that the neck of the bottle used or at least some section of the neck will very often survive both the bottle's shattering and the resultant fire.

range of his or her investigative expertise. The fire scene must be approached in a systematic manner, and fire language must be read to locate the point of origin. Before incendiarism can be determined as the cause of the fire, all accidental causes must be ruled out (see Chapter 6).

References and Selected Readings

Bates, Edward B., *Elements of Fire & Arson Investigation*, Davis, Philadelphia, 1975 (revised 1977).

Battle, Brendan P., and Weston, Paul B., *Arson*, 5th ed., Arco, New York, 1960.

Bromley, James, et al., Cause and Origin Determination, Office of Fire Prevention, Department of State, State of New York, undated.

Carroll, John R., *Physical and Technical Aspects of Fire/Arson Investigations*, Charles C. Thomas, Springfield, Ill., 1979.

Carter, Robert E., *Arson Investigation*, Glencoe, Beverly Hills, 1978.

Fitch, R. D., and Porter, E. A., *Accidental or Incendiary?*, Charles C. Thomas, Springfield, Ill., 1968.

French, Harvey M., *The Anatomy of Arson*, Arco, New York, 1979.

Heidl, James H., *Hazardous Materials Handbook*, Glencoe, Beverly Hills, 1972.

Huron, Benjamin S., *Elements of Arson Investigation*, Dunn-Donnelley, New York, 1963.

Kennedy, John, *Fire and Arson Investigation*, Investigations Institute, Chicago, 1962 (revised 1977).

Kirk, Paul L., *Fire Investigation*, John Wiley and Sons, New York, 1969.

Lewis, B., and Von Elbe, G., *Combustion, Flames and Explosions of Gases*, 2nd ed., Academic Press, New York, 1961.

McKinnon, Gordon P., *Fire Protection Handbook*, 14th ed., National Fire Protection Association, Boston, 1976.

Phillipps, C., and McFadden, D., *Investigating the Fireground*, Prentice-Hall, Englewood Cliffs, N.J., 1982.

Redsicker, David R., personal communication, 1983.

Roblee, C. L., and McKechnie, A. J. *The Investigation of Fires*, Prentice-Hall, Englewood Cliffs, N.J., 1981.

Eliminating
Accidental Causes

6

The elimination of all possible accidental causes of fire is one of the most difficult duties of the fire investigator. Unless all of the relevant accidental causes can be eliminated, the fire must be declared accidental, the presence of direct evidence to the contrary notwithstanding.

Consider, for example, a case where the investigator, during the physical examination of a warehouse fire, believed that a liquid accelerant was splashed on and around several pieces of heavy machinery. He positively identified this section of the warehouse as the area of origin and carefully submitted sections of flooring to a laboratory for analysis. The laboratory technicians identified the accelerant that was used as gasoline. The investigator believed he had an open-and-shut case and declared the fire incendiary. A motive was identified and enough information was developed during the follow-up investigation to connect the warehouse owner to the fire. He was arrested and charged with arson and insurance fraud.

At the first opportunity after the arrest, the investigator discussed the facts and circumstances of the case with an assistant district attorney who would be prosecuting the case. After reviewing the reports and photographs of the scene, the assistant D.A. asked the investigator what measures he had taken to eliminate the various electric motors, switches, junction boxes, and outlets located within the reported area of origin as possible causes of the fire. The investigator, in amazement, answered, "I didn't do anything with them. I just told you, I found gasoline splashed all over the place. Why should I waste my time looking at all the rest of that stuff? Look at this laboratory report! It came back positive!"

During the first hearing, after arraignment, the assistant D.A. advised the judge that the case would not be prosecuted, and recommended that all charges be dropped.

What our fictitious assistant D.A. had recognized was the investigator's failure to positively eliminate accidental causes for the fire. This factor alone would have had dire consequences had a prosecution been attempted. Procedural codes and case law in effect in many states preclude an arson investigator from testifying that a fire was incendiary. In fact, this type of testimony during a trial would amount to reversible error, and a mistrial would be granted. In states where these rules apply, a court-qualified arson expert must first offer testimony suggesting that the fire *was not an accident* by describing the steps that were taken to eliminate accidental causes. He could then go on to describe the conditions of the fire and any items that were found, including accelerants, delayed timing devices, plants, trailers, and so on. He could also offer testimony, based upon his expertise and experience, describing the illegal purposes for which such items are commonly used. However, the ultimate decision as to whether a fire was or was not incendiary rests with the jury.

Some of the typical accidental causes of a fire that may have to be eliminated are listed below:

Electrical malfunction,

Gas or oil service malfunction,

Building furnace or heating plant,

Improper maintenance in the operation of a fireplace or wood stove (*Note:* 20% of all the house fires in New York State are now attributed to the improper operation or maintenance of secondary home heating appliances),

Cooking-related accidents,

Open flame (e.g., candles, burning leaves) or sparks (e.g., static electricity),

Children and pets,

Improper storage of combustibles,

Smoking,

Clandestine laboratories,

Construction, renovation, or demolition (e.g., welding, cement-drying heaters), and

Direct sunlight.

Electrical Fires

A fire investigator must be able to determine conclusively whether or not a fire was caused by electricity. To do this he does not have to be an electrical engineer, but he should have a fundamental understanding

Figure 6.1 An investigator must be well acquainted with the electrical code in force in the state or county in which he is conducting an investigation. Note and photograph all code violations.

of electricity and a working knowledge of the operation of a basic electrical system. He should also be able to differentiate between electrical damage caused internally (within the system) and externally (by flame).

The investigator should note whether each appliance was on or off at the time of the fire. (In a commercial fire, the investigator should examine the types of equipment and appliances common to that occupancy.) At the same time, he should evaluate the particular appliance (or piece of equipment) in terms of its involvement in the initiation of the fire. In so doing, potential accidental causes of the fire may be eliminated, and the investigator can develop an overall opinion as to the possible negligence on the part of the occupant.

The elimination of electrical wiring, appliances, and apparatus as a fire cause has been an area of considerable controversy over the past decade. Recent research indicates that fires of electrical origin do occur, but with far less regularity and extensiveness than previously believed or reported.

Before any fire is declared to be of electrical origin, the investigator should have hard evidence to that effect. The traditional reliance solely upon a visual inspection of electrical components at or near the apparent point of origin of a fire will often lead to an erroneous conclusion and the mislabeling of the fire cause. If, after careful examination, some reasonable doubt exists as to the involvement (or lack thereof) of the electrical components, the fire investigator should seek a second opinion from a qualified electrical expert.

Terminology

In order for an investigator to articulate adequately whatever it is that he finds during his field examination, he must first understand the basic terminology of electricity:

Electron: the fundamental unit involved in electricity. An electron is a negatively charged particle of the atomic structure of matter.

Circuit: an unbroken path through which electricity may pass. When a circuit is interrupted (for example, by opening a switch), it is said to be *open;* when uninterrupted, *closed.* A circuit charged with electricity is said to be *alive;* one free from electricity, *dead.*

Current: the rate at which free electrons pass through a conductor or circuit. Current, which is measured in *amperes* (A), determines the size, diameter, or gauge of the conductor to be used in a given circuit. Too much current flowing through an inadequate conductor will cause it to overheat, possibly starting a fire. *Direct current* (DC) travels only in one direction: out one side (negative) of the circuit and back the other (positive). All batteries are DC. *Alternating current* (AC) reverses its direction many times per second. Standard U.S. house current reverses 60 times per second and is known as *60 cycle.* Because of the constant alternation, the terms positive and negative are inapplicable to the sides of the circuit. When part of a circuit is bypassed, yielding a new circuit of much lower resistance, it is called a *short circuit.*

Potential: the ability of a source of electrons to overcome resistance. Potential is measured in *volts* (V), which are also used to measure differences in electric potential between any two points within an electrical system. The voltage difference between two points determines the insulation required for the conductor(s) connecting them. The greater the difference, the thicker the insulation required to prevent arcing (luminous electrical discharge) and insulation breakdown.

Resistance: the degree of opposition offered by the conductor or circuit to the flow of electricity (passage of electrons). Resistance, which is measured in ohms (Ω), is a form of friction and, as such, dissipates some of the electrical energy as heat.

Ohm's law: the electric current i flowing through a given resistance r equals the applied voltage v divided by the resistance. That is,

$$i = \frac{v}{r}, \qquad r = \frac{v}{i}, \qquad v = ir.$$

The various equations depicted in Ohm's law explain, in readable terms, principles that, though invisible to the naked eye, are measurable with an electric meter. For AC circuits, the law becomes:

$$i = \frac{v}{z},$$

where z is the *impedance* (resistance plus *reactance*, another kind of opposition to current flow).

Watt: a measurement of *power*—electrical energy (in *joules*) consumed per unit time (in seconds).

$$1 \text{ watt} = 1 \text{ joule/sec} = 1 \text{ V} \times 1 \text{ A}$$
$$746 \text{ watts} = 1 \text{ horsepower}$$
$$1 \text{ kilowatt} = 1000 \text{ watts}$$

One kilowatt-hour (kw-h) is a unit of energy equivalent to 1000 watts of power being used for one hour.

Ground: an area used as an arbitrary zero of electrical potential and a common return for an electric circuit; especially, an object that makes an electrical connection with the earth.

Transformer: device that transfers an alternating current or voltage from one circuit to another via *mutual electromagnetic induction*. Changing the current in a given circuit will *induce* a difference in potential in a nearby but unconnected circuit. Transformers can be set up to transfer potentials that are lower (*stepped down*), higher (*stepped up*), or the same as that of the original circuit.

Typical House Service

Normal house service, also referred to as *Edison/single-phase power*, is probably the most common electrical system examined by investigators in the field. A typical house service can be outlined as follows:

1. A local utility company generates power (via a generating plant) at 10,000–20,000 V.
2. The power is distributed via transmission lines.
3. The high voltage carried by the transmission lines is stepped down (via transformer) for distribution to individual customers (residential, commercial, etc.).
4. An overhead service connection (*drop line*) permits voltage to flow from the step-down transformer through the company's meter and into the service main (service panel or fuse box).
5. Within the service panel or fuse box, the power is divided into smaller load-carrying paths called *circuits* or *branch circuits*.
6. Each circuit is protected by an overcurrent protection device (*circuit breaker* or *fuse*). The circuit is comprised of a system of insulated wires or conductors. The power flow through selected sections of the circuit is controlled by switches or devices to open and close the passage of current. Finally, there is an electric *load* or demand for power (e.g., lamp, electric appliance).

One side of a typical house service should be grounded. Usually the

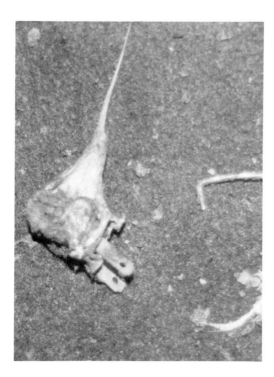

Figure 6.2 This homeowner solved the problem of plugging a three-prong air-conditioner cord into a two-hole receptacle by bending the ground prong out of the way. This condition is far too common. A poorly made ground can overheat when it is carrying too much current and cause an electrical fire.

service (entrance) cable is grounded via the service panel to a water pipe. The voltage (potential) is the same as that of the earth, about zero. Normal resistance is from 0 to 8 Ω. Unless a system is grounded, fuses or circuit breakers will not blow. A poorly made ground can overheat when it is carrying too much current and can cause an electrical fire.

Overcurrent Protection Devices

As previously stated, each circuit should be provided with an *overcurrent protection device*, that is, a *circuit breaker* or *fuse*. The service panel itself is protected by a main circuit breaker. The amperage rating of this breaker usually indicates the total amperage rating for that particular electric service (e.g., 100 A). A fuse box would ordinarily have the same form of protection but, instead of a circuit breaker, would contain a main fuse (usually of the cartridge or blade type) that would also indicate the total rating of the service.

The type of fuse used in any particular circuit should give some indication as to the purpose of that circuit (see Table 6.1). The investigator should count the total number of individual circuits branching

Table 6.1 Type and Rating of Overcurrent Protection Devices

Type	Rating (amperes)
Hexagonal window	15 or less
Round window	20–30
Edison	up to 30
Cartridge (ferrule)	30–60
Blade	60 and up

out from the service panel and note the ratings of the circuit breakers or fuses used. In a typical household fuse box, ratings of 30 A or more should be questioned. The total value of all circuits may exceed the overall service rating, the underlying presumption being that not all circuits will be used at the same time.

The *S-type fuse* is unique in that each rating comes with its own distinct socket to prevent misfusing. Another type is the *time-delay fuse*, normally used with high-horsepower motors. It specifically permits a brief overload on the circuit (via time-delayed response) to allow for the high demand for power when the motor first starts. *Cartridge* or *blade fuses* are normally used to protect the main service panel or for high-demand circuits.

Circuit breakers (CBs) open and close the circuit either by means of internal electromagnets that react to the amount of current flow, or via bimetallic strips (similar to those in a fuse) that, when heated, separate to open the circuit. Switching device circuit breakers (SWDs) should not be used as on/off switches; such improper use causes wear.

Circumvention and Tampering

Someone who wishes to disguise an intentionally set fire as an electrical, accidental one might tamper with a circuit breaker. This requires special knowledge on the part of the person doing the tampering, who would have to know how to reset the calibration screw set by the CB's manufacturer. If the investigator suspects that just such a condition precipitated the fire, he should examine the CB to see whether the plastic seal covering the calibration screw has been removed and replaced.

Fuses are very often circumvented, but the intent is not always criminal. Some people, because of constantly blown fuses, will overfuse a particular circuit. This radically increases the danger of fire in that circuit, since the wire insulation may burn before the (oversized) fuse blows.

Similarly, some people substitute a spark plug for the S-type fuse. Typical means used to circumvent the protection provided by a *properly* sized fuse are as follows:

Water in the fuse: People may intentionally place several fuses into the washing machine with the clothes they intend to wash. In time, the water seeps into the fuse. Once the fuse is full, the water is almost impossible to see except for air bubbles.

Penny behind the fuse: In order for the circuit to open, the penny would have to burn through completely.

Packing with aluminum foil: This requires that the glass on a fuse be broken. The interior of the fuse is then packed with aluminum foil.

Driving a nail through the cartridge: The current passes through the nail, completely bypassing the fuse.

Service Panel/Fuse Box

A fire that originates within a service panel (or fuse box) is usually accompanied by an explosion. This will usually cause the door or cover of the service panel to blow open. When primary supply lines of opposite potential contact each other due to the action of the internal fire, a rather substantial and violent explosion can occur.

Before handling any electrical components of the service panel, the investigator should personally ensure that the utility's meter or clock *has been disconnected* or unplugged. During the inspection of the service panel, the following should be carefully noted:

rating of each fuse or circuit breaker,

gauge of the wire used as compared with the purpose of each circuit,

total rating of the service panel versus total potential load,

how old the service is,

whether the installation is UL approved,

whether the service was converted from fuses to circuit breakers, and

whether service was recently increased (say, from 60 to 150 A).

A fire within a service panel is usually accompanied by deep charring and extensive heat damage in the area immediately surrounding (and especially above) the panel itself. In most cases a clear V pattern is especially visible on the wall to which the panel is mounted. The base of the V will be approximately as wide as the service panel. Substantial arcing within the box may very well be evidenced by the presence of

Figure 6.3 In any case, the electrical service panel must be carefully examined, photographed, and eliminated as a possible cause of the fire. (Photo courtesy of D. Redsicker.)

pop-outs, holes formed by melting in the metal walls and cover of the service panel.

Disguised Use of Accelerants

Several years ago, numerous accelerated fires were mislabeled as having started within the service panel. These fires were classified as accidental, their cause listed as being of electrical origin.

Various radical publications had printed an outline and schematic recommending the suspension of gasoline-filled balloons as close to the service panel as possible. Various delayed-ignition devices were also suggested. The fires that followed this plan were traced back to the area of the service panel, where the deep charring, restricted scope of damage, and the virtual destruction of the service panel itself closely resembled the circumstances that would have followed an accidental fire of electrical origin. Time constraints, due to burdensome caseloads, were probably the chief reason for the ineffective cause and origin determinations in these cases. In any event, the fact is that countless numbers of such fires were misread before an investigator discovered the true cause and published his findings.

Electrical Wiring

Current is carried away from the service panel by insulated conductors (wiring). Local electrical codes mandate the type of wire to be used in any particular region, city, or town. Any electrical code violations observed during the investigation should be photographed, and written notes describing the circumstances should be prepared. The written analysis of the total electrical system should include any and all violations or hazards encountered, regardless of their involvement (or lack of involvement) in the origin of the fire.

A length of standard electrical wiring consists of a conductor (copper or aluminum), an insulated covering surrounding the conductor (designed to prevent conductors of opposite polarity from coming into contact with one another), and an outer covering.

The diameter (*gauge*) of the conductor is determined by the amount of current that it is intended to carry. The amount of current required is, in turn, determined by the purpose of the circuit or line. The thickness of *insulation* is directly related to the line potential: the greater the voltage, the thicker the insulation required to prevent arc-over and insulation breakdown.

Electrical wiring may be sheathed in a variety of different coverings. Armored cable, commonly referred to as BX, is wrapped in rubber and encased in a flexible steel covering. There is also a nonmetallic sheathed cable, commonly called "Romex." Certain electrical codes, depending upon the purpose for the particular line, require that the wire (whether hard- or soft-covered) be encased in rigid metallic conduit. Ordinarily, electrical wiring is color-coded, with the same color denoting the same potential.

Electrical wire diameter is measured in the American Wire Gauge (AWG) system. Each gauge is represented by a numerical value (e.g., 10 or 14 gauge). The higher the number, the smaller the gauge. The carrying capacity, measured in amperes, is directly related to the gauge of the conductor. The recommended maximum current rating for a given gauge is the maximum amperage circuit breaker or fuse that should be protecting that line once energized (see Table 6.2).

As current flows through a length of wire, the individual conductors become hot and anneal. In time, the diameter of the conductors thins and the total length of the wire increases. This accounts for the sagging wires found in the walls of older buildings.

Table 6.2. Wire Gauge and Maximum Current

Gauge (AWG)	Max. current (amperes)	Uses
8	45	House/commercial service
10	30	House/commercial service
12	20	House service
14	14	House service
16	7	Extension cord
18	5	Lamp cord

Aluminum Wire Controversy

In 1979, the National Consumer Product Safety Commission released the results of a comprehensive study that brought a long-debated point to a head. The Commission stated that "for an aluminum-wired home, the risk of having at least one [electrical] receptacle reach fire hazard condition was 55 times as great as for a copper-wired home." The problem with aluminum wire is not that it is a poorer conductor than copper—it is not. Problems seem to result, however, from the method and type of installation and the lack of proper maintenance.

Public awareness was raised by several highly publicized fires whose cause was attributed to aluminum-related electrical fires. Many home owners who lived in aluminum-wired housing developments brought in electricians to correct any electrical problems. Since the cost of rewiring a home with copper wire was prohibitive, *"pigtailing"*—connecting a copper conductor within a receptacle to the aluminum wire buried within the walls—was seen as the only viable alternative. Thus, all the connections (duplex outlets, light switches, etc.) would be copper.

The copper-to-aluminum splice, like any wire connection, should be made with great care. The following factors must be considered:

Aluminum has a coefficient of expansion that is 38% greater than that for copper. Therefore, specially designed connectors must be used. The installation of an improper (all-copper) connector counterpart may create more problems than it prevents. Experts in the field have suggested that the aluminum wire used be one gauge size larger than its copper counterpart.

Aluminum is electrically positive in respect to copper; an aluminum-to-copper connection, in the presence of moisture, acts like an electrolytic cell. The resultant electrolysis can create a situation in which copper salts interact with and corrode the aluminum. The aluminum wire should be elevated in relation to its copper counterpart and coated with an oxide inhibitor.

Copper fuses at approximately 2000°F and aluminum fuses at about 1200°F. As a general rule, and depending on the temperatures reached during a fire, an investigator is likely to find that copper has survived at or near the point of origin more often than aluminum wire.

Electrical Wiring Checklist

Probably 99% of all electrically initiated fires are accidental when viewed from a purely criminal-law standpoint. No mental culpability attaches. Yet although negligence, code violations, and the like may not have criminal significance, these same elements could serve as the basis for a civil trial. A criminal investigator could find himself subpoenaed to testify in civil court about a case which has long been closed.

Wiring problems commonly encountered are listed below.

I. Incorrect and inappropriate use of (flexible) extension cords:
   A. Extension cords are designed to radiate heat to the surrounding air; they should be uncoiled when used.
   B. If damaged or broken, they should be discarded and replaced.
   C. They should not be used in place of permanent or fixed wiring (e.g., snaked through walls).
   D. They should not be spliced.
   E. They should not be exposed to physical hazards by being:
      1. run under rugs and other high-traffic areas where walking, rolling, or pushing objects are likely to damage the wire;
      2. suspended without support;
      3. made accessible to pets;
      4. used in areas where there is tension on or a high risk of impact with wires; or
      5. subjected to sharp bends, knots, twists, pinches, and so on.
II. Poor handling of splices:
   A. mismatched splices;
   B. wires spliced and buried in walls or under floors; or
   C. spliced wires not being protected within a junction box.
III. Other problems, such as:
   A. the familiar "octopus" where more outlets are needed;
   B. nails or staples piercing insulation and contacting conductors; and
   C. junction boxes found buried in walls.

Internal or External Damage?

The most difficult problem when evaluating electrical wiring located at or near the point of origin of a fire is to determine whether the

Figure 6.4 In the course of a physical examination, an investigator may observe serious building or other violations. All such violations should be noted and photographed, even if they have no direct bearing on the cause of the fire. This type of photographic evidence may be used later to depict graphically either negligent or reckless conduct. (Photo courtesy of S. Grennan.)

damage to the wire observed resulted from some (internal) electrical malfunction or was caused by the (external) natural spread of fire. Several factors may be examined in this regard.

Cherry Discoloration.   Heat applied to a copper conductor will normally discolor it to a cherry-red hue. The depth of this cherry discoloration will, to a certain extent, identify the source of the heat. A common pocketknife is sufficient when field-testing a section of involved wiring. Using the blade of the knife, the investigator scrapes the surface of the conductor (carefully—the conductor is likely to be brittle). If after scraping the surface of the wire, the original copper color is visible, the source of the damage was most likely *external*, since the discoloration occurred only on the wire's surface. If, on the other hand, the investigator finds that the cherry discoloration runs throughout the diameter of the conductor, then the source of the damage is most likely *internal*, and may involve an electrical short, arcing, or other internal electrical problem.

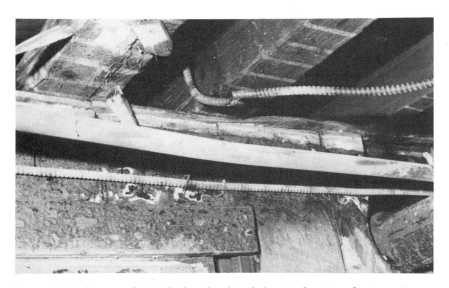

Figure 6.5 Before any fire is declared to be of electrical origin, the investigator should have hard evidence to that effect. The traditional reliance on a visual inspection of electrical components at or near the apparent point of origin alone will often lead to an erroneous conclusion and the possible mislabeling of the fire's cause.

Sleeving.   Rubberized or PVC insulation covering a conductor will react to and move away from a heat source. Therefore, if the insulation is loose on the conductor, the conductor was probably the heat source and the problem was internal. If the insulation is melted to the conductor, however, then the heat source was external.*

Pop-outs.   When a short and arcing occurs within BX cable or sheathed wire, the investigator may find *pop-outs* (holes caused by melting) in the external covering of the wire. If the wire in question is at or near the fire's point of origin, the investigator must determine if the shorting that occurred was due to internal forces or resulted from the normal spread of fire. To make this determination, the ends of the conductors at the pop-outs must be examined. A wire that has been cut by an electrician will have a sharp, pointed end; one that has broken due to an internal electrical short will be rounded (*beaded*) and blunt; and a wire that burned through and collapsed under its own weight will be pointed and annealed.

---

* This particular field test has been recently challenged by experts who question its validity.

Electrical Outlets and Switches

Electrical receptacles are usually rated at 15 A; snap switches may be rated at 5 A. With constant use either of these may become worn, resulting in pitting and arcing on the contact surface—the term *hot switch* is sometimes applied. As the contact surface loses tension, additional resistance may be created, which may cause overheating when used. Foam-type insulation, which was recently banned due to the health hazard it poses, had been widely used in place of fiberglass home insulation. When the foam was introduced into the space between the inside and outside walls of a house, it completely filled the void. However, in so doing, it formed a tight and complete blanket around all junction, switch, and outlet boxes in the wall, preventing these boxes from dissipating heat from their surfaces. The heat that is therefore trapped within the junction boxes may cause premature breakdown in the insulation of those wires housed within them.

Electrical Lighting

Fluorescent Lights

Fluorescent light fixtures should be individually protected with a 3-ampere fuse. The basic components of a fluorescent lighting fixture are a fluorescent bulb, the base, the *ballast* (starter), and a fuse. Older ballasts still in use are considerably more hazardous than the newer, thermally protected ones now required by the electrical code. This protection takes the form of a system of internal bimetallic strips that open and close to alter the flow of current as the ballast heats and cools.

Poor maintenance schedules are one factor in fires started by fluorescent lights. When old fluorescent bulbs are left in fixtures for too long, the ends of the bulbs become dark and eventually black. These older blackened bulbs draw increased voltage, which may cause the ballast to overheat dangerously and possibly ignite. To avoid this condition, fluorescent bulbs should be replaced on a regular basis.

Incandescent Lights

Incandescent bulbs have inadvertently caused many accidental fires. They have also served as the source of ignition for a number of incendiary fires. Many times, tracing the cause of the fire to a light bulb is much easier than determining whether the fire was set or accidental.

New light fixtures, whether they are traditional (e.g., a desk lamp) or distinctive (e.g., a recessed unit), are generally rated by the manufacturer as to the maximum allowable bulb wattage to be used. When

Figure 6.6 (A) A close-up view of the first floor receptacle, revealing the deep burn through the floor and the remains of the beaded Romex cable entering the receptacle. A color television set had been plugged into the receptacle. Note the remains of the TV set to the left and below the outlet. (B) A close-up view of the receptacle revealing the melted and beaded conductors within the receptacle. (C–E) Improper wire splices not only violate national and local electrical codes, but also lead to high resistance, overheating, and eventual fire. The fire and damage pictured in this series of photographs are a prime example of this condition. A view of the wiring suspended (stapled) from the floor joists. Notice the high-resistance short in the Romex cable where it passed up through the floor. Note that the Romex cable tied into the BX cable with no protection. A close-up view of the Romex and BX cables tied together. The splice had been covered with electrical tape. After a detailed examination, this wall outlet was determined to be the point of origin. Note the arcing on the inside of the cover and on the bottom screw of the wall receptacle.

---

this is exceeded, a condition called *overlamping* exists. The danger in overlamping is that the envelope temperature of the oversized bulb may ignite a lamp shade or other nearby combustibles. The excessive temperatures trapped within an installed recessed fixture can cause pyrolysis of the adjacent ceiling joists or actual ignition of certain commonly used ceiling materials or insulation.

In several instances, people have intentionally buried or insulated a bare incandescent bulb in combustible material with the intention of creating a delayed ignition device. In one case, an individual wrapped a 60-watt incandescent bulb several times with toilet tissue, then buried the wrapped bulb in a pile of dry rags and clothing located on an upper shelf in a closet. He then turned on the light switch and energized the bulb. The tissue paper ignited in approximately 25 minutes. Ignition occurred because the bulb's envelope temperature was absorbed by the toilet tissue rather then dispersed into the surrounding air. Table 6.3 illustrates the temperatures associated with various bulb wattage.

Although incandescent bulbs rarely survive fires (or routine fire suppression and overhauling operations), an investigator can readily determine whether or not a particular bulb was energized at the time of the fire by examining the metal components of the bulb's filament. If the bulb was energized (live) when the envelope ruptured, the filament would be blackened by the sudden exposure to the surrounding cooler air. On the other hand, if the filament has maintained a shiny metal appearance, then it was cool (not energized) at the time the envelope ruptured.

Sunlamps and Heat Lamps

Because of their purpose, sun or heat lamps are worthy of special mention. Sunlamps are designed to generate heat rays and are equipped with specially designed bulbs. When energized, a 250-watt sunlamp

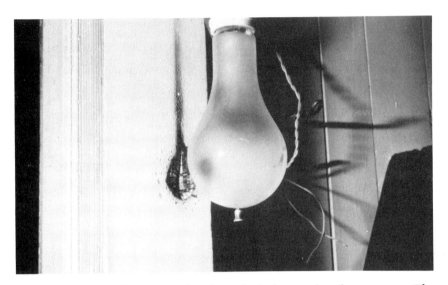

Figure 6.7 An excellent example of pyrolysis from a low heat source. The oversized (150-watt) bulb was installed in a do-it-yourself fixture, too close to combustibles. Notice the charring on the closet door frame. (Photo courtesy of D. Redsicker.)

can have an envelope temperature anywhere between 400° and 700°F. The fixture itself must be equipped with a porcelain or other heat-resistent receptacle because the socket can easily exceed 300°F.

Electric Motors

The operation of an electric motor is based upon the principle of magnetism. Reversing magnetic fields (like and unlike poles) cause the motion in the motor. Magnetic forces are concentrated in an invisible magnetic field that surrounds each pole. The strength of the field is

Table 6.3. Filament and Envelope Temperatures

Wattage (W)	Filament temp. (°F)	Envelope temp. (°F)
100	4000–5000	200–350
200	4000–5000	295–500
300	4000–5000	380–650

directly related to the amount of current carried. Problems can occur when

foreign objects (dust, moisture, metal fillings, etc.) get into the housing;

the motor is subjected to excessive vibration; or

bearings are worn or misaligned.

To field-test an electric motor, spin the motor shaft. If it is stuck, the problem is most likely due to internal damage caused by a breakdown in lubrication and fusing of the ball-bearings (internal friction). Any electric motor should be operated on a separate circuit (have its own circuit breaker or fuse).

Electric Blankets

To eliminate an electric blanket as the source of ignition for a fire, the investigator should examine the contact points within the thermostat for pitting or signs of arcing. Electric blankets should not be

tucked in under the mattress,

left on all the time,

folded up into a ball on the bed, or

insulated or covered with other blankets when on.

Low-Voltage Circuits

Because of their low arc potential, low-voltage circuits are rarely the cause of electrical fires. A typical low-voltage circuit might consist of a step-down transformer connected via 20 or 22 AWG insulated wire to a doorbell or alarm system. Most electrical problems that do involve a low-voltage circuit can usually be attributed to some malfunction in the transformer. Such a malfunction could cause the insulation to burn completely off the light-gauge wire.

Lightning

Lightning, although comparatively rare, has been the source of many accidental fires. The physical signs of a lightning strike will be fairly obvious to the trained investigator: holes blown in concrete, shattered wooden beams, and scorch marks that follow the course of wiring. A lightning strike is usually verifiable through interviews.

An investigator should know that when lightning strikes a transformer, two to three times the normal voltage will go to ground even

Figure 6.8 Lightning, although rare, has been the ignition source for many accidental fires. The physical signs of a lightning strike will be reasonably obvious to the trained investigator and are usually verifiable through interviews. The following sequence of photographs traces the path of, and subsequent fire resulting from, lightning striking a television antenna. (A) Lightning struck this antenna mounted directly outside an attic window. (B) A view of the antenna cable, which had overlapped the gutter, revealing a burn spot on the gutter and on the cable. (C) A close-up view of the fused coaxial antenna cable. (D) Interior view of the attic window revealing the area where the lightning bounced off the antenna cable into the floor, igniting a rug. There was limited extension of the fire, and the damage was reasonably minor.

when lightning resisters are in place. Even so, fuses may not blow. The lightning-induced surge of current is too fast. It has been estimated that the electricity released by one bolt of lightning (if harnessed) could suffice to electrify a small town for three months.

When electrical storms have to be ruled out as a possible accidental fire cause, it is necessary to obtain a certified copy of weather records. They may be ordered from the local National Weather Service or directly from the National Climatic Center.*

Gas and Flammable Vapors

Natural gas, liquid petroleum gases (LPGs), and other flammable vapors have been and continue to be involved in numerous explosions and fires. Experience indicates that most gas- or vapor-initiated fires are accidental. Negligence, human error, simple ignorance, and mechanical defect are the leading contributing factors. Thus, an insurance company may choose to refuse payment at the time a claim is made on the grounds that the fire or explosion was the result of negligence or some unreasonable conduct on the part of the insured. The fact that criminal (arson) charges are not forthcoming does not preclude insurance companies from seeking relief in *civil* court.

Gaseous fuels have, however, been used to accelerate incendiary fires. In such cases, the "torch" is either one of two extremes: *highly skilled* or *blatantly amateurish*. The unpredictability of gaseous fuels and the inherent danger associated with their use virtually preclude their use by professional torches. After all, a torch's intent is to destroy a building, not risk his life. Generally, when a gaseous fuel is used as an accelerant, the investigator should focus the investigation on the

---

* National Climatic Center, Environmental Data Service, NOAA, Federal Building, Asheville, North Carolina, 28801; phone (704) 258-2850, ext. 683.

owner of the property or on the individual who will profit the most from the fire.

Natural Gas

Composition

Commercial natural gas is a mixture of methane (90%–95%), ethane, and other flammable and inert gases. It contains no carbon monoxide (CO) and is, therefore, nontoxic. By itself, it is colorless and odorless. Commercially produced mercaptan, which contains sulfur in place of oxygen, is added as a safety measure. This gives natural gas its distinctive odor and serves as an olfactory warning, protecting against the inadvertent accumulation of natural gas (e.g., due to leakage or appliance malfunction).

Combustion

The combustion of natural gas is clean and smokeless. When oxidized, it should produce a nonluminous flame (Bunsen type) that is blue in color. The inner and outer blue cones of the flame should blend, and yellow flame tips should be absent. A yellow flame indicates an insufficient primary air supply.

The burning of an overrich gas–air mixture results in a condition called *carboning;* as a result of incomplete combustion, carbon in its free state deposits and collects on surfaces surrounding the gas jet (e.g., the burner cap head).

The oxidation of too lean a mixture can also be seen with the naked eye. This condition is indicated by a clear distinction between the inner and outer blue cones that make up the flame, and is usually accompanied by popping noises.

The ideal oxidation of methane is shown by the following formula:

$$7 \text{ air } (O_2 + N_2) + 4CH_4 \rightarrow 7N_2 \uparrow + 2CO_2 \uparrow + 8H_2O \uparrow + 2CO \uparrow .$$

The complete oxidation of one cubic foot (1 ft³) of natural gas produces approximately 1055 Btu (British thermal units).

Residential Gas Service

The local gas/utility company supplies natural gas to their customers through a series of underground transmission lines, commonly referred to as mains. The mains transverse the area serviced in a gridlike configuration. The gas pressure (*service pressure*) in a main can be as low as 1 pound per square inch (PSI) and as high as 35–100 PSI.*

A *house service* line branches off the main and connects the main to the house meter. House service is generally a lower-pressure line than the main; where necessary, a *pressure regulator* is used to reduce the main pressure for house service.

The *gas meter* is a mechanical device that measures, for billing purposes, the flow of gas as it is consumed. Gas meters are generally made either of tin, with soldered joints, or of an aluminum alloy, with screwed joints (the latter is called a *hard-case* meter). A utility's liability generally ends at the inlet cone of the gas meter.

The various gas appliances (*loads*) within the customer's home are connected to the gas meter by rigid gas pipes called *house piping*. The gas requirement for a load (in cubic feet) is determined by dividing its Btu output by 1055 (the maximum Btu output derived from oxidizing 1 ft^3 of methane). The Btu output of a gas appliance, along with the make and model number and other pertinent information, appears on a plate (usually metal) attached to it.

Venting

All automatic gas appliances should be vented. No unvented gas appliance should be operated continuously. Where venting is required, the diameter of the flue pipe used must be properly sized, and its length must not exceed the maximum specified on the appliance or by local code. A flue pipe should also be properly *pitched* (sloped): $\frac{1}{4}$ in/ft is common. Certain appliances, such as a gas clothes dryer, are required to be vented independently and not to an existing furnace chimney.

The oxidation of methane creates large amounts of water vapor as one of its by-products. This moisture can create problems and should be vented. A gas clothes dryer, on average, will evaporate approximately one gallon of water per load in addition to the water vapor created during the oxidation of the fuel.

Liquid Petroleum Gases

In many parts of the country, bottled liquid petroleum gases (LPGs) are used for heating and cooking purposes by residential customers. For example, so-called suburban propane is 90% propane, 5% ethane, and 5% butane. These gases, which include propane, butane, and acet-

---

* Gas pressure is measured with a *manometer*, which is a water-filled, U-shaped glass tube. The manometer is read in terms of inches of water (1 inch H$_2$O = 0.036 PSI). Service pressure is either *low* (below 1 PSI), *medium* (1–15 PSI), or *high* (15–100 PSI).

Table 6.4 Characteristics of Several Common Gases

Gas	Ignition temp. (°F)	Flammable limits (%)	Vapor density	Boiling point (°F)
Methane	999	5.3–14.0	0.6	−259
Propane	871	2.2– 9.5	1.6	−44
Butane	761	1.9– 8.5	2.0	31
Hydrogen	1085	4.0–75.0	0.1	−422
Acetylene	571	2.5–81.0	0.9	−118
Ethane	959	3.0–12.5	1.0	−128
CO	1128	12.5–74.0	1.0	−314

ylene, are also commonly found at the scenes of industrial fires. Their mere presence at the scene of any fire requires that the investigator clearly document and explain whether and how they were involved.

Gas Investigation

To correctly evaluate the role, if any, that gaseous fuel may have played in a particular fire, the investigator must be able to do the following:

identify the suspected gas or vapor,

determine its source, and

locate the point of ignition.

Identifying the Gas or Vapor

A suspected gas can be identified through the laboratory analysis of numerous physical and chemical characteristics. Among others, these include:

ignition temperature,

flammable (explosive) limits,

vapor density, and

boiling point

(see Table 6.4 and the section on Gas, Chapter 4). Once quantified, the values associated with each of these properties serve as a "fingerprint" (set of parameters) that differentiates one gas from another.

The investigator should carefully select and package samples of porous materials, such as cinder blocks, plasterboard, and carpeting. In any fire investigation where evidence or samples are collected, great care should always be taken in the selection process. It should not be done in a haphazard fashion. Consider the following:

Where was the concentration of the suspected gas the greatest?

Many small samples, packaged correctly, are better than a limited number of large (bulk) samples.

Where might I find samples that were least affected by the fire itself or by fire suppression operations?

Determining Source

In any gas-related explosion (pressure release) or fire, the investigator must identify the source of the suspected gas. The type of gases that are most often encountered are natural, propane, methane (sewer, sump), and, on rare occasions, hydrogen.

The accidental sources of *natural gas* and *propane* are similar enough to be discussed together. In general, the pressure of the gas is due to some form of explainable leakage due either to mechanical failure or to defective piping; for example

cracked pipes, especially around threaded fittings, due to sudden impact against or excessive weight placed on the damaged pipe;

improper use of flexible gas tubing (e.g., between floors or through walls); or

malfunctioning or improperly installed gas appliance (e.g., furnace, water heater, dryer, or space heater).

Note that the piping in a gas supply system will *never* unscrew as the result of a fire or explosion. If a threaded pipe *is* unscrewed from a fitting, examine the pipe for fresh tool marks.

Sewer or *sump gas* may be found as the result of a faulty or improperly constructed water (sewer) line: for example, if there is no trap in the plumbing to prevent sewer gases from escaping back into the structure, or if there are cracks in the cast-iron (subterranean) sewer line. In the case of methane gas, an investigator may also have to examine the history of the land on which the structure was built: it might have previously been the site of a landfill (dump), which would account for the presence of methane (sewer gas).

To the best of my knowledge, little is known about the source of hydrogen gas which has infrequently been found in the basements of private homes. In one case, an expert who was called to the scene of a gas explosion in a private home positively identified the cause of the explosion as the ignition of hydrogen gas. However, he was at a loss to determine the source of the gas, other than to state that it may have worked its way up to the surface from some point in the earth.

Locating Point of Ignition

The point of ignition in a gas-related fire or explosion is obvious in some cases, and determined by the investigator's educated presumption in others. When a flash fire results, causing only scorch damage, the burn patterns that remain may indicate the fire's extension away from the point of ignition; backtracking thereby locates the point of ignition. However, when a structure has suffered severe structural or fire damage, the investigator may develop a list of several probable points of ignition. Some of the more typical ones include the following:

heated machine parts, due to friction;

spark or arc from some nearby piece of electrical equipment or other electrical installation; and

gas-fired furnace or water heater suddenly "kicking on."

In one actual case, the point of ignition was determined to be a short circuit in an energized doorbell. A neighbor testified that when he rang his neighbor's doorbell, the house literally blew up.

Gas-Related Hazards

During the postfire evaluation, an investigator must determine if any hazards related to the provision or use of natural gas service contributed to, caused, or existed before the fire. During the step-by-step process required to complete this evaluation look for the following:

signs of tampering at the meter,

evidence of tampering (e.g., tool marks) at any connection of the house piping,

improper installation of appliances,

misapplication of equipment,

incorrect burner adjustments,

code violations (e.g., improper use of flexible pipe),

improper or inadequate venting,

missing or loosened house piping components (Note: Under no circumstances will a threaded fitting unscrew. This includes caps or plugs on pipe endings.),

appliances used in inappropriate locations (e.g., in the presence of flammable or explosive vapors or dusty atmosphere), and

auxiliary (e.g., portable) heaters used as the primary heat source.

The investigator must also document and evaluate the building's history:

Have there been complaints alleging gas odor?

What do the utility's records show for calls for service at that address?

How do meter readings compare over time? Are there unusual volumes or recent changes in use?

Role of the Gas Company

Most utility companies maintain well-trained investigative units. These units are on call and will respond to any fire where gas is suspected, since any such fire represents a substantial financial liability to the parent company. In my experience, these investigative personnel are very professional and eminently qualified in the analysis of gas-related incidents.

Such "in-house" investigative staffs are not restricted by personnel and budgetary constraints, as are their state and municipal counterparts. They examine and document every scene where gas is suspected with an eye toward eventual court presentation. Their laboratory results, photographs, and investigative reports are usually available to other interested investigative units. (Any investigative results obtained from the company should, of course, be double-checked for accuracy.)

A typical utility-run investigation includes the following procedures:

Inspect every gas fueled appliance.

Note dial settings (whether on or off).

Examine piping and connections.

Check local fire department records for number of false alarms.

Check for thermostat failure.

See if copper or plastic inserts are needed in the feedline. *

Photograph burn patterns and/or damage due to explosion.

Identify gas-related scorch pattern.

Determine whether the explosion was soft (gas) or high order (explosives, etc.).

Identify point of ignition and source of ignition.

Trace source of gas.

---

* Because of the effects of moisture, the cast iron feedlines from the main to the house have been known to become porous. To correct this condition, copper inserts (inner sleeves) were used. However, because of the value of copper, such inserts have sometimes been stolen, leaving the feedline in disrepair. More recently, plastic inserts have been used to discourage such thefts, but these are still subject to vandalism.

Building Furnace or Heating Plant

As a general rule the investigator should locate and examine the building's furnace or heating plant. This should be done even in those cases where the fire does not involve the heating plant. In every case, the investigator should be able to positively describe (at trial) the steps taken in eliminating the heating plant or furnace as the cause of the fire. Local utility companies are usually very cooperative in assisting the investigator in the evaluation of a furnace or boiler.

The most common type of *oil burner*/furnace used is the *gun* or *pistol-type pressure burner*, in which oil is pumped under pressure into the burner. Internally, pressurized oil is sprayed through a nozzle in a fine mist and mixed with air supplied by an electric fan. The combination of oil particles and air is ignited by an electric spark.

There are several different types of safety device that, when installed in an oil boiler/furnace, shut down the oil pump to prevent excess oil from being forced into the combustion chamber, causing it to overflow. Excess oil in the combustion chamber or an oil overflow could cause a fire or explosion when the system reignites. One of these safety devices is the *stack control* or *stack relay control*. It is a small electric sensing device mounted on the chimney, flue pipe, or side of the furnace. The stack control is designed to operate as hot gases from the furnace's internal combustion pass through the smoke or chimney pipe. If no hot gases pass through the chimney, indicating no combustion, the stack control relay shuts off the oil pump motor.

A second safety device installed in oil-fired steam boilers is the *low-water safety*. This device automatically shuts off the oil pump when the water level in the steam boiler falls below a predetermined level.

In a *gas-fired furnace* or boiler, natural gas is fed into a burner assembly via a gas supply line equipped with an electric control valve. Gas within the burner assembly passes through gas jets and is ignited by a pilot light flame. The safety device in a gas furnace/boiler is a *thermocouple*: a thin metal sensor, one end of which rests in the pilot light flame while the other is attached to the gas control valve. The pilot light flame heats the thermocouple, which converts this heat into a small electrical current. This current holds the electric gas valve in the gas supply line open. If the pilot light flame goes out, the thermocouple cools, no current is produced, and the gas valve closes.

For a discussion of gas as an accidental cause, see the section on Gas and Flammable Vapors.

Auxiliary Home Heating Devices

Approximately 20% of the residential fires in New York State are the direct result of the improper installation, operation, or maintenance of auxiliary heating devices. The tremendous increase in the price of home heating fuels, brought on by the Arab oil embargo of 1973, has

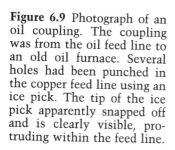

Figure 6.9 Photograph of an oil coupling. The coupling was from the oil feed line to an old oil furnace. Several holes had been punched in the copper feed line using an ice pick. The tip of the ice pick apparently snapped off and is clearly visible, protruding within the feed line.

created an almost frenzied interest in supplementary heating units. Millions of home owners turned to wood and coal stoves, kerosene heaters, electric space heaters and the like in an effort to save on home heating costs. Their presence at the fire scene warrants thorough investigation. Problems associated with use of these heaters include the following:

death from asphyxiation due to unvented or improperly vented operation;

improper installation—location in proximity to combustibles,
  failure to follow minimum clearances,
  improperly sized flues, and
  poorly made chimney connections;

incorrect operation—
  improper storage of flammable fuels,
  spillage and overfilling,
  overheating,
  improper choice of fuels,
  use of heater to dry out clothes, and
  use of spot/area heaters as a primary heat source.

improper maintainance—
  failure to replace worn or damaged components routinely, and
  failure to clean and/or inspect components on a regular basis.

Figure 6.10 Creosote will quickly accumulate in any chimney that is not adequately maintained and cleaned regularly. Creosote is a major fire hazard.

Note that auxiliary heaters may be used as incendiary devices.

Cooking-Related Fires

Most kitchen fires start as cooking accidents and are preventable. Thoughtlessness and panic are the two human characteristics that are chiefly at fault. People thoughtlessly leave pots cooking on the stove and roasts baking in the oven. When a minor fire starts, they panic in their attempt to extinguish it. For example, people try to carry a flaming pot from the stove to the sink, and one of three things inevitably occurs:

1. They drop the flaming pot on the floor after burning their hands.
2. They make it to the sink and set the kitchen window curtains on fire.

Figure 6.11 (A) View of a kitchen counter. The lowest point of burning is on the right end of the counter next to the refrigerator. A V pattern can be seen on the kitchen wall above that point. The holes in the wall and ceiling were cut by fire fighters checking on possible fire extension. (B) The point of origin was cleaned, and a toaster found on the kitchen floor was put back in its proper place. (C) A view of the interior of the toaster revealed internal flame damage and the residue of a molten, tacky substance. Investigation revealed that a fruit-filled pastry had apparently jammed when being toasted. A child had forgotten about it and had gone outside the house. The pastry ignited and the fire extended to the wall.

A

B

C

3. They pour water on the flaming grease or oil and find that small droplets of flaming grease "spit" about the room.

Here are some typical accidental causes of cooking-related fires:

barbecue grill left burning next to home or in garage until tank is empty;

food left heating in toaster ovens and counter-top broilers;

shortening, vegetable, or similar cooking oils overheating and igniting in the pan, or boiling over and igniting on the cooking surface;

ignition of grease built up in a kitchen exhaust fan; and

dish towels and oven mitts (insulated mittens used to protect the hands when moving hot roasting pans, etc.) thoughtlessly dropped on or close to hot cooking grills.

Exposed or Unprotected Flames and Sparks

Exposed or unprotected flames and sparks cause many fires, most of which are accidental. However, after close scrutiny, some evince gross neglect or reckless conduct of such a nature as to warrant civil if not criminal sanctions. Common sources of exposed flame and sparks include:

candles (decorative or religious),

chimney exhaust,

welding equipment (arc or acetylene torch),

static electricity (discharge can produce gas-igniting sparks),

electric motors and equipment (sparks from friction or electric discharge), and

open burning (leaves, rubbish, bonfires).

Children and Pets

Children, household pets, and farm animals may recklessly knock over candles, kerosene heaters, or other auxiliary heating units, accidentally starting a fire. In one case, a family dog either carried or dragged a large throw pillow from the living room couch, while the family was sleeping, and dropped it against the protective screen of a smoldering fireplace. A spark ignited the pillow. Fires caused by children playing with matches are an all too common occurrence. In New York State, children under the age of seven years are considered to be infants and not criminally responsible for their conduct. However, the child's parents may be held to be civilly liable for any damage.

Improper Storage of Combustibles

All too often warnings printed on packages or simple commonsense considerations are ignored when storing and handling combustible materials. Some examples of *improper* storage follow:

Combustibles are stored close to heat sources (e.g., furnace, heat vent, or auxiliary heater).

Pool chemicals or metallic sodium and potassium are stored in damp, moist areas. Magnesium slowly oxidizes in moist air.

Oxidizing agents or acids (e.g., sulfuric, nitric, hydrochloric acids) are stored too close to combustibles.

Phosphorus may be stored in a damaged container or otherwise exposed to possible contact with the atmosphere.

Vinyl acetate used in paint or other monomers may be stored in close proximity to peroxides or other catalysts.

The U.S. Department of Transportation publishes numerous periodicals that list literally hundreds of hazardous and flammable/explosive substances. Any investigation that involves large numbers of unknown or suspect chemicals may require the involvement of outside experts.

Spontaneous Combustion

All things being equal, spontaneous combustion (defined in Chapter 4) will progress more rapidly and efficiently in a warm or hot atmosphere (say, preheated by the sun's rays) than in a cold (wintery) atmosphere. For spontaneous combustion/ignition to occur, at least three factors must exist:

1. The fuel mass or materials involved must be subject to spontaneous combustion; for example, fresh-cut sawdust, grass clippings or hay, soft coal or coal dust, charcoal, or rags or paper soaked with linseed oil (boiled oil).
2. Oxidation (heat production) within the fuel mass must be slow, and sufficient heat must be generated to reach and initiate ignition.
3. The self-heating core of the fuel mass must be insulated well enough to prevent the generated heat from dispersing into the surrounding atmosphere.

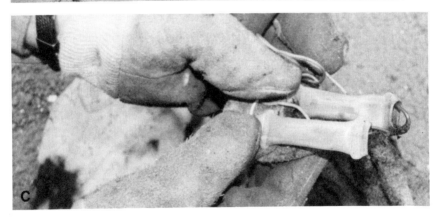

Figure 6.12 (A) View of a reconstructed bed that had been removed from the room of origin. Notice that the headboard had almost totally burned away. The fire was ruled accidental, caused by careless smoking in bed. (B) All other accidental causes had to be ruled out, including an electric heater and an electric blanket. (C) Note the close-up of the contact points.

The preheating qualities of direct sunlight (i.e., the greenhouse effect) may very well be a factor in expediting spontaneous combustion.

Smoking

Cigarettes, cigars, and pipe ash improperly discarded have been responsible for many structural, vehicular and forest/brush fires and countless deaths. However, it is also true that smoking products have long been the scapegoat in cases where no cause of the fire could be determined. Detailed and extensive experimentation conducted over the past decade has painted a much clearer picture of the true role of smoking products in the creation of fire. Research conducted by David Redsicker of the New York State Fire Academy indicates that careless disposal of smoking material is highly overrated as an accidental cause. The average burn time for cigarettes is between 5 and 15 minutes— an additive to cigarette tobacco aids in sustaining glowing combustion. Cigars, which do not have such an additive, rarely sustain burning for more than a couple of minutes. Stick matches will burn for 35 seconds, and cardboard matches for only 25 seconds.* Meanwhile, the average time span from the smoldering phase to open-flaming combustion is at least one hour. In addition, the increased use and effectiveness of flame-retardants has significantly reduced the frequency of such incidents.

Clandestine Laboratories

A *clandestine laboratory* can be defined as a place where controlled substances (i.e., drugs) are illegally prepared or processed. Many of the *precursors* (substances from which others are formed) used in the preparation of illegal drugs can be categorized as dangerous flammable materials. In addition, the gaseous by-products resulting from the cooking, baking, or mixing phases in the drug-making process result in the creation of a critical (explosive) atmosphere in the apartment, basement, or garage where the lab is hidden. A careless act can easily cause a disastrous and/or fatal explosion.

The huge demand for illicit drugs on the open market and the exorbitant profits associated with their manufacture and sale has lead to the creation of many such illegal labs. Narcotic investigators speculate that thousands are operating throughout the nation, many under the cover of a legitimate business.

---

* Values are for matches in *horizontal* position, as they might be if accidentally left or carelessly tossed away. Respective burn times for vertical are 70 and 47 seconds; held down at 30° angle, 12 seconds for both.

Figure 6.13 The fire that devastated this top-floor apartment was caused by an explosion due to the faulty operation of an "urban still." (Photo courtesy of D. Calderone.)

If, as an investigator, you inadvertently discover such a lab facility, *proceed with extreme caution.* Several law enforcement officers have been killed and/or seriously injured by explosions at clandestine labs. Follow the same procedures as you would at the scene of a natural gas emergency. If you discover a lab as the result of an explosion or fire, immediately contact the local narcotics investigation unit or the regional Drug Enforcement Administration office. They may supply the technical personnel and expertise necessary to complete the investigation safely.

The presence of any of the following may be due to the operation of an illicit drug laboratory.

Odors
  burnt almonds
  ether
  peppermint (often burned to cover the ether)
  gas (especially if passersby or nearby residents constantly
     complain of such an odor)

Equipment
  gas (Bunsen) burners
  electric mixers and grinders

gas, electric, or portable ovens
electric hot plates
plastic welding machines
pharmaceutical scales or other measuring and weighing devices

Controlled substances
heroin (from morphine or morphine base)
cocaine
THC (cannabis extract)
mescaline (peyote, trimethoxyphenethylamine)
methadone
amphetamines
methamphetamines
LSD (lysergic acid diethylamide)
DMT (dimethyltryptamine)
DET (diethyltryptamine)
PCP (phencyclidine, "angel dust")
STP/DOM (methyl-dimethoxy amphetamine)

Precursors
acetone (propane)
acetonitrile (methyl cyanide)
ammonium chloride
benzene
chloroform (liquid)
dimethylamine
dimethylformamide
diphenylacetonitrile
ethyl alcohol (ethanol)
ethyl ether
hexane
hydrochloric acid
lithium aluminum hydride
methanol (methyl alcohol)
methylformanilide
nitraethane
potassium permanganate
propane
sulfuric acid
tetrahydrofuran

Construction, Renovation, and Demolition

Many construction or demolition fires involve the use of electric or gas welding or cutting torches without having first followed minimum safety standards. Molten metals may come in contact with combustibles, starting a fire. In some cases, the inexperienced or untrained welder inadvertently permits the torch flame to touch nearby combustibles, or rests the still-hot torch (after use) on combustible material.

Propane heaters, which are either used to heat a workplace or to dry cement work quickly during winter months, may malfunction and result in a flash fire or explosion.

A common sight at construction and demolition sites during the winter is workers feeding wood scraps into flaming 55-gallon drums to stay warm. Sparks and burning embers carried aloft by the heated gases and smoke may come to rest on combustibles elsewhere in the structure and start a fire.

Direct Sunlight

Under unique conditions, the sun's rays may strike a curved section of auto or window glass in such a way that the refracted (bent) or distorted rays passed through the section of glass are slightly more concentrated than they might be ordinarily. This type of condition could not occur with standard flat or sheet glass. An exceptional combination of factors is required before any type of ignition is possible:

1. the room or car interior must be preheated (a greenhouse effect would be sufficient);
2. the fuel to be ignited must be of small mass with a low ignition temperature; and
3. the slightly concentrated light energy must strike the fuel mass for the length of time required to cause ignition.

A working knowledge of the unique combination of conditions required to cause ignition through the action of direct sunlight clearly justifies its infrequent linkage to or listing as the accidental cause of fire. However, children playing outdoors with magnifying glasses have been known to start both structural and brush or forest fires.

References and Suggested Readings

Beland, B., "Examination of Electrical Conductors Following a Fire," *Fire Technology*, November 1980.

Beland, B., "The Overloaded Conductor," *Fire and Arson Investigator*, International Association of Arson Investigators, April–June 1981.

Beland, B., "Arcing Phenomenon as Related to Fire Investigation," *Fire Technology*, August 1981.

Beland, B., "The Overloaded Circuit as a Fire Cause," *Fire and Arson Investigator*, International Association of Arson Investigators, July–September 1981.

Beland, B., "Electricity . . . The Main Fire Cause?," *Fire and Arson Investigator*, International Association of Arson Investigators, January 1982.

Beland, B., "Insulated Heat Source as a Fire Cause," *Fire and Arson Investigator*, International Association of Arson Investigators, June 1982.

Beland, B., "The Breaker on a Cold Wall—A Fire Cause?," *Fire and Arson Investigator*, International Association of Arson Investigators, December 1982.

Beland, B., "Comments on Fire Investigation Procedures," *Journal of Forensic Sciences*, January 1984.

Brannigan, F. L., Bright, R. G., and Jason, N. H., *Fire Investigation Handbook*, Handbook No. 134, National Bureau of Standards, Washington, D.C., August 1980.

Carter, E. R., *Arson Investigation*, Collier MacMillan, London, 1978.

Ettling, B. V., "Electrical Wiring in Building Fires," *Fire Technology*, November 1978.

Ettling, B. V., "Arc Marks and Gouges in Wires and Heating at Gouges," *Fire Technology*, May 1981.

McPartland, J. F., "All These Electrical Fires? Hogwash!!!," *Electrical Construction and Maintenance*, January 1981.

Roblee, C. L., and McKechnie, A. J., *The Investigation of Fires*, Prentice-Hall, Englewood Cliffs, N.J., 1981.

Investigating Fatal Fires

7

The impact on society from unchecked incendiarism is most often delineated in economic terms. Arson is described as one of the predisposing causes of the economic blight so evident in our urban centers. Its costs are frequently measured in terms of the dollar value of shrinking tax revenues, the high cost of insurance premiums, and the increased burden of welfare benefits. This price-tag approach, although accurate, is blatantly deficient in describing the grief and suffering of the individual burn victim, or the loss to society, family, and friends of a fellow human being.

This year alone, arson will dramatically impact upon the livelihood and well-being of millions of Americans. More importantly, well over 1000 people will die and ten times that number will be injured or frightfully disfigured. Every arsonist, regardless of motive, is a potential mass murderer.

Six-Phase Investigative Approach

The multiplicity of problems confronting an investigator at the scene of a fatal fire is not always obvious. The underlying investigative dilemma is the separation, with absolute certainty, of those incidents that are tragic accidents from those that require detailed criminal investigation.

During the initial stages of the investigation, numerous questions will be raised that may be hours or even days away from credible answers:

Was the fire intentional or accidental?

Was the victim alive or dead before the fire? (Arson is sometimes employed in an attempt to disguise a crime scene or to destroy evidence of criminality; see the section on Crime Concealment, Chapter 2.)

Who last saw the victim alive?

Who discovered the fire?

Can enough solvability factors be identified to warrant an aggressive prosecution?

The answers to these and similar questions provide the investigative blueprint for determining the truth.

The following six-phase approach is presented as an aid to the investigator in a fatal fire case:

1. fire incident,
2. examination of the body,
3. cause and origin/investigative canvass,
4. investigative procedure,
5. follow-up investigation, and
6. arrest and trial.

The strategy used in this approach is applicable in every case involving a fire fatality. However, the information to be collected during each of the phases may be tempered by unusual or unique conditions. The utility of each phase must be evaluated in light of the facts and circumstances presented in the case at hand.

Fire Incident

The first phase in the process deals with the duties and responsibilities of the first fire-fighting units to respond to a fire in which a person dies or is seriously injured and likely to die. It begins at the time the fire is discovered, and ends with the arrival of the fire/police investigator. The ultimate responsibility for this phase rests with the fire officer in command of the scene. If the fire is considered suspicious, the officer should immediately request the assistance of a fire investigator. In the case of a fatal fire, he should also request the assistance of a *police* investigator; the investigation of unusual or unnatural deaths generally falls within the jurisdiction of the local Police Department.

Maintenance of the Fire Scene

The credibility of the scene investigation and, to a great extent, any future prosecution is directly affected by the extent to which the fire scene has been disturbed. The person responsible for preserving the integrity of the fire scene until the first investigator (fire/police) arrives is the chief fire officer. A chronologic list of all authorized persons entering the crime scene should be maintained and given to the assigned investigator when he arrives. Those authorized to enter the fire scene would include police and fire officials assigned to investigation, the medical examiner or medical investigator, the district attorney/prosecutor or his representative, and so on. In the case of a fatal fire, the scene, in its entirety, should remain *intact* until the medical examiner arrives. Therefore, line fire fighters and other emergency personnel should be prevented from removing a dead human body found in the charred debris. There are some obvious and reasonable exceptions to this rule:

any doubt as to whether the person is, in fact, dead,

danger of fire-structure collapse or falling debris creating a serious hazard,

a serious threat that the body will be further damaged by the spread of flames, and

the continued presence of the body being a serious hindrance to fire-fighting operations.

However, in the absence of circumstances, the body and its immediate surroundings should be left as originally found.

If the responding fire/police investigator is nearby, the overhauling process should be delayed until he is present. This is to prevent the inadvertent destruction of any evidence near where the body was found or at the point of origin.

Arrival of the Investigator

An experienced investigator should be aware of the fact that the timeliness of his response to the scene can, to a great extent, make or break the investigation. Survivors of and people with an interest in the fire may be present, and fire fighters with first-hand knowledge of conditions within the building during the fire may still be available. In addition, a rapid response—one made before the Fire Department releases the building to the owner—can preclude certain legal problems regarding crime scene searches (see Chapter 14).

Upon arrival at the scene, an investigator must make a conscious effort to maintain his professional objectivity and avoid getting caught up in the confusion and hysteria that will immediately confront him. Other uniformed personnel (fire and police) will be looking to him for direction. Rather than jumping headlong into a case, an investigator must pause long enough to assess the situation and develop a preliminary plan of action. One way to secure the needed time is for the investigator to maintain a low profile upon arrival. This will give the investigator a few minutes in which to record some basic information and collect his thoughts.

The type of information to jot down initially includes:

the exact address of the fire (which may differ from that received from a dispatcher),

the time you arrived at the scene, and

general observations (weather conditions, lighting, entrances, exits, etc.).

The next step is to ensure that "pedigree" (detailed background) information on all the persons injured or evacuated is being recorded by subordinate uniformed personnel. This should be done even if the injured are to be treated at the scene and released. Also to be noted are the names of the ambulance attendants, paramedics, and Red Cross volunteers who are treating and transporting the injured; pertinent information regarding the ambulances; and the hospital(s) or other emergency center(s) to which the injured are being moved. Everyone displaced and all the injured will have to be interviewed when the investigator has finished at the scene. The paramedics and attendants should also be interviewed to see whether any of the people being transported made statements while in the ambulances. These statements could be material to the case or may contradict statements already noted. (The reasons for and an analysis of such contradictory statements is covered in Chapter 12.)

Once the investigator has had a chance to evaluate the situation and is satisfied that the necessary background information has been recorded, he should identify himself to the chief fire officer or his aide. The chief or his aide can then fill the investigator in on what transpired at the scene before his arrival, as well as confirm whatever information he may have received up to that point. Other information that should be sought at this time includes the identity of anyone missing or unaccounted for, an estimate of the fire damage, and whether or not the fire's cause is suspicious (and the rationale for this classification).

Remember that this scene involves a death investigation. It is crucial to determine anything that transpired before the investigator's arrival and that may impact on the investigation. The fire scene is to be treated as a *crime* scene, even thought it is not yet known whether a crime has, in fact, been committed.

Chief's Report

The ranking officer will prepare a fire report describing the actions taken to extinguish the fire. A copy of this report is usually available to the fire/police investigator. This after-action report will include, among other things, a determination as to whether the fire's origin and/or cause were suspicious.

A fire may be declared suspicious for a variety of reasons. The fire report should list and explain any factors that led to such a determination. Some common factors are the following:

The rate of burning was not consistent with the type of combustibles present in the fire building.

A person died in the fire.

There were questionable or multiple points of origin.

The cause of the fire could not be readily ascertained.

Fire fighters noticed an odor of gasoline or other accelerant.

Examination of the Body

The second phase of the investigation involves the visual inspection and physical examination of any dead human body discovered during phase 1. In most jurisdictions, the office of the *medical examiner* or *coroner* is responsible for ensuring that both an investigation at the scene and a subsequent autopsy on the body of the victim are conducted. The autopsy should be conducted by a *forensic pathologist,* but the scene investigation is usually carried out by either a medical examiner's or coroner's representative or a physician (nonpathologist) who holds the title of *medical investigator.* Although it is frequently preferable for the pathologist to visit the scene, the vast number of medical examiner cases, from all sources, and the scarcity of forensic pathologists do not currently permit this except in unusual cases.

The fire/police investigator should advise the local medical examiner's office as soon as possible as to the known facts and circumstances relating to the fire and victim(s). In all fire cases where a body is found, a medical investigator should respond to observe the scene, the condition of the body, and its relationship to the origin of the fire.

There are four main tasks facing an investigator during phase 2:

1. recording the scene,
2. identifying the victim (to whatever degree possible),
3. determining (tentatively) whether the fire occurred ante- or post-mortem (i.e., whether the victim was dead prior to the start of the fire or died as a result of the fire), and
4. examining and collecting whatever physical evidence may be present that would corroborate a finding in tasks 2 or 3 and would assist the pathologist performing the autopsy.

Recording the Scene

Photographs of the body *in situ* (i.e., in its original position) and of the room or area in which it is found will prove to be very valuable later in the investigation. These photographs, along with investigative notes and any rough sketches prepared at the scene, are to serve the purposes outlined below:

1. To provide an overview of the body and its surroundings so that its relative position can later be established.
2. To provide close-up photographs of any evidence that indicates (a ruler should be used for true size comparison):
   a. the identity of the victim;
   b. circumvented alarm or fire-suppression systems;
   c. point(s) of forced entry or exit;
   d. another (underlying) crime or signs of a struggle;
   e. the presence of gas cans, trailers, plants, and so on.
3. To clarify the condition of the body regarding:
   a. the extent of burning or cremation;
   b. the flow of fire patterns on the body and whether they are consistent with the extent of damages to the surroundings (Was a victim who died on the second floor found buried in an ash-filled basement because of the collapse of the interior structural members?);
   c. whether the body was found face up or face down, and the degree to which it insulated the floor below it (or failed to do so).
4. To identify furnishings (e.g., bed, coffee table, desk) in the area where the body was found.
5. To indicate the relative position of the body in relation to the point(s) of origin.
6. To identify any other factors of importance to technical or forensic procedures.

In some cases, especially where the victim is found quite a distance from the point of origin of the fire, it is necessary to trace the connection between the fire and the resultant death. The connection may seem obvious when the investigator is at the scene, but while on the witness stand some 12 or 15 months later, the connection may not be as clear. To illustrate this problem, let us examine the particulars of a fire that occurred in the Bronx, New York, late in 1978.

At 5 A.M., a fire started in the basement of an abandoned five-story walkup. The adjoining buildings were fully occupied and were evacuated by the responding fire units. One of the evacuees was a 9-year-old, mentally retarded boy. During the ensuing confusion, the boy was separated from his parents and, apparently frightened by the crowd, sought the safety of his room. The boy's father, searching for his son, found him under his bed. The boy had died from carbon monoxide asphyxiation.

The fire damage to the abandoned building was extensive, but did not communicate to the adjoining buildings. The boy's body was found one building away and four stories above the source of the carbon monoxide that caused his death. The investigators involved in the case traced and (wisely) photographically documented the path that the billowing smoke and gases took between the source and the boy's room.

On occasion, the medical examiner will, after autopsy, refer a case to a police investigator for further investigation. The autopsy may have revealed insufficient and/or contradictory data or may have raised additional questions that the medical examiner wants to have clarified before signing a death certificate. These cases are referred to as *CUPPIs* (Circumstances Undetermined Pending Police Investigation). If the crime scene was processed and recorded accurately, the investigator, in many cases, should be able to review the crime scene data and provide the medical examiner with satisfactory answers. (See Chapter 10 for more on crime scene documentation.)

Psychological Profiling

If, during the course of the investigator's crime-scene analysis, it appears that the fire was set to conceal the scene of an especially gruesome or sex-related homicide, the investigator should evaluate the evidence collected and the documentation of the scene in terms of their possible value in the development of a psychological assessment.

> The purpose of the psychological assessment of the crime scene is to produce a profile; that is, to identify and interpret certain items of evidence at the crime scene which would be indicative of the personality type of the individual or individuals commiting the crime (Ault and Reese 1980, p. 23).

The following are necessary in order for a psychological profile to be conducted properly:

1. Complete photographs of the crime scene, including photographs of the victim, if it is a homicide. Also helpful are some means of determining the angle from which the photographs were taken and a general description of the immediate area.
2. The complete autopsy protocol including, if possible, any results of lab tests which were done on the victim.
3. A complete report of the incident to include such standard details as date and time of offense, location, weapon used (if known), investigating officer's reconstruction of the sequence of events (if any), and a detailed interview of any surviving victims or witnesses. Also included in most

investigative reports is background information on the victim(s). (Ault and Reese 1980, p. 24)

The background information on the victim should be as detailed as possible.

Information provided by such a profile may include the following:

1. the perpetrator's race;
2. sex, age range, and marital status;
3. general employment;
4. reaction to questioning by police;
5. degree of sexual maturity;
6. whether the individual might strike again;
7. the possibility that he/she has committed a similar offense in the past; and
8. possible police record (Ault and Reese 1980, p. 24).

If the investigating officer's agency or department does not have the trained personnel to develop a psychological profile, then the assigned investigator should contact the nearest Federal Bureau of Investigation field office. The agents assigned to the field office may be able to evaluate the submitted material in terms of its applicability to the profiling process. If the field office does not offer this service, the investigator should forward his request directly to the Behavioral Science Unit, FBI Academy, Quantico, Virginia.

In light of the FBI's success in this field, some of the larger state, county, and municipal law enforcement agencies in the country may well develop their own procedures in this area. Many law enforcement agencies already have the personnel on staff (studying the effects of stress on job performance and conducting preemployment psychological testing) who could conceivably provide this service.

The role of psychological profiling is covered in more detail by Geberth (1983).

Identifying the Victim

Determining the identity of a fatality discovered at the fire scene can be a difficult job involving the efforts of several specialists. The investigator must, therefore, collect any items that might directly or indirectly facilitate the proper identification of the victim (e.g., remains of the victim's clothing or objects found on or near the body). Some obvious questions should also be answered:

Who was most likely to have been within the fire structure when the fire started?

Who was observed entering the structure during the fire?

Who, among these people, is missing or unaccounted for?

If these preliminary avenues of investigation seem to make the identity of the victim clear, the field investigator should make every effort to identify and record the names, addresses, and phone numbers of relatives and friends of the deceased. This information should be supplied to the office of the medical examiner. Many victims are identified by these relatives and friends during a viewing of the body conducted at the morgue. Such visual identification is referred to as *gross identification*. The feasibility of such a viewing is obviously determined by the condition of the body.

The degree of destruction of a body depends largely on the intensity of the fire and on how long the body was exposed to it. In extreme cases, the body may be so badly damaged that it is impossible to determine even sex or race, let alone identity and cause of death, prior to autopsy. Position of the body relative to the fire is another significant factor: Suspension over flames (e.g., on a bed, couch, or reclining chair) will lead to more complete bodily destruction because body fat and tissue fuel the fire.

The investigator should know that in most fires, the body is almost never totally consumed and is usually recognizable as human even if the sex, race, and so on are undiscernible due to massive charring. This is because it is extremely difficult to maintain the open burning of a human body. Even when a body is cremated—burned for approximately two hours at 2000°F—teeth and dental work are rarely destroyed.

Beyond gross identification, there are several other approaches to victim identification available. One is by means of *fingerprint comparison*. Palm and sole prints should also be made at the time fingerprints are taken. These are all forwarded to the Federal Bureau of Investigation for comparison with prints already on file. The value of finger, palm, and sole prints for identification purposes is limited, of course, by the condition of those areas to be printed. If a complete set of prints cannot be taken, the incomplete set and tentative identification should be forwarded to assist in the comparison.

Another method of positive identification is the use of dental records. As mentioned earlier, teeth and dental work are usually found intact. Furthermore, the shrinking of the victim's facial skin and the swelling of the tongue tend to protect not only the teeth, but also the inner mouth. This means that a *forensic odontologist* can identify three or four times as many points of identification as can a fingerprint technician. These include the shape of the fillings, sinus cavities, nerve paths, signs of root canal work, and so on.

At autopsy, the odontologist takes dental x-rays and then removes the upper and lower jaws for charting purposes. These charts are then compared with prior x-rays and charts based on any tentative identi-

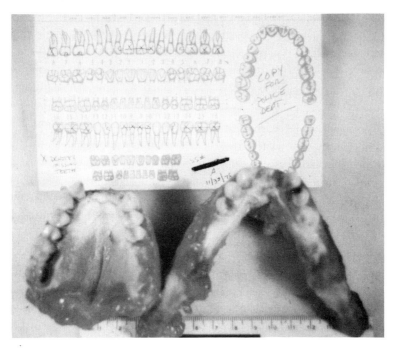

Figure 7.1 Fire victims are very often identified through an examination of antemortem and postmortem dental records. As seen here, the victim's jaws were removed during the autopsy, and a dental chart was prepared. This chart and x-rays are compared with the antemortem records of suspected victims. (Photo courtesy of Dr. A. Goldman.)

fication. If no tentative identification is available, the odontologist can at least greatly narrow down the possibilities by identifying the *style of dentistry* (e.g., type of materials used in fillings). This may help identify the socioeconomic class of the victim.

A fourth method of identification is based on information discovered during the medical/physical examination and autopsy. These factors include:

tattoos and scars;

evidence of prior surgical procedures or prior fractures;

unique or unusual deformity;

sex, race, build, features, and approximate age; and

personal papers, jewelry, clothing, and so on.

Time of Death: Before or During the Fire?

One of the most important issues in any fatal fire investigation is the question of time of death. Was the victim alive or dead prior to the fire? This piece of information, coupled with the cause of the fire and the cause of death will set the tone of the entire investigative process that is to follow (as we shall see in phase 4).

The police, fire, and medical investigators, working as a team, may be able to make certain tentative determinations regarding the status of the victim during the fire, based on an analysis of ante- or post-mortem burns and injuries. Any determination made at the scene is obviously tentative; the precise analysis of ante- and postmortem injuries can only be determined and interpreted at autopsy.

In some jurisdictions, an investigator may have to wait several days to receive the final disposition of an autopsy. This is a crucial factor in any investigation. It is, therefore, incumbent upon the investigator to initiate and pursue whatever investigative data are available on the basis of his initial, on-site investigation.

In many cases, the medical investigator, with the assistance of the police and fire investigators, is able to develop a defensible and medically accurate conclusion as to whether death occurred before or during the fire, based upon what he sees at the scene. There are several factors that, when analyzed, can provide the empirical data upon which to base such a conclusion. These factors examined separately (like the pieces of a puzzle) can be misleading; but when compared and connected chronologically, they can provide a reasonably clear picture of what occurred.

The first thing that the investigator should note during the physical examination is whether the victim is face up or face down. Except for those found in bed or on a couch, most victims are found face down. A person who succumbs while staggering or crawling through a smoke-filled room can usually be expected to fall forward and thus, be found face down. However, it is reasonable to expect to find a person sleeping face up in bed or on a couch. The fact that a body is found face up elsewhere is not in and of itself necessarily suspicious, but it does warrant additional attention and inquiry.

If the victim was alive during the fire, he or she may have inhaled quantities of smoke and soot. If so, the body should show signs of soot and smoke particles (*carbonaceous material*) in and around the mouth and nose, indicating that breathing continued during the fire.

Certain physical changes occur after death or when varying degrees of heat and flame are applied to a dead human body. These effects, in most cases, are natural phenomena and should not be misinterpreted by an investigator as indicative of foul play.

Postmortem Lividity

The natural settling of the blood after death is called *postmortem lividity*. This is due to the gravitational pooling of the blood, and it is usually purplish to blue-black in color. Its location is dependent on the position in which the body rests after death. Although it begins *at* death, lividity becomes *visible* from 30 minutes to 4 hours later. Over the next 8 hours, it becomes fixed. It is during this latter period (before lividity becomes permanent) that *secondary lividity* may occur. If a body is turned from the position in which it originally rested—as might occur if a body were moved several hours after death and positioned differently—lividity will develop in this second position. The medical investigator arriving at the scene will note the presence of lividity corresponding to two positions (Gross, undated, p. 5). Unless the repositioning can be attributed to structural collapse or operational intervention, secondary lividity would seem to indicate foul play.

Concentrations of carbon monoxide in the blood cause postmortem lividity to be pink to cherry-red in color. Redness of the lividity might, therefore, indicate that the victim was alive and breathing at the time of the fire. Should the examination of the body take place before lividity has had a chance to develop, the pink to cherry-red color may appear in the victim's lips and eyelids.

Pugilistic Attitude

A victim may be found in what appears to be a defensive boxing pose or fetal position. This is called the *pugilistic attitude*. This condition occurs when the stronger muscles in the limbs are exposed to high temperatures over a prolonged period of time. The intense heat causes the large muscles in the arms and legs to contract, thereby pulling the limbs toward the torso. In addition, the hands may be cupped (clawlike) as the fingers are drawn toward the palms. This movement is a gradual one, and not a spasmodic or jerking action.

The absence of the pugilistic attitude in a body that has been exposed to ample stimuli may very well be questionable. One possible reason for its absence might be that the body was in rigor mortis prior to the start of the fire. *Rigor mortis* is the stiffening of the body after death due to the postmortem contraction of the muscles as the result of changes in protein content. It first develops to completeness in the muscles comprising small tissue masses and is, therefore, first visible in the face, jaws, and hands. It develops in about 2–4 hours, becomes complete over a period of 12–24 hours from death, and remains for another 24–48 hours before it begins to disappear.*

---

* The onset of rigor mortis may be hastened by the presence of heat or cold. It may even develop instantaneously in the case of a fatal head injury. Its disappearance is accelerated in a warm environment and with the development of putrefaction.

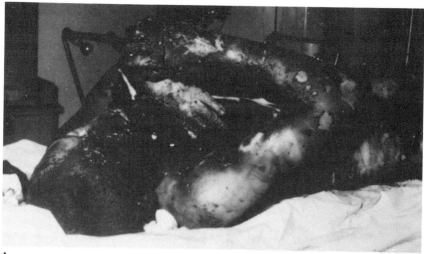

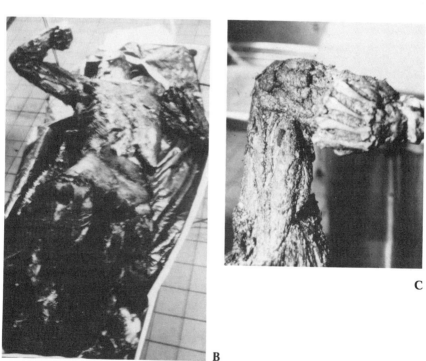

Figure 7.2 (A–B) The body pictured appears to be in a defensive boxing pose. This condition is called "pugilistic attitude." It is a natural phenomenon of fire. (C) The close-up of the victim's right arm illustrates how the limbs are drawn toward the torso and the fingers are cupped. The extent of the burning makes fingerprint identification impossible. (Photos courtesy of Dr. A. Goldman.)

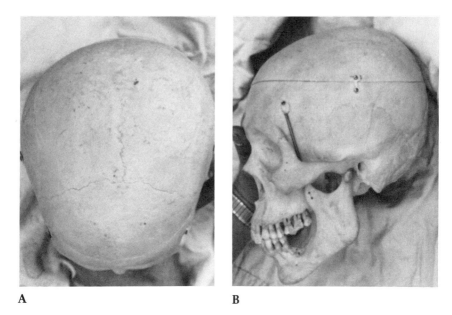

A   B

Figure 7.3 (A) Photograph illustrates the natural suture appearing on the skull. (B) A side view of a normal human skull. (Photos courtesy of Dr. A. Goldman.)

A body in rigor mortis prior to the start of the fire will develop only a limited pugilistic attitude or none at all, depending on the time and extent of rigor mortis.

The pugilistic attitude might also not occur if the heat necessary to cause the muscle contraction was not sufficiently long or intense. This might be the case in a flash fire. Regardless of the suspected cause for the lack of pugilistic attitude, the responding medical investigator should routinely examine the body for rigor mortis.

Skull Fracture

Another factor that may easily be misconstrued is the discovery that the victim's skull is fractured. Care must be taken to determine whether the fracture is implosive or explosive. An *implosive fracture* may have been caused by a fall, may be evidence of a prior felonious assault or homicide, or may result from a collapsed structural member. The exact cause will be determined at autopsy and evaluated during the follow-up investigation. An *explosive fracture*, however, is usually a natural consequence of fire. The extreme heat may cause the fluids in and around the brain to boil and expand. The resulting steam produces pressure sufficient to cause an explosive (pressure-release) reaction. The fracture(s) that result usually follow the natural suture lines of the skull. In extreme cases, the cranium may burst, causing the expelled brain and skull matter to form a circular pattern around the head. This is more common in children than in adults: The *fontanel*, or membrane-covered opening between the uncompleted parietal bones, is the weakest point in a fetal or young skull. The resulting circular pattern (0–12 inches from the skull) is signficant when compared with the type of splattering that might result from a shotgun blast or high-order explosion.

Blistering and Splitting of Skin

The unfamiliar investigator may be somewhat apprehensive in attempting to evaluate the effects of heat and flame on the skin of the victim. The medical investigator is in the best position to render a judgment in this area.

The formation of blisters (*vesicles*) is part of the body's natural defense system. The exact distinction between ante- and postmortem blistering can only be made at autopsy. There are however, certain signs that a medical investigator can evaluate in the development of a hypothesis. *Postmortem blisters* are generally limited in size and may contain only air or air mixed with a small amount of body fluid. *Antemortem blisters* are larger in size and contain a complex mix of body fluids. The precise determination of the fluids requires microscopic analysis. A blister surrounded by a pink or red ring can be considered as having occurred before death; the reddish ring is the result of an antemortem inflammatory reaction.

Note that in some instances, temperatures may not have been sufficiently high to produce blistering. Likewise, if the skin is burnt off or otherwise heavily damaged, blistering will not be in evidence.

The heat and flame inherent in the fire also cause the skin to shrink or tighten and ultimately split. The splitting or lesions may be seen on the arms, legs, and torso. At first glance this condition, coupled with pugilistic attitude, could be misinterpreted as indicating defense wounds.

Note that, in some cases, a seriously burnt person survives the fire and is removed to a local burn center. In an effort to save the person, the medical staff at the center may attempt to duplicate the natural splitting of the skin with a surgical technique known as an *escharotomy*. This technique is used to help foster circulation and to prevent the onset of gangrene. Should the burn victim expire some time after the fire, these splits should not be misinterpreted as fire-induced.

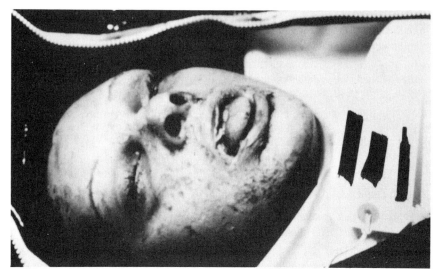

Figure 7.4 Photograph illustrates the effects of varying degrees of heat and flame on human skin. The victim's skin is sloughing or separating from the tissue below and has experienced some charring. (Photo courtesy of Dr. A. Goldman.)

Figure 7.5 The skin on the victim is split or ripped. (Photo courtesy of David Redsicker.)

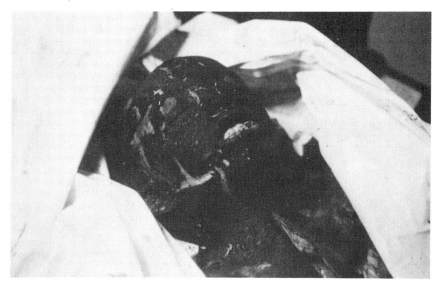

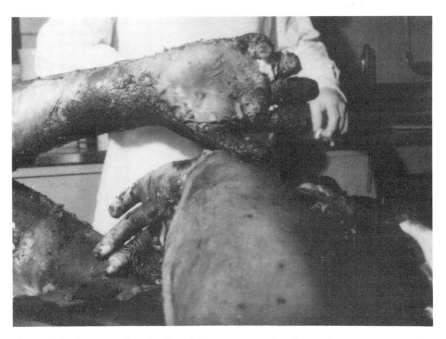

Figure 7.6 Victim's skin is sloughing or separating from tissue.

Cause and Origin/Investigative Canvass

In this third phase of the inquiry, two separate investigative operations take place simultaneously. The *fire investigator*, who is responsible for determining the fire's cause and origin, begins the physical examination of the structure (or automobile salvage in the case of a vehicular fire). The *police investigator*, who is responsible for the death investigation, begins an investigative canvass.

Also at this stage, the medical investigator authorizes and supervises the removal of the body and the associated debris. This debris may contain evidence that would resolve the circumstances of death and the possible origin of the fire (e.g., remnants of a charred mattress). The body itself is a germane part of the physical evidence, and a chain of custody must be maintained. Remember, too, that the body may be heavily charred and very fragile. Special care must also be taken to ensure that personal items that might aid in the identification process (e.g., dentures, jewelry, clothing) are not lost. No attempt should be made to separate these items from the body prematurely; this should be done at the morgue where the autopsy is to be conducted.

Cause and Origin

Determination of cause and origin is covered in detail in Chapter 5, and automobile salvage is covered in Chapter 8. However, several additional points deserve mention at this time in that fire fatalities call for the generation of many additional reports and their eventual referral to the medical examiner's office.

The medical examiner's interest in the results of the physical examination or automobile salvage will focus on several narrowly circumscribed factors.

1. He will want to know the cause of the fire (accidental or incendiary), since this may provide information regarding the circumstances of death.
2. He will want to know if the use of an accelerant (e.g., gasoline or kerosene) is suspected and the possible type(s) of material(s) that were ignited. At autopsy, the pathologist may then order additional toxicologic analyses of the victim's blood and lung residue to test for the presence of the appropriate flammable vapors or toxic gases. (If this is the case, then the location of the point(s) of origin in relation to the location of the body at the scene would also be considered.)
3. A third area of interest, especially if the victim died during the fire, is *survivability*. The medical examiner will be concerned with any fact that would provide insight into the victim's failure to escape safely.

Investigative Canvass

Interview and interrogation strategies and the investigative canvass are covered in detail in Chapter 12. The investigator conducting a canvass must remember that the neighbors and friends of the victim, who may themselves have just escaped the flames, may make threatening and accusatory statements that they will rarely make or repeat at a later date. The investigator must learn to make use of the tension and stress apparent in and manifested by the fire survivors as a motivating factor to elicit information.

Determining Investigative Procedure

In phase 4, all of the information amassed from the investigative steps already completed (phases 1–3) is assembled and analyzed by the medical examiner, together with the results of the autopsy (cause of death). The product of this synthesis serves as a blueprint determining how the follow-up investigation (phase 5) is to be conducted.

Medicolegal Autopsy

After the body is removed from the fire scene (phase 3) but before investigative procedure can be determined, an autopsy must be performed. The *medicolegal autopsy* is a systematic examination of a dead body, following standardized procedures, conducted for multiple purposes. The predominant purpose for a medical examiner's autopsy is usually to determine the cause of death. Many other factors are considered in the course of the examination, some of which are a continuation of examinations initiated at the scene:

identification,

time of death,

circumstances of death,

correlation of injuries,

evidence, and

survivability (Gross, undated, p. 8).

Although the external areas of the body may be very heavily charred, in most cases the internal organs will be relatively undamaged.

X-rays

The forensic pathologist's first action will be to x-ray the body and the associated debris. By examining the x-rays, the pathologist will be able to isolate and identify any foreign objects (e.g., spent bullets, cartridges, knife blades) that may be present. If an explosion preceded the fire, shrapnel may have been blown into the body and may, indeed, be the cause of death.

Carboxyhemoglobin

Carbon monoxide (CO) is an odorless, colorless gas present at hazardous levels in all structural fires. Carbon monoxide asphyxiation is probably the single most common cause of death in fires. Exposure to as little as 1.3% carbon monoxide can cause unconsciousness after only two or three breaths, and death in a few minutes. As we have already seen, CO causes the cherry-red color of postmortem lividity (as well as that of internal organs and muscle tissue).

At autopsy, the pathologist will test the victim's blood for the level of *carboxyhemoglobin*—carbon monoxide present in the pigment of the red blood cells. Carbon monoxide has an affinity for red blood cells that is approximately 210 times greater than that of oxygen. The concentration of carbon monoxide in the blood is a very important element in determining if the victim was alive before and during the fire. Its concentration is quantified in terms of a percentage of saturation. Because carbon monoxide in the blood is generally due to the inhalation of CO during the fire, the absence of CO in the red blood cells (less than a 10% saturation) would be rather conclusive evidence that the victim was dead prior to the fire.*

Alcohol and Controlled Substances

At autopsy, the pathologist should routinely test a sample of the victim's blood for the presence of alcohol or drugs (controlled substances). The purpose of this test is threefold.

1. The first objective is to determine if the presence of alcohol and/ or drugs was a relevant factor in the death, due to the *synergistic* (enhanced-effect) reaction between alcohol or drugs and carbon monoxide. When a person is "high" on alcohol or drugs, the available oxygen carried to the brain is restricted. When that same person inhales carbon monoxide, the CO quickly replaces the already restricted oxygen in the blood, and unconsciousness and death quickly follow.
2. The second purpose is concerned with the question of survivability. Did the presence of alcohol or drugs in the victim have any bearing on the fact that the victim failed to escape safely?
3. It affords the investigator and district attorney an opportunity to evaluate and prepare for a possible contention by a defense attorney that the victim himself accidentally started the fire while in a drunken stupor.

Toxicology

If the fire investigator or fire marshal has reason to suspect that an accelerant was used, he should advise the medical examiner of this fact. Based on the information supplied, especially the distance between the point of origin and the body, the medical examiner may choose to send blood and lung residue samples to the lab for gas chromatographic or mass spectrophotometric analysis. The lab would both analyze and attempt to identify any flammable vapors present in these samples. If flammable vapors were found, this would both indicate that the victim was alive and breathing these vapors during the fire and corroborate the suspicion and findings of the fire marshal.

---

* It is possible for a charred body to absorb small quantities of CO, which accounts for the low levels (10% or less) of CO found in a body proved to have been dead before a fire occurred.

Cause of Death and Investigative Procedure

During the course of the autopsy, the pathologist will make a determination as to the cause of death. Death may have resulted from a single factor or from several contributing factors. The cause(s) may include, but are not limited to, the following:

burns,

burns plus CO asphyxiation,

spasm of the epiglottis,

acute alcoholism plus CO asphyxiation,

edema,

shock,

gunshot wound or stabbing.

After fixing the cause or contributing causes of death and evaluating the circumstances of death, the medical examiner will generally classify the case and refer it to the local police department. As shown in Table 7.1, the medical examiner's classification is usually the determining factor in how a case will be investigated.

Follow-up Investigation

The responsibility for conducting the follow-up investigation of a fatal fire rests with the police investigator. The purpose of this investigation is to resolve cases referred by the medical examiner's office. The investigative procedure proposed by the medical examiner in phase 4 is normally used as the basis for cataloging cases earmarked for further action.

In many cases, a preliminary follow-up investigation will have commenced at the time of the fire incident, based on the tentative findings from the examination of the body and the officially listed cause of the fire.

In situations where the death is an obvious homicide (e.g., apparent shooting or stabbing victim, victim's hands and/or feet bound, or ligature tied around the neck of the victim), the investigation should be well documented by the time supporting data are received from the medical examiner. Here, the motive for the homicide (e.g., domestic, robbery, narcotics, sex crime) becomes a key issue in identifying a suspect. The fire, if of incendiary origin, was most probably set either to prevent or impede the identification of the victim; to conceal wounds and injuries; or, as is the case in certain sex crimes, to purge or purify the site where, to the psychopathic mind, something evil was

Table 7.1. Determining Investigative Procedure

Cause of fire	Cause of death	Investigative procedure
Accidental	CO asphyxiation No additional factors (accidental)	Close case during follow-up investigation
Incendiary	CO asphyxiation No additional factors (homicidal)	Investigate as an arson/ homicide Motive for the fire important
Accidental	Gunshot, stabbing, manual or ligature asphyxiation, blunt force trauma, etc., prior to the fire (homicidal)	Investigate as a homicide Reevaluate physical examination of fire scene
Incendiary	Prior to fire (homicidal)	Investigate as a homicide Fire used to conceal Motive for homicide is important
Accidental	CO asphyxiation plus other natural illness (accidental)	Close case during follow-up investigation
Accidental	CO asphyxiation Additional injury (implosive skull fracture) (CUPPI)	CUPPI Review crime scene photos and reports Prepare report for medical examiner with results of follow-up investigation
Incendiary	CO asphyxiation Additional injury (implosive skull fracture) (homicidal)	Investigate as an arson/ homicide Fire to conceal prior assault or attempted homicide
Incendiary	CO asphyxiation Additional factors (burns/shock) (possible suicide)	CUPPI Results of investigative canvass crucial Prepare report for medical examiner Check possible suicide (rare)

committed. (See Chapter 2 for a discussion of Arson Motives and Pathology.)

The investigation of an arson/homicide or felony murder is measurably different from that of a homicide in which the fire was set to conceal the crime. The two investigations are similar only in that, in both cases, numerous sources of information and associates of the victim will have to be identified and interviewed. The greatest distinction between the two is in the intent of the actor. In the investigation of an arson/homicide, the key element is the identification of the motive for the fire. The investigator may discover that the fire was indeed set to kill the victim; this would, however, be an exception rather than the rule. In most cases, the arsonist does not intend to kill. There may be no connection whatever between the motive for the fire and the death that results; the death is an unintended consequence.

An important point to consider when investigating any incendiary fire, regardless of motive, is the level of sophistication or technical knowledge exhibited by the fire setter. An investigator can, at times, extrapolate enough data in and from the point or area of origin to speculate on such factors as:

whether a fire was planned or an impulsive act,

possible age differentiation (adult versus child) by target chosen, and

whether the torch was an amateur or professional.

To address these questions, the investigator would have to consider:

the source of ignition (sophisticated, delayed timing devices versus a common match),

the first material ignited (were chemicals or other liquid accelerants carried into the premises or were commonplace combustibles simply piled and ignited?),

whether any measures were taken to circumvent fire-alarm or -suppression systems, and

other conditions or circumstances peculiar to the case at hand.

CUPPI Follow-up

Perhaps the best way to explain the investigation that follows a CUPPI (Circumstances Undetermined Pending Police Investigation) referral from the medical examiner is to examine a hypothetical example.

Referral from Medical Examiner: The Case of John Doe

On Tuesday, July 9, 1982 at 0200 hours, there was a one-alarm fire at 123 Main Street, Garnerville, New York. During the search and rescue operations, the body of a white male, 53 years of age, was recovered in the bedroom of apartment 4B. The fire was brought under control at 0225 hours. There was extensive water and smoke damage on the fourth floor, but limited fire damage.

The fire was declared accidental by Fire Marshal Jones, Shield No. 30764, at 0500 hours of July 9, 1982. The cause of the fire was traced to an overloaded electrical circuit in apartment 3C. All other residents of the building escaped safely.

At autopsy, the victim was positively identified as John Doe. The cause of death was determined to be carbon monoxide asphyxiation. The victim also suffered an implosive fracture on the right side of the head, just above the right ear.

CUPPI: How did the victim sustain the fracture to the right side of the skull? Determine if the victim was the victim of an assault.

Facts: Cause of fire—accidental/electrical; cause of death—CO asphyxiation; problem—implosive fracture to the right side of the skull.

Investigative Follow-up on John Doe Case

Results of interviews: Mr. John Doe had lived alone at 123 Main Street, Apartment 4B, for the past 17 years. His sister and her husband, Mr. and Mrs. Thomas Smith of 129 Broadway, Bronxville, New York, had had dinner with the victim at his apartment at 8 P.M. on the night of the fire. They stated that the victim was alone when they left him at 11 P.M. The first firemen at the scene stated that the front door to apartment 4B was locked from the inside, and that they had to force entry.

Review of crime scene data indicates that the victim was found face up on the bedroom floor, next to a two-drawer night table, approximately 3 feet from his bed. The victim was dressed in nightclothes, and it appears, from all available evidence, that the victim was most probably asleep at the time of the fire.

An analysis of all available evidence indicates that the victim awoke in his smoke-filled bedroom. While suffering from carbon monoxide intoxication, he stumbled, fell, and struck the right side of his head on the corner of the night table. The injury took the form of an implosive fracture. After striking his head, the victim fell to the floor, face up.

There is no evidence to indicate that the victim was the subject of a prior assault or any form of foul play. Recommend that the case be closed.

CUPPI: Suicide by Fire

The investigation of a fire death, particularly where suicide by fire is suspected, is a complex exercise. The final determination relating to the circumstances of a suicide by fire can only be made by the medical examiner.

The medical examiner will generally refer such a case to the local police detective unit for additional follow-up investigation. The purpose of this CUPPI referral is to amass as much background information on the victim as possible. This information may then be referred to a forensic psychologist or psychiatrist for evaluation, the purpose of which is to develop an antemortem psychological profile of the victim. This type of diligent, integrated investigation is absolutely necessary for two reasons:

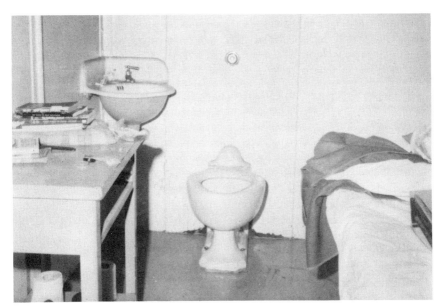

A

B

Figure 7.7 (A) Photograph of an unburned cell in the same cellblock. (B) Young male victim who committed suicide by setting fire to his jail cell mattress. (Photos courtesy of D. Redsicker.)

1. To accurately classify the death as a suicide.
2. To verify and document all the available information that may be necessary to defend the classification of death in any future litigation.

Suicide by fire is rare in our culture, but fire/arson investigators must be aware that it does occur and be alert enough to recognize it when it happens.

A case in point is that of Mr. Joseph M., an 80-year-old retired fire lieutenant. His body was found tangled in the remains of his bed in the heavily damaged bedroom of his two-family home. The first firemen at the scene thought the body was bound with wire and advised their chief, who contacted both fire and police investigators. A closer examination revealed that the victim had become tangled in the remains of an electric heating blanket and was not bound as was first thought.

The scene investigation uncovered an empty one-gallon gasoline can in the rubble next to the bed, and an undated, yellowed newspaper headline taped to the wall in the living room. The headline read, "Fire Chief Dies In Blaze." No suicide note was found.

The interviews of relatives and neighbors conducted the same day, provided a penetrating portrait of the victim. Mr. M. was a widower and had no children. His wife of 38 years had died two years earlier. The victim was pensioned from the fire department on a disability, after 24 years of service. He had not worked in the 22 years since his retirement. Soon after his wife passed away, he was diagnosed as having cancer. Since that time, he had undergone at least two operations. Relatives stated that the victim has suffered terribly and had been despondent for the past several months.

Mr. M.'s death was ultimately classified as a suicide by fire. In this case, the diligence of the investigators both during the scene examination and the follow-up investigation brought the matter to a proper conclusion.

Victim Identified as Fire Setter

A fire investigator must be alert to the fact that a body (or one of the bodies) found at the scene may be that of the fire setter. Many inexperienced fire setters, including the home owner or businessman turned torch, seriously injure or kill themselves while setting a fire. This seems either to be due to a lack of knowledge of fire behavior and combustibility, or to be indicative of poor planning. The inordinate reliance upon and excessive use of highly flammable liquid accelerants probably accounts, more than any other reason, for the injury and death of the amateur torch.

The investigator must keep this thought in mind when conducting the follow-up interviews of the injured. These interviews generally take place at the hospitals to which the injured have been transported. It is important that the investigator pinpoint through questioning the actions and locations of the injured up to and at the time they state they were injured. The investigator can then compare these statements with the information developed during the physical examination.

In one particular case, a building superintendent stated that he was awakened by smoke at about 5:30 A.M. and was injured moments later when he opened a basement door, located in a front hallway in his apartment house. He stated that when he opened this particular door he was "hit in the face with a blast of flame and heat."

An analysis of the already completed physical examination indicated that the fire had started in the rear storage area of the basement and that an accelerant (gasoline) had been used. In addition, it was known that the fire extended into a rear airshaft and that the lateral spread to the front of the basement came much later in the fire. It was, therefore, impossible for the superintendent to have been injured at the time and location he stated. A determination was made that the superintendent was either chronologically confused or lying. Following a well-developed line of questioning, the investigator was able to get him to admit that he had been in the basement when he was injured. He later made statements that led to his arrest: The superintendent "victim" was in fact the torch.

Arrest and Trial

As the case approaches the stage where sufficient probable cause exists to warrant the arrest of one or more suspects, the investigator, working closely with the local district attorney or prosecutor, must carefully consider the options governing the *method of arrest*. This is not a question of tactics, although all arrests do involve some tactical considerations; the method of arrest refers to the authority or agency authorizing or ordering the arrest. A law enforcement officer in the United States has only two options:

1. arrest based on probable cause, or
2. arrest with a warrant.

Arrest Based on Probable Cause

Probable cause, also referred to as *reasonable cause to believe,* is the minimum level of proof required legally to effect an arrest. The experienced investigator should realize that there are serious weaknesses inherent in choosing to make a summary arrest.

The first shortcoming involves some confusion on the part of the investigator as to his or her obligation to see that the case comes to fruition. The investigator, as previously stated, would be operating at the minimum level of proof necessary to justify an arrest; whereas the district attorney, who is to prosecute the case, must prove every element of the crime beyond a reasonable doubt in order to secure a conviction. It does not serve society to have an arsonist and/or murderer hastily taken off the streets and then freed because of the state's failure to prosecute. Thus, although the initial purpose of the investigation was merely to determine the facts, specific ancillary objectives become important for the investigator as the case builds:

To identify the suspect(s).

To gather and present sufficient evidence to carry the case to a successful conclusion.

To ensure continuity, the investigator should coordinate efforts with the local prosecutor's office. In this way, weaknesses or problems in the case can be identified and corrected before an arrest is made. The district attorney's office is also the route through which the investigator can gain access to electronic surveillance, eavesdropping, or search warrants, should these become necessary.

A second area of concern when a summary arrest is made is the possible problem of civil liability. Many arson cases (because of the nature of the crime) are based largely on circumstantial evidence. The legal principle of "exclusive opportunity" is commonly at issue, and there may not be any hard or direct evidence positively to place the defendant at the fire scene. At arraignment, in such cases, the arresting officer must be eloquent enough to explain the steps that led to the development of probable cause satisfactorily. However, the arresting officer may very well then be the subject or respondent of a civil suit charging false arrest. The arresting officer, if an agent of any federal, state, or municipal agency, may then be the subject of a federal suit for violation of civil or constitutional rights (U.S. Code, Title 18, Sects. 241–242; Title 42, Sect. 1983).

Arrest with a Warrant

A second option available to the investigator, while working closely with the local district attorney, is to effect an arrest under the authority of an arrest warrant issued by a state supreme court or district court judge. An arrest warrant both authorizes and orders the arrest of the person(s) named on the face of the warrant. Such a warrant can be obtained in one of two ways, regional policy or practice notwithstanding.

In one situation, the district attorney presents the case before a sitting grand jury. The members of the jury consider the testimony and physical evidence and vote on the issue. If an indictment results, the district attorney files the indictment (accusatory instrument)* with a local superior court and requests that an arrest warrant be issued.

A second method, which is also a powerful investigatory and prosecutorial tool, is for the district attorney to present the case directly to a superior court judge after filing an accusatory instrument, such as a felony complaint. This method is especially useful in a case where there are a large number of suspects. The investigator and prosecutor can pick one of the defendants, usually the weakest link in the case, and attempt to "turn" him. Using the threat of an indictment and trial on the major count as an inducement, the chosen subject may decide to cooperate with the investigation and testify for the state. This method is often used to build a stronger case against the remaining subjects. In return for cooperation and testimony, the defendant turned informer is listed as an unindicted coconspirator and is given immunity from prosecution.

Trial

The details of the investigator's responsibility during an arson trial are covered in detail in Chapter 13. An arson/homicide trial tends to be far more complex, and is, therefore, worthy of special mention. In addition to the points that must be proven in an arson trial—

1. that crime (arson) was committed and
2. that the defendant committed the crime—

there is the additional burden of proving

3. that the actions of the defendant led to the death of the victim.

Additional witnesses, including the medical examiner, serologist, and toxicologist, will be called to testify.

As in the arson trial, the defense attorney's primary attack will focus on the handling and examination of the fire scene. He will challenge the officially listed cause and origin of the fire. If the defense counsel is able to discredit either the qualifications of the fire scene technician or the actual scene examination itself, the people's case against the defendant will come to an abrupt end; if the fire is ruled the result of some accidental cause, then the death that resulted from it was also accidental.

---

* In New York State, the right to counsel immediately attaches with the filing of an accusatory instrument.

The opening of this chapter described the underlying dilemma faced by every investigator during the investigation of a fatal fire: to separate tragic accidents from criminal matters. The greatest tragedy occurs when, because of investigative laziness or oversight, an arsonist and murderer goes free.

References and Selected Readings

Adelson, Lester, *The Pathology of Homicide*, Charles C. Thomas, Springfield, Ill., 1974.

Ault, Richard L., Jr., and Reese, James T., "A Psychological Assessment of Crime: Profiling," *FBI Law Enforcement Bulletin* 49(3) (March) 1980.

Geberth, Vernon J., *Practical Homicide Investigation*, Elsevier Science Publishing Co., New York, 1983.

Gross, Elliot M., "The Role of the Medical Examiner in Homicide Investigation," course material, Homicide Investigation Course, NYPD, undated.

Harris, Raymond I., *Outline of Death Investigation*, Charles C. Thomas, Springfield, Ill., 1962.

Hughes, D. J., *Homicide Investigative Techniques*, Charles C. Thomas, Springfield, Ill., 1974.

Kennedy, John, *Fire and Arson Investigation*, Investigations Institute, Chicago, 1962 (revised 1977).

Kirk, Paul L., *Fire Investigation*, John Wiley and Sons, New York, 1969.

O'Hara, Charles E., *Fundamentals of Criminal Investigation*, 5th ed., Charles C. Thomas, Springfield, Ill., 1980.

Snyder, LeMoyne, *Homicide Investigation*, 3rd ed., Charles C. Thomas, Springfield, Ill., 1977.

Spitz, Werner U., and Fisher, Russell S., *Medicolegal Investigation of Death: Guidelines for the Application of Pathology to Crime Investigation*, Charles C. Thomas, Springfield, Ill., 1973.

Investigating
Vehicular Fires

8

There are tens of millions of motor vehicles on the highways and streets of America. Over the next 12 months, millions of these will be involved in accidents. Approximately one million vehicles will be reported stolen. Thousands more will be abandoned, their derelict frames dotting the landscape. Additionally, each year throughout the nation, hundreds of thousands more will burn. Annually, close to 20,000 of these are classified as vehicular arson.

Although accidental fires do occur in vehicles, the overwhelming majority of vehicular fires are intentionally set. People seem to burn their automobiles, vans, and mobile homes for the very same reason that they burn their homes. The primary motive seems to be economic. For the most part, this motive can be described as "selling it to the insurance company."

Some enterprising individuals who have decided to rid themselves of their motor vehicles do so in a rather unique fashion: by driving them into a ghetto area, one well known for its high crime rate and representing a low socioeconomic class of people. The driver simply parks his or her car anywhere in the area and walks away. In a matter of days, the vehicle is usually stripped of its tires, radio, and anything else of value. Soon after that, it may be set on fire, perhaps by a roving band of juveniles who have nothing better to do. Meanwhile, soon after abandoning the vehicle, the owner contacts the local police and reports the vehicle as stolen.

The investigation of a vehicular fire requires a two-part approach. The first involves the completion of a detailed postfire *automobile salvage examination* to determine the cause and origin of the fire. The second, which hinges upon the determination made during the first,

Figure 8.1 Upon arrival at the scene, fire fighters found the passenger compartment of this vehicle fully involved. An accelerant had been poured on the front seat, and the driver's door had been left open to provide oxygen and accelerate burning.

involves the interviewing and/or interrogation of the vehicle's owner (see Chapter 12 on Interviewing and Interrogation). If the cause of the fire is determined to be incendiary and the investigator has reason to suspect the owner, then the purpose of the follow-up interview and/or interrogation is to elicit statements that would implicate the vehicle owner.

This chapter is concerned with the investigation of vehicular fires and the commensurate responsibility of an arson investigator to investigate and classify properly the cause as either accidental or incendiary.

Local Policy

The degree and amount of emphasis placed on the investigation of vehicular fires varies widely throughout the country. Certain communities consider vehicular arson as a very serious offense, requiring a diligent, in depth investigation. Other jurisdictions only investigate vehicular fires that involve some other mitigating circumstance (for example, death or an organized crime connection). This kind of approach is usually a policy decision mandated by competing interests vying for limited resources. After all, if a specific community is experiencing a major upsurge in certain "part 1" crimes (e.g., homicide, rape), how much emphasis, in terms of personnel and equipment, can realistically be devoted solely to the investigation of vehicular fires?

Role of the Insurance Industry

The primary motivating force behind the heightened interest in the investigation of vehicular arson has been the insurance industry. Traditionally, it has suffered the greatest overall losses in this area from unwarranted or fraudulent insurance claims. The truth is that we, the motoring public, ultimately pay for the insurance losses sustained, which are passed down and distributed among all policy holders in the form of higher premiums.

Because of the insurance industry's interest, an investigator conducting a vehicular arson investigation can, in almost all cases, expect full industry cooperation.

Notification Response

Once a fire/arson investigator is notified of a vehicular fire, the decision as to whether or not he will respond to the scene is usually based upon several factors:

preliminary determination made by the fire officer who directed the fire-suppression operations;

number and type of other arson cases under investigation that require active follow-up (e.g., arson homicide, structural fire);

personnel available;

time of day—most vehicular fires occur at night in remote areas where lighting conditions are poor, whereas the type of detailed examination required necessitates daylight; and

mitigating circumstances—a body or contraband (narcotics, weapons, etc.) is involved, the vehicle is connected to a member of organized crime or to the commission of some other serious crime, and classification of the vehicle as abandoned or derelict (in which case a fire/arson investigator would not ordinarily respond to the scene).

All telephone or written reports of vehicular fires should be maintained in a separate log, so as not to confuse these incidents with other calls for service. The log serves as a ready reference and source of data for monthly or quarterly reports, aids in the preparation and updating of related crime analysis reports, and ensures the equitable distribution of cases among the assigned investigators.

If a vehicular fire has been declared suspicious, or if the fire/arson investigator has been requested to respond, the vehicle must be safe-guarded and protected until his arrival. Under *no* circumstances should the vehicle be returned or released to the owner without the prior approval of the assigned investigator.

Single Vehicle Collisions

The vehicular fires addressed here do not ordinarily include those that are the result of collisions (especially multiple vehicle collisions). The investigation of such accidents is highly specialized, and generally is conducted by special units attached to local, state, or federal law-enforcement agencies. One common exception, however, is the case of a fire in a vehicle supposedly involved in a *single vehicle collision*. Certain mitigating circumstances, when carefully considered, may well heighten an investigator's interest in a particular case.

Location of incident (populated versus desolate area). Did the purported accident and fire occur at a location where it was highly unlikely for anyone to have witnessed it?

Collision evidence. Although the vehicle may show signs of collision damage, is there any physical evidence at the scene, independent of the vehicle, that would tend to support the driver's contention? This type of scrutiny is necessary to avoid the possibility of a prior (unre-ported) multiple vehicle accident now being reported as a single-vehicle accident, with the fire designed to disguise this fact.

Time of incident (daylight versus nighttime hours). Did the purported accident and fire occur at a time when it was highly unlikely for anyone to have witnessed it?

Driver's description of incident. Care must be taken to evaluate carefully statements made by the driver to the first fire or police units to arrive. Can any incriminating or inconsistent statements be identified?

Vehicle Identification and Owner Information

On arrival, the investigator should first record a complete and accurate description of the vehicle including:

color, make, and year of manufacture,

license plate number (registration),

Figure 8.2 Was the vehicle reported stolen? Note the vehicle identification number (VIN). Since 1971, the VIN number has been located on the upper left side of the dashboard of all U.S.-manufactured and most foreign automobiles.

vehicle Identification Number (VIN),*

engine serial number, and

state inspection code number (if appropriate—located on inspection sticker).

This information should be transmitted to the state department of motor vehicles, the local police auto squad, and the national auto theft bureau. These agencies will provide the following:

identity (name and address) of the last registered owner;

verification of color, make, and year of manufacture, and/or code number;

name of insurance company; and

pedigree on vehicle, including:

    vehicle history,

    dealer information,

    prior accidents (if reported) and whether vehicle was the subject of a prior insurance settlement (salvage),

    correlation of the engine and vehicle data (the 9-digit engine serial number is incorporated in the 13-digit VIN),

    verification of registration and vehicle data (e.g., whether incorrect license plates are on vehicle), and

    possible identification of state-registered inspection.

---

* Since 1971, the Vehicle Identification Number (VIN) has been located on the upper left side of the dashboard of all U.S.-manufactured automobiles and most foreign vehicles.

If the vehicle has been reported as stolen, then the investigator should compare the approximate time and date of the fire with the time and date of the reported theft.

Salvage Examination

The salvage examination is completed in two separate stages: exterior and interior. The investigator should fully examine the exterior of the vehicle before starting the interior examination.

Exterior Examination

The investigator should first direct attention to the exterior of the vehicle and to the area immediately surrounding it. During this stage he should pay particular attention to the following:

tires (extent of burning, condition, rims, lug nuts, hub caps, tool marks);

gas tank (tank, flange, cap filler tube);

suspension system (springs/shock absorbers, sagging, annealed);

glass (in place, missing, softened, fused, window frames, windows open or closed during fire);

catalytic converter;

roof panel (collapsed or concave, condition of paint);

engine and trunk hoods (collision damage, condition of paint);

fenders (collision damage, burn pattern in paint, extent of burn pattern in paint);

grill (collision damage);

bumpers (collision damage, pushed or towed to site);

doors (collision damage, burn pattern on paint, open or closed during fire);

lights (collision and fire damage); and

license plates (registration/inspection stickers).

All information derived and investigative actions taken should be

---

Figure 8.3 During the exterior examination, the investigator should photograph the exterior of the vehicle and the area surrounding the vehicle. Note the general condition of the vehicle, including collision damage. Is the vehicle burned "bumper to bumper?" If an accelerant was used, it may be possible to see where the accelerant dripped from the vehicle to the ground.

Figure 8.4 Fire fighters risk injury fighting vehicle fires in which the vehicle owner's intention was to "sell the car to the insurance company." In this photograph, gasoline had been poured in the passenger compartment and the vehicle was set ablaze. The vehicle had been intentionally placed in a very secluded area. Note the snow tires mounted on the front wheels of a rear-wheel-drive automobile. The subsequent investigation revealed that the burnt auto had been towed to the scene.

documented in the investigator's notes and by means of photographs and sketches. Any collision damage should be photographed. The total extent of fire damage should be noted. Any vehicle fire in which fire damage extends from "bumper to bumper" should be considered highly suspicious. Such a burn pattern is indicative of a highly improbable fire extension. An investigator must realistically consider what parts of a vehicle are combustible: rubber hoses, wire insulation, tires, rubber belts, grease and oil, floor mats, carpeting, upholstery and seat padding, undercoating, ornamentation, and personal property. A fire that accidentally starts in one of the three interior compartments will tend to stay in that compartment. If the visible exterior fire damage is localized to the area surrounding one of the interior compartments, the investigator would be fairly safe in presuming that the fire started in that compartment.

Tires

A person intending to burn his or her car may remove good tires and replace them with old or worthless tires before starting the fire. What is the condition of the tires and tire tread? How much of a tire was burned? Even when a tire burns, there is usually a section left between the rim and the ground; from this, the investigator should determine whether the tires were bald or recapped. The lug nuts and hub caps

Figure 8.5 Examine the gas tank, gas filler tube, and gas cap. Was the drain plug in the gas tank, was it removed to allow gasoline to pool under the vehicle, or was it blown free if the tank exploded?

should also be checked. If the hub caps are not on the rims, are they lying nearby? Are the lug nuts missing? Are there any tool marks on the lug nuts indicating that the tires were recently changed?

Gas Tank

The investigator should examine the gas tank, the gas tank filler tube, and the gas cap. Is the gas cap on the car? If not, is it lying nearby? Does the gas cap flange show signs that it was blown off during the fire (as by an explosion)? Was the drain plug in the gas tank in place or had it been removed to allow the gasoline to pool below the vehicle? Are there any tool marks on the drain plug? Is the drain plug collar in place? If the collar is in place and the drain plug is missing, then it is virtually impossible for an explosion to have displaced the drain plug: experience indicates that had an explosion occurred, both the plug and collar probably would have been blown free. Note that when a gas tank does explode, it usually ruptures at its weakest points, along the seams.

Some knowledgeable vehicle owners may introduce certain easily obtainable chemicals into the gas tank to induce an explosion. This may be done by putting the chemical first into a balloon, which will dissolve in the gasoline. When the chemical comes into contact with the gasoline, a violent explosion will usually cause the gas cap to blow off, leaving behind the flange of the filler tube exhibiting the tell-tale outward flaring typical of an explosion. Upon arrival, the fire department will usually flood the gas tank with water to extinguish the fire and obviate the possibility of reignition. In so doing, they may inadvertently destroy any evidence of the chemicals' presence in the gas tank.

Suspension System

The failure (sagging) of the vehicle's suspension system, as indicated by the annealing of the chassis (leaf/coil) springs or by the collapse of the shock absorbers due to the fusing of internal bushings, strongly suggests that these components were subjected to intense heat. The high temperature ranges required to cause a chassis spring to lose its tension means that an accelerant was most probably used. The annealing of such a spring is a function of and in direct proportion to the following factors:

Temperature: How much heat was the particular component exposed to? Steel will soften at approximately 1000°F, and may fail between 1500° and 1700°F.

Duration: How long was the particular component exposed to the high temperature?

Mass: What are the measurements of the component (diameter, weight, and size)?

Glass

Examine the windshield and other glass. If the glass is intact, check for tape or tape residue on the windows. This may indicate that "for sale" signs had been displayed.

Safety plates or bonded glass (windshield) will crack (craze) at approximately 800°F, soften at about 1000°F, and fail at about 1400°F. The bonding material itself will, under certain conditions, release a flammable gas. The kind used in most cars bubbles and softens at about 250°F.

The type and amount of soot on the inside of the windows may also give some insight into the type and magnitude of the fire. Is the glass checkered, cracked, or fused? These factors can indicate heat ranges and serve as heat indicators (see Glass as an Indicator, Chapter 5). An examination of windows and doors should also show whether they were open or closed during the fire.

Catalytic Converter

The *catalytic converter* was introduced with the advent of unleaded gasoline. It refines automotive emissions into mostly harmless products by chemically filtering out impurities. This filtering process can generate temperatures in the 1500°F range when operating properly. A single fouled plug or improperly operating engine may increase temperatures to 2500°F.

Because of this high temperature potential, the catalytic converter represents an additional point of reference during the investigation of a vehicular fire. This is especially true in the case of an off-road fire. The converter is an additional factor that must be eliminated as an accidental cause in suspected cases of arson. The owner's manual that accompanies every new automobile carries a specific warning about avoiding contact between the exhaust system and flammable materials, such as dry grass, paper, and rags.

Multiple Points of Origin

The presence of either separate (distinct) or primary and secondary burn patterns on the vehicle's exterior is highly suggestive of intentional damage. Primary and secondary burn patterns may indicate that the original fire may have burnt itself out, possibly due to a lack of oxygen, and either the windows and/or doors were opened to supply additional oxygen or a second fire was started in the same area. These same distinctive burn patterns may indicate that two fires were burning at the same time in different compartments. If both the engine hood and the trunk lid show signs of fire damage but there is no fire damage to the roof of the vehicle (over the passenger compartment), this would indicate that the fire did not communicate or extend from one compartment to the other. Two separate fires on the same vehicle, where it cannot be shown that one fire precipitated the other, are a definite indication of arson.

Accelerant Splatter

The investigator should examine the exterior for the presence of the distinctive finger patterns indicative of accelerant splatter or splash. If an accelerant was poured on the exterior of the vehicle and ignited, the pattern of burning will correspond to the path or flow that the liquid followed as it spread over the vehicle's body. If a sufficient

Figure 8.6 Note discolored chrome around windows.

amount of the accelerant was used, it may be possible to see where the accelerant dripped from the body to the ground. If this is the case, soil samples should be taken from this area, correctly packaged in airtight containers, and forwarded to a laboratory for analysis.

Flashback

Examine the ground under and around the vehicle for any signs of a *flashback* (unintentional recession of flame). Such evidence would indicate either that:

1. an accelerant poured within the vehicle's interior may have dripped to the ground beneath the car and ignited, or
2. while pouring the accelerant on the vehicle, the arsonist may have inadvertently spilled some on the ground around the vehicle.

If there seems to have been a flashback, the investigator should take soil samples from the suspected area.

Heat Indicators

It is a well-known fact that chrome discolors when different temperatures are applied to it (see Table 5.2). Chromed fittings around the windows as well as chromed fixtures within the car may serve as heat indicators.

The higher-temperature or lighter colors will probably not remain in the metal after it cools, but may be indicated by a series of concentric circles of the darker colors.

Second Vehicle

The investigator should also be conscious of additional tire tracks and footprints in the area surrounding the suspected vehicle. These may suggest that the vehicle was pushed or towed to the scene where it was burned, or may indicate the presence of a second auto. If the vehicle was pushed or towed to the scene, the investigator may find recently made scratch marks on the rear bumper or on the frame below the front bumper. A second auto, possibly driven by a friend or the suspect's spouse, may have been used to drive the arsonist away from the scene.

Panic Stop

The investigator should look for skid marks or any indications of a panic stop. Their absence may be used later to impeach or attack a suspect's statements relating to the incident. This would be especially true if the suspect claims to have been driving when the car suddenly burst into flames. A normal person confronted with these circumstances might well be expected to hit the brakes, pull off the road, and expeditiously leave the vehicle. If the suspect makes such a claim, he should be asked to describe and explain his actions.

Does it appear that any attempt was made to extinguish the fire? Is the dirt or sand next to the vehicle disturbed to the extent that it appears likely that they may have been utilized as extinguishing agents?

Roof Panel

A mistakenly rigid interpretation has been fostered over the past decade concerning the condition of the roof panel in a vehicular fire. For years, the connection between a concave or sunken roof panel and the use of an accelerant was made almost automatically. This contention still has some limited credibility, depending upon the year of manufacture of the vehicle under investigation, particularly if it predates 1969. Today, though, modern engineering concerns for gas economy, wind resistance, and lightweight construction have affected the burning characteristics of more recently released models. The ever-increasing use of fiberglass, aluminum, and a wide range of plastics in automotive bodies, interiors, and accessories has altered the significance of the roof panel in vehicular fire investigations.

Figure 8.7 An investigator can no longer rigidly interpret the role of a vehicle's roof panel in the total evaluation of a vehicular fire. Modern engineering considerations have affected the burning characteristics of vehicle models produced since 1969.

Interior Examination

Upon completion of the exterior examination, the investigator's attention is next directed toward the examination of the three compartments that comprise the vehicle's interior: the engine, passenger, and trunk compartments.

Engine Compartment

The investigator should pay particular attention to the engine and its components. Are any parts of the engine missing, such as the:

carburetor,

starter,

battery,

valve covers,

alternator/generator,

air breather, or

engine hoses?

Is the insulation burnt off the electrical wiring? Are the belts (fan, alternator/generator, air conditioner/power steering) missing or burnt? Are there any tool marks on the engine, indicating that work was recently completed? Are the bolts on the manifold and head missing or loose?

Examine the fuel line and carburetor. The investigator should know that there is less than one cup of gasoline available in the carburetor and fuel line located within the engine compartment. Any burning in the area of the radiator is highly suspicious.

Check the radiator solder. Melting indicates extreme temperatures and is highly suspicious. In addition, any burning in the area of the motor mounts (rubber cushions) is also unusual and should be considered highly suspicious.

Remove and examine the engine dipsticks (oil and transmission). Are they dry or do they show any sign of fire damage? Is the engine block cracked, as evidenced by water in the oil? Have the engine hood hinges annealed or lost their tensile strength, indicating unusually high temperatures?

If the fire appears to have started within the engine compartment, isolate the point of origin. Use the exhaust manifold as the midpoint of the engine, dividing the engine compartment into a top and bottom. An apparent point of origin below the exhaust manifold is highly improbable, considering the available fuel sources. If this is the case, absent some explainable (unique) circumstance, look for an external source of fire.

Passenger Compartment

The investigator should record the total mileage indicated on the odometer and check whether the odometer has been tampered with. He should also check the frame of the driver's door and ascertain if any gas station or mechanic stickers are located there. These may be traced to the station that performed the work. In this way, the investigator might be able to document the condition of the vehicle prior to the fire, should that become necessary.

One of the items that the investigator should look for is the ignition key. If it is in the ignition or lying in the debris, this fact alone may be enough to rebut a statement or claim that the vehicle had been stolen.

While examining the interior of the passenger compartment, the investigator should also note the condition of the floor mats, carpeting, headliner, and seats. Note and photograph the condition of the seats, including the upholstery, padding, and springs. If the springs have annealed, collapsed, and lost their tension or tensile strength, high tem-

Figures 8.8 and 8.9 Have the seat springs and other metal components annealed or collapsed under their own weight? Are they brittle? Is the electrical wiring fused under the dashboard? You must rule out any possible electrical cause for the fire.

peratures are indicated. Note, however, that this does not imply the use of an accelerant. The foam rubber and other plastic products used extensively in automobile interiors may burn at temperature ranges approaching those of most common accelerants (1700°F and up).

The investigator should carefully examine the wiring system (see Electrical Fires, Chapter 6), checking for signs of electrical shorts and noting the condition of the insulation. Also check for signs of wire beading and determine whether any damage to the wiring was caused internally or externally.

The glove compartment and the rest of the interior of the vehicle should be examined for personal items. These can later be compared with the list of personal items that the vehicle's owner may claim were lost in the fire. Inconsistencies may be used to attack the credibility of the owner at a later interview or during a trial.

Trunk or Luggage Compartment

The trunk or luggage compartment should be examined for fire damage, personal items, and other items normally associated with the operation of a motor vehicle (spare tire, jack, tools, etc.). Tools should be ex-

Figure 8.10 Examine trunk or luggage compartment for fire damage, personal items, and tools.

amined in detail, and photographs should be taken of their bearing surfaces. A vehicle owner about to burn his or her car may first remove expensive parts (e.g., customizing) or equipment (e.g., stereo components). Photographs may help match the tools to marks found on the vehicle itself.

If the connection between the gas tank and the gas tank filler tube failed during the fire, the investigator can expect to find extensive fire damage in the rear area of the vehicle. Gas tanks are normally located in the rear portion of American-made vehicles, and once the gas fumes are liberated they tend to burn vigorously and cause extensive damage.

Elimination of Accidental Causes

Electrical malfunction: As in the case of structural fires, it is necessary to eliminate positively all possible accidental causes of vehicular fires. Typical accidental causes are as follows: Look for signs of beading, burn through, sleeving, cherry discoloration, electrical shorts. Differentiate between internal and external damage. Check for fusing or blown fuses. See whether the battery is charged or dead and damaged by explosion of fire or leaking acid. If the electrical system was overloaded, the battery will be dead. Otherwise, the battery will still have some charge even after a fire. Also eliminate accessories added as an afterthought by the owner.

Fuel system malfunction: Check carburetor, fuel lines, and fuel tank. Look for tool marks and signs of tampering. Have holes been punched in the gas tank? Are the drain plug and collar in place? Has the gas tank ruptured or exploded?

Smoking: Lit cigarettes (cigars, pipes, etc.) may be flicked or tossed out a front window only to be blown back in through an open rear window. On occasion cigarettes have been flicked into *closed* windows (on the assumption they were open).

Catalytic converter: This may ignite grass or paper once the car has pulled off the road.

Dragging a foreign object: Once lodged under the vehicle, a foreign object may overheat from friction with the road surface and either ignite or cause sparks.

Typical Vehicular Arson

In a *typical* vehicular arson case, the owner of the vehicle and the arsonist are the same person. Statistically, the arsonist will be a male. Although roughly half of the drivers in America are women, they account for less than 2% of vehicular arsonists. The vehicle will be driven, towed, or pushed to a remote or isolated, relatively traffic-free location so that the fire can be accomplished away from the view of interested bystanders. The fire will occur at night. If an accelerant is used, it will most probably be gasoline. If an ordinary combustible is used, it will most likely be paper (e.g., newspaper) stuffed under the seats and ignited. The vehicle will be privately owned, insured, and financed. If the burning is accomplished a long distance from the arsonist's home, a second vehicle will be involved. The motive for the fire will most probably be economic (insurance fraud).

Driver Injuries and Burns

Any time the driver of a vehicle sustains or is treated for burns associated with a vehicular fire that is under investigation, the investigator should make a diligent effort to get a doctor's or other official diagnosis regarding the extent, degree, and location of such burns. If an accelerant, such as gasoline, was used to enhance the fire, the person pouring or splashing the accelerant may have burned or at least singed himself when igniting the accelerant. The inexperienced torch usually is not aware of the role of flammable vapors and their relation to fire. The persons who mistakenly believe that it is the liquid that burns may place themselves in a position where their safety is in jeopardy. When ignited, vapors from the accelerant that may have been splashed in, on, and around the vehicle may produce a vapor explosion, thereby causing injury to the inexperienced arsonist.

References and Selected Readings

Kennedy, John, *Fire and Arson Investigation*, Investigations Institute, Chicago, 1962 (revised 1977).

Kirk, Paul L., *Fire Investigation*, John Wiley and Sons, New York, 1969.

National Institute of Law Enforcement and Criminal Justice, *Arson and Arson Investigation (Survey and Assessment)*, Law Enforcement Assistance Administration, U.S. Department of Justice, Washington, D.C., October 1977.

Arson Evidence

9

Evidence may be defined as anything that is legally seized and submitted to a court of law for consideration in determining the truth in a matter. Investigators have traditionally viewed evidence as anything that a suspect leaves at or takes from a crime scene, or anything that may be otherwise connected to the crime under investigation. The value of legally seized evidence is directly related to the role it plays in the solution of the case at hand.

When called to the scene of a suspicious fire, an investigator's first interest is to determine the cause and origin of the fire. If he determines that the fire was intentionally set, his concern shifts to the discovery of evidential material that will support his contention and prove the elements of the crime of arson in a court of law. Throughout the investigative process, the investigator will be seeking evidence to identify and connect a suspect to the commission of the crime, as well as any documentation tending to expose a possible motive. Evidence, regardless of its form or type (business records, photographs, sketches, incendiary devices, etc.), must be identified, collected, and correctly packaged throughout the case-building process.

As mentioned in Chapter 5, the overhaul and general cleanup operations should have been halted or delayed until the officer in charge and the investigator have had an opportunity to examine the scene. Even if these operations take place in an area that seems remote from the point of origin, they may still destroy evidence vital to the investigation.

Figure 9.1 Gasoline had burned on the tongue-and-groove flooring pictured here. Note the puddling effect.

Direct Versus Circumstantial Evidence

Direct evidence is evidence with such individualized or identifying characteristics that it tends to prove the fact without the support or corroboration of evidence of any other fact. This evidence can be positively identified as having come from a specific source or person if sufficient identifying characteristics or microscopic or accidental markings are present. Examples of direct evidence are few, but include fingerprints, palm prints, teeth, and certain ballistic materials.

Circumstantial evidence is evidence with class characteristics only. This evidence, no matter how thoroughly examined, can only be placed into a class; a positive source cannot be identified. Examples include soil, blood, hair, and flammable vapors (i.e., when vapors are identified as flammable but, due to topping or weathering,* the exact type or liquid source cannot be identified). Circumstantial evidence tends to prove the fact only with the intervention of evidence of other facts. It is evidence that falls into the logical progression of events and from which inferences can be drawn.

---

* *Topping* is the oxidation of low boiling point fractions of an accelerant, leaving only the high boiling point fractions to show up in analysis. *Weathering* is the altering of composition or form by the actions of the elements (e.g., rain, wind) and, for our purposes, the fire-fighting operation (water, walking, etc.).

Evidence that substantiates a motive for arson includes:

Lack of inventory, empty shelves, etc., in a commercial/retail business.

Business books and records that, when audited, identify an arson-for-profit or insurance fraud scheme.

Files and office cabinets left open to expose records to the ravages of the fire.

Accelerant residue (identified by the medical examiner) on the charred remains of a homicide victim, confirming the investigator's belief that the fire was set to conceal the homicide.

Suspect and Motive Identification

An analysis of all the available physical evidence in conjunction with information revealed through interviews and interrogations can lead to the positive identification of individuals responsible for an arson. In some cases, where positive identification cannot be made, the investigator may still be able to narrow the scope of the investigation by eliminating possible suspects. The types of evidence that assist in the identification of a suspect include the following:

fingerprints found on a discarded gasoline can;

positive identification, by tenants or other witnesses of an individual observed fleeing the building at the time of the fire;

identification of a unique modus operandi (MO), which would permit the investigator to use data from one crime scene for another investigation; and

evidence developed during the course of the investigation that may confirm or discredit an alibi proposed by a suspect.

If an arrest has been made at the fire scene, *under no circumstance* should the suspect be brought back inside the scene of the fire before his footwear and trousers have been vouchered as evidence and suitable replacement garments supplied. If this is not done, future laboratory examination, which might discover the presence of a flammable liquid on the defendant's clothing or footwear, would be of no value. After all, a defense attorney could easily argue that the trace evidence discovered on the defendant's clothing and/or footwear resulted from the investigator taking the defendant into the scene.

Chain of Evidence

The term *chain of evidence* refers to the chain of custody (possession) of an item of evidence from the point in time that it was first discovered until the time that it is offered as an exhibit in court. Any break in the chain of evidence will preclude the use of the item as evidence in any future court presentation. Every time a piece of evidence passes from one person to another, the identities of the individuals involved in this exchange *must be documented*.

The chain of custody *must* be maintained, even if this creates some procedural difficulties. The scene should be protected to prohibit the entry of unauthorized and unnecessary persons and to prevent the inadvertent or intentional contamination, removal, or alteration of evidence. Serious problems can arise when a fire fighter inadvertently removes an item of evidence (e.g., a gas can) found during the fire-fighting operation. This piece of evidence may lie in a storage locker back at the firehouse for several days before someone remembers to contact a fire investigator. If this item is eventually vouchered as evidence, a defense attorney (claiming a break in the chain of evidence) may successfully prevent its admission into court.

In order to account properly for evidence from the time it is found to the time it is produced in court, an investigator must adhere to strict guidelines during each stage of the evidential procedure. The stages of evidential procedure are:

1. discovery,
2. collection and identification,
3. packaging,
4. vouchering and transmittal,
5. laboratory analysis, and
6. court presentation.

Discovery

During the course of the on-scene examination, the investigator must be ever vigilant in order to recognize the potential evidential value of any items, documents, or burn patterns that he is likely to discover. Every piece of physical evidence discovered should be photographed in place, exactly as it was found. In addition, each such discovery should be well-documented in the investigator's crime-scene notes and carefully located on a crime-scene sketch. Only after these steps have been taken should the evidence be disturbed or removed for closer examination and identification.

Collection and Identification

The investigator should remove from the scene any items, samples, specimens, or other form of evidence that would tend to prove an element of the crime or indicate the motive for the crime. He should

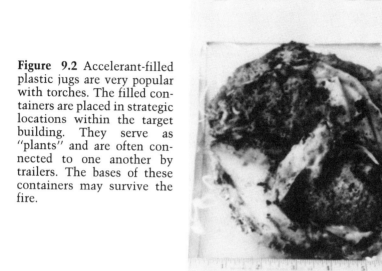

EVIDENCE

Figure 9.2 Accelerant-filled plastic jugs are very popular with torches. The filled containers are placed in strategic locations within the target building. They serve as "plants" and are often connected to one another by trailers. The bases of these containers may survive the fire.

photograph those items or areas that support his findings, and document fire patterns, heat indicators, and unusual circumstances.

The identification of items of evidence is an integral part of the investigative process. The action of writing or scratching a badge or shield number, one's initials, or some other individualized identifying mark on an item of evidence initiates the chain of custody for that item. The mark itself serves as a point of positive identification in any forthcoming court presentation.

Items such as weapons, documents, and delayed-timing devices present few problems in terms of handling and packaging. On the other hand, the selection process involved in the collection of charred or burnt flooring or debris suspected of containing an accelerant residue is one that requires prudence and discretion. When dealing with any item where accelerant vapor or residue is suspected, care must be taken to select samples that afford the greatest potential for securing a positive laboratory analysis. The thoughtless and indiscriminate taking of charred samples in the vain hope that some laboratory technician will perform a technical miracle is, in most cases, a total waste of investigative and laboratory time. The computer term *GIGO* (garbage in–garbage out) could very well apply; if you send bad samples to the laboratory for analysis, you will receive inconclusive laboratory results.

Where within the suspected area does the investigator take samples that are most likely to result in a positive laboratory finding? Experience is the best teacher in this area. Given that most of the suspected liquid accelerant has burned away and that whatever is left has been deluged with thousands of gallons of water (during the fire-fighting operations), the investigator must realize that, at best, he will be selecting weathered and topped samples. Therefore, realizing that a liquid will flow (depending on the slope of the floor) and be affected by the forces of gravity (seek its lowest point), the investigator should select samples (e.g., flooring, rug, trim) after considering the prevailing conditions. Where within or near the suspected area is it likely that the liquid flowed and for any reason failed to ignite? Where is it likely that a portion of the liquid was absorbed in its original state?

Hydrocarbon detectors or *"sniffers"* are often used to narrow the scope of or pinpoint those areas where the best possible (accelerant) evidence samples may be collected. To be effective, these units should be calibrated by laboratory personnel to limit (as much as possible) reactions to nonflammable hydrocarbons.

Once charred samples have been taken, the investigator must then take *control samples* of the same items. These are usually taken in the same room as the evidence samples were, but in an area away from the point of origin.

Next, the investigator must seriously consider the tools that will be used to collect both the evidence and control samples. There are problems inherent in the use of certain tools. If a power tool (e.g., chain saw) is used to remove sections of the floor, the investigator must consider what effect, if any, the lubricants used on the blade or chain will have on the samples removed. The investigator should record in his notes the type of tools involved and the types of lubricants used. When the evidence and control samples are submitted to the laboratory, the investigator should advise the lab personnel that certain lubricants used may affect the results of the lab analysis. Such notification is given to avoid a defense argument that the evidence was contaminated and that the positive results from the lab tests were the result of the lubricants and not any suspected accelerant. Most lubricants are petrochemical derivatives and will chemically react as hydrocarbons.

If a quantity of a suspected liquid accelerant is found, the investigator may choose to field-test a small portion of it. This is done by pouring it on the pavement outside the building and igniting it in the presence of a *reliable witness*—a person (upstanding citizen) chosen at random

Figure 9.3 When evidence is collected at the scene of a suspicious fire, it should be packaged in airtight containers. Pictured here is a 1-gallon metal evidence can with an evidence label affixed.

from the crowd (not someone in any way connected to the incident)—who can attest to the flammability of the sample.

Packaging

Each piece of evidence should be packaged separately to avoid cross contamination. In order to adequately package evidence that is to be sent to a laboratory, the investigator should have a quantity of airtight containers and various cardboard boxes. Acceptable airtight containers would include *new* (unused) metal cans and glass jars. Gallon- and pint-size metal cans and quart-size mason jars are ideally suited for this function.

As new supplies of these containers are received from the manufacturer, random samples should be selected from each shipment and sent to a laboratory for analysis. This precautionary measure is intended to ensure that the containers are free from any form of contaminants that might adversely impact upon later cases. It would also tend to "short-circuit" any future defense argument that the containers used for evidence samples and presented at the time of the trial were coated with some substance that caused the laboratory technician to render a positive finding.

Cardboard boxes could be used to package nonvolatile pieces of evidence such as the following:

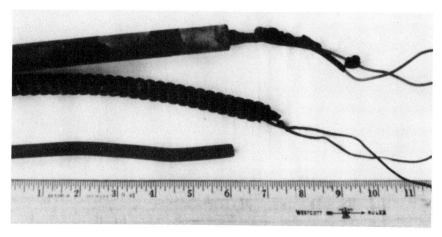

Figure 9.4 Sections of electrical wiring; when evidence photographs are taken, some form of reference scale should be used.

sections of electrical wiring or electrical appliances that exhibit signs of tampering or failure;

books and papers (documents, records);

remains of electrical timing devices; and

fused heat indicators, indicating that an unusually high temperature range existed.

Vouchering and Transmittal

An evidence voucher is simply an administrative form on which the investigator lists all of the physical evidence that has been collected in a particular case. The voucher usually contains a background section that, when accurately prepared, identifies the case, the assigned investigator, other pertinent information, and a brief statement as to the origin and history of the evidence listed thereon. The voucher acts as a medium to prevent the inadvertent destruction or misplacement of vital pieces of evidence and documents the chain of evidence.

Laboratory Analysis

The investigator should know beforehand the types of laboratory services and analyses that can be performed by the laboratory to which he is forwarding evidence samples. Where possible, the investigator should visit the laboratory and observe technicians conducting actual

Figure 9.5 Molotov cocktails are still popular devices with amateur arsonists. An investigator should be aware that the neck of the bottle used or at least some section of the neck will very often survive both the bottle's shattering and the resulting fire.

specimen tests. In this way, the investigator gains an understanding both of the facility and of the problems confronting the technician.

Some of the most common types of evidence analysis available, either through law enforcement agencies or private laboratories, are outlined below.

Individualizing evidence
identification or comparison of
fingerprints,
palm prints, and
sole (foot) prints.
Class evidence
handwriting and typewriter comparisons on documents;
identification of accelerants or flammable/combustible vapors via:
gas-chromatographic analysis,
infrared (IR) spectrometry,
mass spectrometry, or

ultraviolet (UV) light;
hair and fiber analysis;
blood and body-fluid grouping and analysis; and
the full line of criminalistic analyses (tire or sneaker tracks, etc.).

Court Presentation

Most arson trials involve substantial amounts of circumstantial evidence. Direct evidence may clearly document that the fire was incendiary, but the evidence connecting the defendant to the commission of the crime will be largely circumstantial.

An investigator should expect a diligent attack by a defense attorney against any form of evidence offered at trial that tends to establish the guilt of his client. Case law on evidence and the rules of evidence are strictly adhered to by courts throughout the nation. Any evidence that is suppressed during any of the several pretrial motions, no matter how damaging to the defense case, cannot be brought into evidence during the trial.

Summary

The value of items to be used as physical evidence hinges directly on several factors involved in the identification, collection, and packaging of those items.

An investigator's field experience and prior training are, to a great extent, the key factors involved in his ability to recognize the evidential value of items found at the scene of a fire. In this regard, the investigator will be evaluating colors, smells, temperature ranges, natural and unnatural fire spread patterns, and so on. The investigator's expertise in reading burn patterns and fire spread, coupled with his willingness to dig or shift manually through the debris, will determine the quantity and value of items he will find.

The investigator must decide which items will be removed from the scene for transport to a laboratory, and which will be photographed (*in situ*) and left at the scene.

The size of the samples to be taken and the areas within the scene from which they are removed are important issues that must be carefully considered. If the investigator suspects that a liquid accelerant was used, he should take samples of the suspected area and forward them to the laboratory for analysis. The size of the samples to be taken is governed by the available packaging materials and by testing facilities at the lab to which they are sent.

References and Selected Readings

FBI *Handbook of Forensic Science*. U.S. Department of Justice, Federal Bureau of Investigation, Washington, D.C., 1979.

Kennedy, John, *Fire and Arson Investigation*, Investigations Institute, Chicago, 1962 (revised 1977).

Kirk, Paul L., *Crime Investigation*, 2nd ed., John Wiley and Sons, New York, 1974.

Kirk, Paul L., *Fire Investigation*, John Wiley and Sons, New York, 1969.

National Institute of Law Enforcement and Criminal Justice, *Arson and Arson Investigation (Survey and Assessment)*, Law Enforcement Administration, U.S. Department of Justice, Washington, D.C., October 1977.

APPENDIX: REQUESTING LABORATORY ASSISTANCE*

The information under this caption as well as that contained elsewhere in this section under the particular type of examination or assistance desired should be consulted to facilitate the submission of requests to the Laboratory Division.

Requests for Examination(s) of Evidence

All requests should be made in a written communication, in triplicate, addressed to the Director, Federal Bureau of Investigation, with an attention line in accordance with instructions below and contain the following information:

A. Reference to any previous correspondence submitted to the Laboratory in the case.

B. The nature of and the basic facts concerning the violation insofar as they pertain to the Laboratory examination.

C. The name(s) and sufficient descriptive data of any subject(s), suspect(s), or victim(s).

D. The list of the evidence being submitted either "herewith" or "under separate cover." (Note: Due to evidential "chain of custody" requirements, all evidence sent through the U.S. Postal Service (USPS) system must be sent by registered mail and not by parcel post or regular mail. If United Parcel Service, Federal Express, or air freight is used, utilize their "acknowledgment of delivery," "protective signature," "security signature," or any other such service which provides the same protection as USPS registered mail.)

   1. "Herewith": This method is limited to certain small items of evidence which are not endangered by transmission in an envelope marked clearly as containing sealed evidence, and attached securely to the written communication which should state "Submitted herewith are the following items of evidence. . . ."

* Reprinted, with permission, from the Federal Bureau of Investigation's *Handbook of Forensic Science*.

2. "Under separate cover": This method is generally used for shipment of numerous and/or bulky items of evidence. The written communication should state "Submitted under separate cover by (list the method of shipment, be it USPS Registered, United Parcel Service, Federal Express, or air freight) are the following items of evidence." For further information concerning the preparation of packages sent under separate cover see Packaging Chart elsewhere in this section.

E. A request. State what types of examinations are desired, to include, if applicable, comparisons with other cases.
   1. Evidence will not be forwarded by the Laboratory Division to the Latent Fingerprint Section, Identification Division, for latent fingerprint examination unless specifically requested to do so in the written communication.

F. Information as to where the original evidence is to be returned as well as where the original Laboratory report is to be sent.

G. A statement, if applicable, as to whether
   1. The evidence has been examined previously by another expert in the same technical field.
   2. Any local controversy is involved in the case.

H. Notification of the need and the reason(s) for an expeditious examination; bearing in mind this treatment should not be routinely requested.

Attention Lines for Communications and Packages

The following guidelines should be adhered to as closely as possible to avoid any unnecessary delay in the routing of mail at FBI Headquarters.

A. Requests for Laboratory examination *only*, should be marked "Attention: FBI Laboratory."

B. Requests for a fingerprint examination *only*, should be marked "Attention: Identification Division, Latent Fingerprint Section."

C. Requests for *both* a fingerprint examination and Laboratory examination of any type should be marked "Attention: FBI Laboratory."

Shipment of Evidence

The following steps should be followed to properly prepare a package for shipment of numerous and/or bulky items of evidence. (Note: Comply with steps A through I if a cardboard box is used and step J if a wooden box is used):

FEDERAL BUREAU OF INVESTIGATION

Washington, D. C. 20537

REPORT

SAMPLE LETTER

of the

SAMPLE LETTER

LATENT FINGERPRINT SECTION

IDENTIFICATION DIVISION

YOUR FILE NO. 12-741   March 22, 19_ _
FBI FILE NO.   95-67994
LATENT CASE NO.
                          A-73821   REGISTERED

TO: Mr. James T. Wixling
     Chief of Police
     Right City, State (Zip Code)

RE: GUY PIDGIN:
     EMPALL MERCHANDISE MART
     RIGHT CITY, STATE
     MARCH 16, 19_ _
     BURGLARY

REFERENCE: Letter March 17, 19_ _
EXAMINATION REQUESTED BY: Addressee
SPECIMENS: Piece of bent metal, Q5
                 Ten transparent lifts
                 Fingerprints of Guy Pidgin, FBI #213762J9

Four latent fingerprints of value were developed on the piece of metal,

Q5. Seven latent fingerprints of value appear on three lifts marked "safe door"

and five latent fingerprints of value appear on two lifts marked "side window."

No latent prints of value appear on the remaining lifts.

A. Take every precaution to preserve the items of evidence as outlined in the applicable sections of the Evidence Chart as well as afford appropriate physical protection of the latent fingerprints thereon to include identification with the word "latent."
B. Choose a cardboard box suitable in size.
C. Wrap each item of evidence separately to avoid contamination.
D. Do not place evidence from more than one investigative case in the same box.
E. Pack the evidence securely within the box to avoid damage in transit.

The four latent fingerprints developed on the piece of metal, designated Q5, have been identified as finger impressions of Guy Pidgin, FBI #213762J9.

The remaining twelve latent fingerprints are not identical with the fingerprints of Pidgin.

Photographs of the unidentified latent fingerprints have been prepared for our files and will be available for any additional comparisons you may desire.

Should you desire the assistance of one of the FBI's fingerprint experts in the trial of this case, we should be notified in ample time to permit the necessary arrangements. This report should be used, however, if legal considerations permit, in lieu of the appearance of our expert in any pretrial action such as a preliminary hearing or grand jury presentation. Our representative cannot be made available to testify if any other fingerprint expert is to present testimony on the same point, namely, that the impressions in question are identical.

The lifts and the fingerprints of Pidgin, which should be retained for possible future court action in this case, are enclosed.

The results of the laboratory examinations, as well as the disposition of the piece of metal, Q5, are the subjects of a separate report.

Enclosures (11)

Page 2
LC #A-73821

F. Seal the box with gummed tape and clearly mark the outer portions of the box with the word(s) "evidence." (Note: If any of the evidence in the box is to be subjected to a latent fingerprint examination, also clearly mark the outer portions of the box with the word "latent.")

G. Place a copy of the original written request for the examination(s) in an envelope marked "invoice" and securely affix this envelope to the outside of the sealed box.

H. Enclose the sealed box in wrapping paper, seal the wrapping paper with gummed tape, and address the package to the Director, Federal

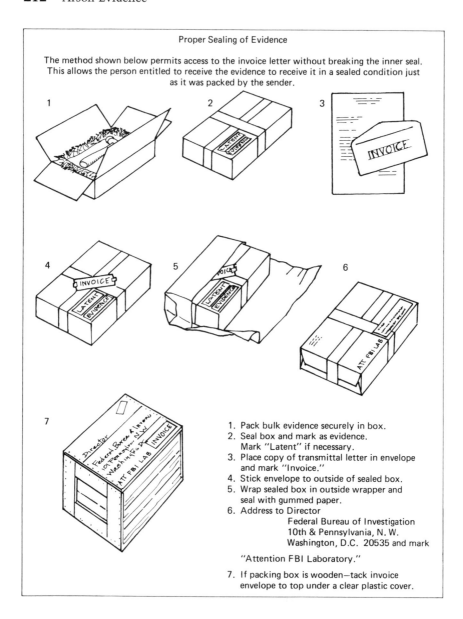

Proper Sealing of Evidence

The method shown below permits access to the invoice letter without breaking the inner seal. This allows the person entitled to receive the evidence to receive it in a sealed condition just as it was packed by the sender.

1. Pack bulk evidence securely in box.
2. Seal box and mark as evidence.
   Mark "Latent" if necessary.
3. Place copy of transmittal letter in envelope and mark "Invoice."
4. Stick envelope to outside of sealed box.
5. Wrap sealed box in outside wrapper and seal with gummed paper.
6. Address to Director
   Federal Bureau of Investigation
   10th & Pennsylvania, N. W.
   Washington, D.C. 20535 and mark

   "Attention FBI Laboratory."

7. If packing box is wooden—tack invoice envelope to top under a clear plastic cover.

Bureau of Investigation, Washington, D.C. 20535, with the proper attention line as outlined above.

I. Ship the package via U.S. Postal Service, Registered Mail, United Parcel Service, Federal Express, or air freight.

J. Choose a durable wooden box suitable in size and
   1. Comply with the above steps A, C, D, and E.
   2. Securely fasten the lid on the box and address it to the Director,

Federal Bureau of Investigation, Washington, D.C. 20535, with the proper attention line.

3. Place a copy of the original written request for the examination(s) in an envelope marked "invoice," place the invoice envelope in a clear plastic cover, and tack it to the box.

4. Comply with step I above.

Evidence Chart

The following chart [Table A.1] is provided to give assistance in the collection, identification, preservation, packaging, and sending of evidence to the laboratory. This chart should be used in conjunction with similar evidence information contained elsewhere in this section under each type of examination desired. This evidence information and chart are not intended to be all-inclusive.

Hazardous Materials

Over 3,000 items, including flash paper, live ammunition, explosives, radioactive materials, flammable liquids and solids, flammable and nonflammable gases, spontaneously combustible substances, and oxidizing and corrosive materials are currently considered as hazardous materials. All require special packaging, and the amount of each item which can be shipped is regulated. Therefore, the applicable action listed at the top of the opposite page is to be taken:

A. Flash paper: Contact the FBI Document Section for shipping instructions *each and every time* this item is to be submitted to the Laboratory.

B. Live ammunition: For shipping instructions see paragraph regarding Live Ammunition.

C. Other hazardous materials: Contact the FBI Explosives Unit for shipping instructions *each and every time* any hazardous material, except flash paper or live ammunition, is to be submitted to the Laboratory.

Nonhazardous Materials

If evidence of this type is not found in this chart or elsewhere in this section, locate a specimen which is most similar in nature and take the appropriate actions or call the Laboratory at 202-FBI-4410 for general instructions.

Table A.1

Specimen	Amount Desired		Send by
	Standard	Evidence	
Abrasives, including carborundum, emery, sand, etc.	Not less than one ounce	All	Registered mail or Federal Express
Acids	250 milliters (ml.)	All to 250 ml.	Contact FBI Explosives Unit for instructions
Adhesive tape	Recovered roll	All	Registered mail
Alkalies—caustic soda, potash, ammonia, etc.	250 ml. 100 gm.	All to 250 ml. All to 100 gm.	Contact FBI Explosives Unit for instructions
Ammunition (cartridges)			
Anonymous letters, extortion letters, bank robbery notes		All	Registered mail
Blasting caps	(Contact FBI Explosives Unit for instructions)		

Identification	Wrapping and Packing	Remarks
On outside of container: Type of material. Date obtained. Name or initials	Use containers, such as ice-cream box, pillbox, or plastic vial. Seal to prevent any loss.	Avoid use of envelopes.
Same as above	Plastic or all-glass bottle. Tape stopper. Pack in sawdust, glass, or rock wool. Use bakelite or paraffin-lined bottle for hydrofluoric acid.	Label acids, glass, corrosive.
Same as above	Place on waxed paper or cellophane.	Do not cut, wad, or distort.
Same as above	Plastic or glass bottle with rubber stopper held with adhesive tape	Label alkali, glass, corrosive.
Same as above		Unless specific examination of cartridge is essential, do not submit.
Initial and date each unless legal aspects or good judgment dictates otherwise.	Place in proper enclosure envelope and seal with "evidence" tape or transparent cellophane tape. Flap side of envelope should show 1) wording "Enclosures(s) to FBIHQ from (name of submitting office)," 2) title of case, 3) brief description of contents, and 4) file number, if known. Staple to original letter of transmittal.	Do not handle with bare hands. Advise if evidence should be treated for latent fingerprints.

(continued)

Table A.1 *(continued)*

Specimen	Amount Desired		Send by
	Standard	Evidence	
Blood:			
1. Liquid known samples	Two tubes each (sterile) 5cc, 1 tube—blood only. 1 tube—EDTA and blood or heparin and blood.	All	Registered airmail special delivery
2. Small quantities: a. Liquid questioned samples		All	Registered airmail special delivery
b. Dry stains, not on fabrics		As much as possible	Registered mail
c. For toxicological use		20 cc. (Blood and preservative mixture)	Registered airmail special delivery
3. Stained clothing, fabric, etc.		As found	Registered mail, Federal Express, United Parcel Service (UPS)
Bullets (not cartridges)		All found	Registered mail

Identification	Wrapping and Packing	Remarks
Use adhesive tape on outside of test tube, with name of donor, date taken, doctor's name, name or initials of investigator.	Wrap in cotton, soft paper. Place in mailing tube or suitably strong mailing carton.	Submit immediately. Don't hold awaiting additional items for comparison. Keep under refrigeration, *not* freezing, until mailing. *No* refrigerants and/or dry ice should be added to sample during transit. Fragile label.
Same as above	Same as above	If unable to expeditiously furnish sample, allow to dry thoroughly on the nonporous surface, and scrape off; or collect by using eyedropper or clean spoon, transfer to nonporous surface and let dry; or absorb in sterile gauze and let dry.
On outside of pillbox or plastic vial: type of specimen, date secured, name or initials.	Seal to prevent leakage.	Keep dry. Avoid use of envelopes.
Same as liquid samples	Medical examiner should use a standard blood collection kit.	Preservative desired (identify preservation used). Refrigerate. *Can freeze.*
Use tag or mark directly on clothes: type of specimens, date secured, name or initials.	Each article wrapped separately and identified on outside of package. Place in strong box placed to prevent shifting of contents.	If wet when found, dry by hanging. *Use no heat to dry.* Avoid direct sunlight while drying. Use no preservatives.
Initials on base, nose, or mutilated area	Pack tightly in cotton or soft paper in pill, match or powder box. Label outside of box as to contents.	Unnecessary handling obliterates marks.

(continued)

218

Table A.1 *(continued)*

| Specimen | Amount Desired | | Send by |
	Standard	Evidence	
Cartridges (live ammunition)		All found	
Cartridge cases (shells)		All	Registered mail
Charred or burned documents		All	Registered mail
Checks (fraudulent)		All	Registered mail
Check protector, rubber-stamp, and/or date-stamp known standards. (Note: send actual device when possible.)	Obtain several copies in full word-for-word order of each questioned check-writer impression. If unable to forward rubber stamps, prepare numerous samples with different degrees of pressure.		Registered mail
Clothing		All	Registered mail, Federal Express, or United Parcel Service (UPS)
Codes, ciphers, and foreign language material		All	Registered mail
Drugs: 1. Liquids		All	Registered mail, UPS, or air express

Identification	Wrapping and Packing	Remarks
Initials on outside of case near bullet end	Same as above	
Initials preferably on inside near open end and/or on outside near open end	Same as above	
On outside of container indicate fragile nature of evidence, date obtained, name or initials.	Pack in rigid container between layers of cotton.	Added moisture, with atomizer or otherwise, not recommended.
See anonymous letters.	See anonymous letters.	Advise what parts questioned or known. Furnish physical description of subject.
Place name or initials, date, name of make and model, etc., on sample impressions.	See anonymous letters and/or above.	Do not disturb inking mechanisms on printing devices.
Mark directly on garment or use string tag: type of evidence, name or initials, date.	Each article individually wrapped with identification written on outside of package. Place in strong container.	Leave clothing whole. Do not cut out stains. If wet, hang in room to dry before packing.
Same as anonymous letters	Same as anonymous letters	Furnish pertinent background and technical information.
Affix label to bottle in which found, including name or initials and date.	If bottle has no stopper, transfer to glass-stoppered bottle and seal with adhesive tape.	Mark "Fragile." Determine alleged normal use of drug and if prescription, check with druggist for supposed ingredients.

(continued)

Table A.1 *(continued)*

Specimen	Amount Desired		Send by
	Standard	Evidence	
2. Powders, pills, and solids		All to 30 gms.	Registered mail, UPS, or air express
Dynamite and other explosives	(Contact FBI Explosives Unit for instructions.)		
Fibers	Entire garment or other cloth item	All	Registered mail
Firearms		All	Registered mail, UPS, or Federal Express
Flash paper	One sheet	All to 5 sheets	Contact FBI Technical Evaluation Unit for instructions.
Fuse (safety)	(Contact FBI Explosives Unit for complete instructions.)		
Gasoline	500 ml.	All to 500 ml.	Contact FBI Explosives Unit for instructions.
Gems		All	Registered mail, insured
General unknown 1. Solids (nonhazardous)	500 gms.	All to 500 gms.	Registered mail

Identification	Wrapping and Packing	Remarks
On outside of pillbox, name or initials and date.	Seal with tape to prevent any loss.	
On outside of sealed container or on object to which fibers are adhering.	Folder paper or pillbox. Seal edges and openings with tape.	Do not place loose in envelope.
Mark inconspicuously as if it were your own. String tag gun, noting complete description on tag. Investigative notes should reflect how and where gun marked.	Wrap in paper and identify contents of packages. Place in cardboard box or wooden box.	Unload all weapons before shipping. Keep from rusting. See Ammunition, if applicable.
Initials and date	Individual polyethylene envelopes double-wrapped in manila envelopes. Inner wrapper sealed with paper tape.	Fireproof, place in vented location away from any other combustible materials, and if feasible, place in watertight container immersed in water. Mark inner wrapper "Flash Paper Flammable."
On outside of all-metal container, label with type of material, name or initials, and date.	Metal container packed in wooden box.	Fireproof container
On outside of container	Use jeweler's box or place in cotton in pillbox.	
Name or initials, date on outside of sealed container	Same as drugs	If item is suspected of being a hazardous material, treat as such and contact FBI Explosives Unit for shipping instructions.

(continued)

Table A.1 *(continued)*

Specimen	Amount Desired		Send by
	Standard	Evidence	
2. Liquids (nonhazardous)	500 ml.	All to 500 ml.	Registered mail
Glass fragments		All	Registered mail, UPS, or air express
Glass particles	All of bottle or headlight. Small piece of each broken pane.	All	Registered mail
Glass wool insulation	1″ mass from each suspect area	All	Registered mail
Gunshot residues 1. Cotton applicator swabs with plastic shafts *(do not use wood shafts)*		All	Registered mail
2. On cloth		All	Registered mail
Hair	Dozen or more full-length hairs from different parts of head and/or body	All	Registered mail
Insulation (See glass wool insulation.)			
Handwriting and hand printing, known standards			Registered mail

Identification	Wrapping and Packing	Remarks
Same as for liquid drugs	Same as drugs	Same as above
Adhesive tape on each piece. Name or initials and date on tape. Separate questioned and known.	Wrap each piece separately in cotton. Pack in strong box to prevent shifting and breakage. Identify contents.	Avoid chipping and mark "Fragile."
Name or initials, date on outside of sealed container	Place in pillbox, plastic or glass vial; seal and protect against breakage.	Do not use envelopes.
Same as above	Sealed container	
On outside of container, date and name or initials. Label as to name of person and which hand.	Place swabs in plastic containers.	Do not use glass containers.
Attach string tag or mark directly: type of material, date, and name or initials.	Place fabric flat between layers of paper and then wrap so that no residue will be transferred or lost.	Avoid shaking.
On outside of container: type of material, date, and name or initials	Folded paper or pillbox. Seal edges and openings with tape.	Do not place loose in envelope.
Name or initials, date, from whom obtained, and voluntary statement should be included in appropriate place.	Same as anonymous letters	

(continued)

Table A.1 *(continued)*

| Specimen | Amount Desired | | Send by |
	Standard	Evidence	
Matches	One to two books of paper. One full box of wood.	All	UPS or Federal Express
Medicines	(See Drugs.)		
Metal	One pound	All to one pound	Registered mail, UPS, or air express
Oil	250 ml. together with specifications	All to 250 ml.	UPS
Obliterated, eradicated, or indented writing		All	Registered mail
Organs of the body		200 gms. of each organ	UPS, air express, or registered airmail special delivery
Paint: 1. Liquid	Original unopened container up to 1 gallon if possible	All to 1/4 pint	Registered mail, UPS, or air express
2. Solid (paint chips or scrapings)	At least 1/2 sq. in. of solid, with all layers represented	All. If on small object, send object.	Registered mail, UPS, or air express

Identification	Wrapping and Packing	Remarks
On outside of container: type of material, date, and name or initials.	Metal container and packed in larger package to prevent shifting. Matches in box or metal container packed to prevent friction between matches.	Keep away from fire. Use "Keep away from fire" label.
Same as above	Use paper boxes or containers. Seal and use strong paper or wooden box.	Melt number, heat treatment, and other specifications of foundry if available. Keep from rusting.
Same as above	Metal container with tight screw top. Pack in strong box using excelsior or similar material.	*Do not use dirt or sand for packing material.* Keep away from fire.
Same as anonymous letters	Same as anonymous letters	Advise whether bleaching or staining methods may be used. Avoid folding.
On outside of container: victim's name, date of death, date of autopsy, name of doctor, name or initials	Plastic or glass containers. Metal lids must have liners.	"Fragile" label. Keep cool. Send autopsy report. Add no preservatives to the organs. Use dry ice in the package.
On outside of container: type of material, origin if known, date, name or initials.	Friction-top paint can or large-mouth, screw-top jars. If glass, pack to prevent breakage. Use heavy corrugated paper or wooden box.	
Same as above	If small amount, round pillbox or small glass vial with screw top. Seal to prevent leakage. Envelopes not satisfactory. Do not pack in cotton.	Avoid contact with adhesive materials. Wrap so as to protect smear.

(continued)

Table A.1 *(continued)*

| Specimen | Amount Desired | | Send by |
	Standard	Evidence	
Plastic casts of tire treads and shoe prints	Send in shoes and tires of suspects. Photographs and sample impressions are usually not suitable for comparison.	All shoe prints; entire circumference of tires	Registered mail, UPS, or air express
Powder patterns (See gunshot residues)			
Rope, twine, and cordage	One yard or amount available	All	Registered mail
Saliva samples	1 1/2" diameter stain in center of filter paper	All	Registered mail
Safe insulation	Sample all damaged areas	All	Registered mail, UPS, or air express
Shoe print lifts (impressions on hard surfaces)	Photograph before making of dust impression.	All	Registered mail
Soils and minerals	Samples from areas near pertinent spot	All	Registered mail
Tools		All	Registered mail, UPS, or air express

Identification	Wrapping and Packing	Remarks
On back before plaster hardens: location, date, and name or initials.	Wrap in paper and cover with suitable packing material to prevent breakage. Do not wrap bags.	Use "Fragile" label. Mix approximately four pounds of plaster to one quart of water. Allow casts to cure (dry) before wrapping.
On tag or container: type of material, date, name or initials.	Wrap securely.	
On outside envelope and on filter paper put type of sample, name of donor, date of collection, and collector's initials or name.	Seal in envelope.	Stain should be circled in pencil for identification. Filter paper available from hospitals and drug stores. Allow to dry.
On outside of container: type of material, date, name or initials.	Use containers, such as pillbox or plastic vial. Seal to prevent any loss.	Avoid use of glass containers and envelopes.
On lifting tape or paper attached to tape: name or initials and date.	Prints in dust are easily damaged. Fasten print or lift to bottom of a box so that nothing will rub against it.	Always secure crime scene area until shoe prints or tire treads are located and preserved.
On outside of container: type of material, date, name or initials	Pillbox or plastic vial.	Avoid glass containers and envelopes.
On tools use string tag: type of tool, identifying number, date, name or initials	Wrap each tool in paper. Use strong cardboard or wooden box with tools packed to prevent shifting.	

(continued)

228

Table A.1 *(continued)*

Specimen	Amount Desired		Send by
	Standard	Evidence	
Toolmarks	Send in the tool. If impractical, make several impressions on similar materials as evidence, using entire marking area of tool.	All	Registered mail, UPS, or air express
Typewriting, known standards			Registered mail
Urine	Preferably all urine voided over a period of 24 hours	All	Registered mail
Vaginal samples 1. Slides (microscope)		Minimum of two slides	Registered mail
2. Swabs	Two unstained swabs from same package as stained	Minimum of two swabs	Registered mail
Water	2 liters	2 liters	Registered mail
Wire (See also toolmarks.)	Three feet (Do not kink.)	All (Do not kink.)	Registered mail
Wood	One foot or amount available	All	Registered mail

Identification	Wrapping and Packing	Remarks
On object or on tag attached to or on opposite end from where toolmarks appear: name or initials and date.	After marks have been protected with soft paper, wrap in strong wrapping paper, place in strong box, and pack to prevent shifting.	
Place name or initials, date, serial number, name of make and model etc., on specimens.	Same as anonymous letters	Examine ribbon for evidence of questioned message thereon.
On outside of container: type of material, name of subject, date taken, name or initials.	Bottle surrounded with absorbent material to prevent breakage. Strong cardboard or wooden box.	Use any clean bottle with leakproof stopper.
Same as for saliva samples	Use commercial slide box.	Slide box available at hospitals. Doctor should not fix slides. No cover slips. Air dry.
Same as above	Seal in envelope.	Allow swabs to dry before packaging.
Same as for urine	Same as for urine	Same as for urine
On label or tab: type of material, date, name or initials	Wrap securely.	Do not kink wire.
Same as above	Wrap securely.	

Documenting the Crime Scene 10

The proper inspection and accurate documentation of a crime scene is the most important initial step in any investigation. The notes, photos, and sketches generated to document the scene and discovered evidence serve as an aid and ready reference for the investigator throughout the investigation. More importantly, they provide the foundation for any criminal prosecution or civil action that follows.

Fire scenes have traditionally been one of the most poorly documented and underrated classifications of crime scene. The chief reason for this lack of documentation has been the investigator's traditional reliance on sketchy notes and personal recollection when preparing official reports or describing the circumstances of the fire to a jury or other judicial body. Other reasons for the lack of proper documentation include:

ignorance of proper crime-scene techniques,

lack of equipment (e.g., cameras, film),

time constraints,

shortage of qualified personnel, and

lack of motivation (e.g., laziness, poor attitude, apathy).

The fact that fire scenes are unique and their analysis time-consuming and sometimes arduous does not relieve the investigator of his responsibility to adhere to proper crime-scene techniques.

Crime Scene

In a fire investigation, the crime scene should include the area surrounding the location where a crime (arson) may have been committed and where evidence pertaining to the investigation of that crime may

Figure 10.1 Every scene of a serious crime, regardless of the nature of the crime, should be documented by means of photographs, crime scene sketch, detailed notes, and a thorough search for evidence.

be found. It should include all entrances and exits or paths to and from the scene.

Under normal circumstances, a criminal investigator is called to the scene of a crime (e.g., homicide) that has occurred. However, a fire investigator is called to the scene of a *suspicious fire*, where a crime may or may not have been committed. That determination is to be made (tentatively) upon the completion of the physical examination, but what the fire investigator sees and hears at the scene may be the basis for the entire case. The treatment of all suspicious fire scenes as crime scenes is purely a precautionary measure.

"Seat" of the Crime

The "seat" of the crime is the area of the crime scene evincing the greatest impact between the criminal and the commission of the crime. In an arson investigation, this would be the point of origin. In a fatal fire, it is the area of greatest impact among the criminal, the victim, and their surroundings. If the fire was set to conceal a homicide, the seat of the crime is the area around and including the body. If the victim died as a result of the fire (arson/homicide), the seat of the crime is the point of origin of the fire.

Protecting the Crime Scene

An investigator must realize that mistakes made during certain phases of the preliminary investigation may be rectifiable (say, by reinterviewing witnesses), but errors made in the processing of the crime scene can never be corrected. Once the scene has been left unprotected for any length of time or released to the owner, reentry to the scene must be made with a search warrant or with the consent of the owner unless the structure has been abandoned and the owner no longer has a reasonable expectation of privacy. In any case, the admissibility of any evidence found during the later entry is at best questionable due to the break in the chain of custody (see Chapter 9).

The responsibility for protecting the fire scene varies nationally according to local custom, size and setting of the municipality (rural or urban), and availability of personnel (paid or volunteer fire department versus police department). Regardless of local custom or procedure, however, the ultimate responsibility for the preservation of the fire scene (until an investigator arrives) lies with the chief or line officer (volunteer or paid) who declared the fire suspicious. This issue is rarely addressed in fire officer's training programs conducted by municipal, regional, or county fire-training academies.

Several investigative and legal questions would be simplified if a fire fighter were left at the scene. It would also be beneficial if the fireman who is left to protect the scene was from one of the first fire units to respond. This would maintain the fire department's presence at the scene and prevent the unintentional release of the building back to its owner. It would also afford the responding investigator the opportunity to interview an individual who has first-hand knowledge of conditions in the structure during the actual fire-fighting operations. Should the investigator arrive while fire-fighting operations are still in progress, the questions of chain of custody and scene protection become moot.

The guarding officer must avoid unnecessary conversations with reporters or people who may congregate at the scene, especially at a fatal fire. Reporters should be told that the matter is under investigation and be referred to the investigator assigned to the case for further information.

Documentation Sequence

There is a specific five-step sequence to be followed in documenting a crime scene:

1. visual inspection,
2. note taking,
3. photography,
4. sketches, and
5. search for evidence.

Step 5 has already been discussed in Chapter 9; steps 1–4 are treated in the following sections.

Visual Inspection

The visual inspection of a fire scene uses the investigator's ability to read the observable burn patterns and "push the fire back" to its point(s) of origin. The investigator should try to reconstruct mentally what occurred and be constantly looking for and aware of the unusual, such as:

unnatural lateral spread of fire;

evidence of plants, trailers, and accelerants;

unlikely relationship between the point(s) of origin and the body (a fatal fire);

heat indicators; and

evidence of a delayed ignition device.

Note Taking

One of the most important operations mandated by proper crime-scene techniques is the preparation of a written record of the investigator's observations and impressions at the crime scene. This operation is known as *note taking*. An investigator should not rely on memory alone; information left to memory is easily forgotten. If the case goes to trial months or years later, the notes prepared at the fire scene are accessible to a defendant's attorney and will be used by the investigator to refresh his memory while testifying. The notes will also be scrutinized by the district attorney who will be preparing and prosecuting the case. With these considerations in mind (and to avoid embarrassment), the crime-scene notes should be arranged and prepared in a deliberate manner. Several principles govern the preparation of these notes:

make entries accurately and promptly,

give observations in chronologic order,

avoid indiscernible codes and cryptic abbreviations,

be clear, and

make decisions as to what is really important.

In addition to being useful when preparing for court, crime-scene notes will be of value in the following ways:

providing ready reference for reports to be prepared,

highlighting points of conflict to be resolved,

refreshing the memory of witnesses,

yielding new information to be evaluated,

aiding in the development of logical and pertinent questions for interviews and interrogations,

identifying recurring names, and

ensuring that important data are not omitted.

Included in the investigator's written record of observations and impressions should be the following:

time of the investigator's arrival,

exact address of the fire,

weather conditions,*

identity of persons present,

statements made (verbatim, if possible),

odors detected at the scene,

extent of damage and room or area of origin,

anything unusual (e.g., dead pet, lack of furniture in a supposedly occupied apartment), and

anything else that the investigator may feel is important.

The original handwritten notes prepared by the investigator while walking through the fire scene *should be kept* in the case folder. Too many investigators, upon completion of the required follow-up reports, discard or otherwise destroy the handwritten notes. A defense attorney who, during questioning, discovers that the investigator's original notes have been destroyed, may suggest that information beneficial to

---

* The reference to weather conditions is a subtle way of pointing out the investigator's concern in the preparation of the notes. The underlying impression suggested is that the level of diligence carries over to the rest of the investigation.

the defendant was included in those notes (that being the reason the investigator destroyed them). Such an argument may have a persuasive effect on the jury.

It is becoming increasingly popular and effective to use cassette recorders for note taking at the scene. These taped notes are transcribed. In lieu of original handwritten notes, the audiocassette(s) should be filed. Removing the two little plastic tabs on the *top* edge of the cassette will prevent anything from being recorded on the same tape (or over the notes).

Photography

The fire scene should not be disturbed before the crime-scene photographs are taken. Every piece of evidence should be photographed in place (long-shot and close-up) before it is removed for processing.

It can be very difficult to photograph a fire scene. Pictures of a building's interior can be especially hard to take because of poor lighting conditions and extensive carbonization. Regardless of the difficulty, such documentary photographs have become an absolute necessity. Juries have come to expect them (slides and prints), and prosecutors rely on them for graphic corroboration of verbal testimony. The technical language of fire science can be disquieting to a jury. Such intricate testimony can be better deciphered if its essence is clarified or illustrated photographically.

An investigator should be prepared to take photographs both in color and in black and white (B&W). During a trial for arson/homicide, a judge may admit B&W photos of the victim into evidence after refusing to admit color photos of the same victim on the grounds that the latter may be prejudicial to the defendant.

The first photos taken should be of the exterior of the building. At least one exterior photo should include the address of the building. The sequence of photos that follows should take the viewer into the building, then gradually to the room of origin, and ultimately to the point of origin. This sequence should closely resemble the steps taken by the investigator during the physical examination to determine the cause and origin of the fire.

Certain precautionary measures should be taken by the investigator to ensure that the photographs taken at the scene will be admitted into evidence. The investigator should list in written notes or on the back of the actual photograph the following information:

type of camera used and its serial number,

type of film used,

ASA number (film speed),

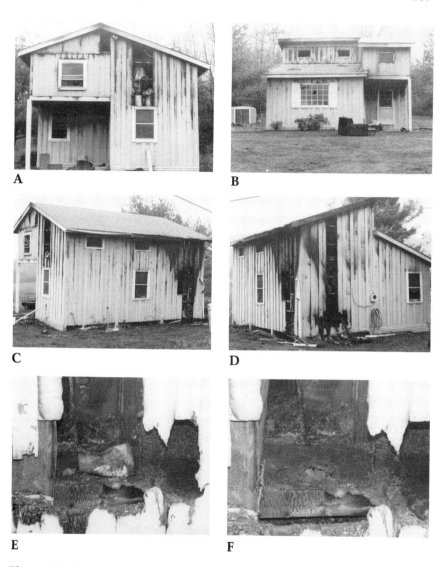

Figure 10.2 (A–D) The exterior of a fire-damaged building should be documented photographically. The following photographs illustrate the value and necessity of a detailed external fire scene examination. (A) and (B) show little exterior damage. (C) and (D) isolate the area of greatest damage. The lowest area of burning and a distinctive V pattern are clearly illustrated. (E) Looking into the structure through the exterior damage. The remains of an electric heater are visible on the floor in the center of the photograph. (F) During the interior examination, the area where the electric heater was found was determined to be the point of origin. The area was carefully cleared of debris. A second photo was taken through the exterior wall isolating the point of origin.

lens setting (*f* stop),

name and shield/badge number of photographer,

case number (if assigned) and address, including apartment number of location photographed, and

number of the photo in chronologic sequence.

The investigator should also record in written notes the amount of film he had available and the total number of photographs that were taken. For example, an investigator photographs a scene using a Polaroid camera. He has two packets of film with him, which means that he can take a total of 16 photos of the scene. During the course of the physical examination he took 12 photos. This fact, although seemingly minor, *should be documented* in his notes for two reasons:

1. it reinforces the notion of the investigator's diligence, and
2. it precludes a defense argument (at trial) that the reason the investigator cannot account for the unused film is that the investigator *intentionally destroyed* certain photographs that depicted factors or evidence that the investigator knew proved the innocence of, or were beneficial to, the defendant.

This kind of argument by the defense attorney is made as much to discredit the investigator in the minds of the jurors as it is to seek a favorable ruling from the trial judge regarding suppression of the evidential photographs. Its effectiveness is thwarted, if not precluded, by responsible documentation of the use of film.

Whenever possible, photograph the scene during daylight hours. If the scene must be processed at night, follow these suggestions:

If conditions permit (i.e., electricity or battery pack available), use floodlights.

If floodlights cannot be used and there is insufficient light by which to focus clearly, attempt to focus the camera on a specific object within a given area (zone-focusing technique) or direct an assistant to shine a flashlight beam into the area as a focusing point for the camera.

Use a 2 × 2 or $2\frac{1}{4}$ × $2\frac{1}{4}$ (-inch) format, twin- or single-lens reflex camera equipped with an electronic flash unit. (The larger the negative, the better the print.)

Bracket each photo (reshoot at an *f* stop higher and lower); remember that a light meter may be useless.

Consider using high-speed film.

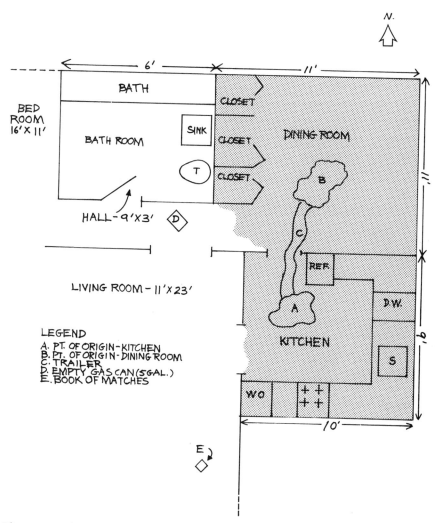

Figure 10.3 (A) Rough sketch—proportional; measurements exact.

Sketches

The drafting of a thorough and accurate crime-scene sketch is the next essential step in the documentation of a crime scene. The purposes of the sketch are several:

to provide orientation, showing the relationship of objects to each other;

to give an overall view of the scene that cannot be correctly depicted by photographs;

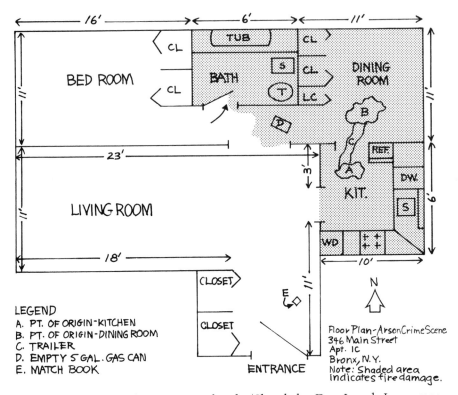

Figure 10.3 (B) Rough projection sketch. (Sketch by Det. Joseph Long, measurements by Chief Jones, 3rd Battalion, 9/15/83–0600 hr.)

to eliminate clutter and items not important to the investigation;

to clarify issues and refresh the memory of witnesses during interviews, and

to avoid unnecessary and, at times, legally prohibited return trips to the scene.

While at the scene, the investigator should draft a rough sketch. To complete this, the investigator will need paper, pencil, a ruler or straight edge, and a measuring tape. Sketching material should include ¼-inch graph paper.

A *rough sketch* is drawn *in proportion* to the shape of the room, not to scale. However, measurements taken of the room and to locate evidence in the room must be exact. The rough sketch will serve as the basis for a finished sketch, which will be drafted later in the investigation and drawn to scale. Items of evidence depicted in the sketch

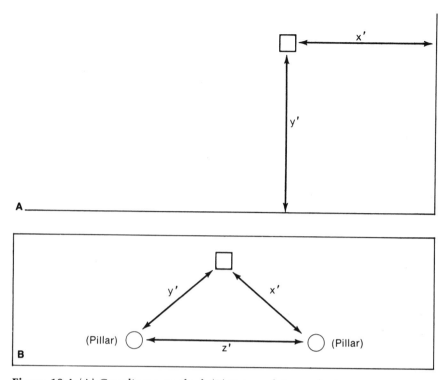

Figure 10.4 (A) Coordinate method. (B) Triangulate method.

should be lettered and listed separately in a legend. *Every* item should be included in the sketch; unnecessary items can be deleted later. An arrow labeled *N* should be included to indicate north (as on a map).

To show relationships involving movable objects, the investigator should use either the coordinate method or the triangulate method. The *coordinate method* is most often used to locate movable objects in a room or other small area. Two measured perpendicular lines are drawn from the object to the nearest walls (Fig. 10.4A). The *triangulate method* is most often used to locate movable objects in large buildings such as warehouses or factories and also at outdoor crime scenes. Three measured lines (Fig. 10.4B) are drawn. The investigator selects two fixed objects (structural pillars, telephone poles, trees, etc.) and measures the distance between each of them, and the item to be located as well as the distance between the two fixed objects themselves.

The *finished sketch* (Figure 10.5) is drafted to scale (usually 1 inch equals 4 feet) and is generally prepared for court presentation. The investigator may also have to prepare a *projection sketch*, used when

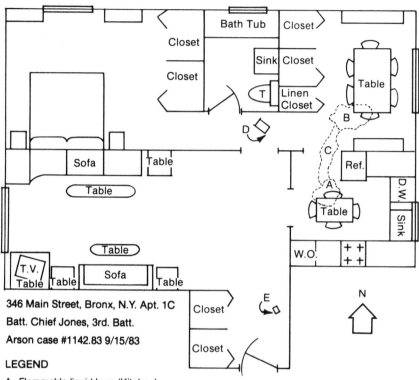

346 Main Street, Bronx, N.Y. Apt. 1C

Batt. Chief Jones, 3rd. Batt.

Arson case #1142.83 9/15/83

LEGEND

A. Flammable liquid burn (Kitchen)
B. Flammable liquid burn (Dining room)
C. Burned newspapers
D. Empty 5 gallon can (metal)
E. Book matches

Figure 10.5 Finished sketch. Note: There is no indication or phrasing on sketches that tends to draw conclusions for jury. Do not use terms like "trailer," "incendiary device," "accelerants," etc. It is acceptable, however, to refer to these items as "burned newspapers" instead of "trailer," or "flammable liquid burn pattern" rather than "accelerant pour." (Sketch prepared by Det. Joseph Long, 9/15/83–1030 hr. Measurements by Det. Vincent Farry.)

the investigator wants to focus attention on a particular location or area. A dotted line is normally used to indicate motion. Photographs are located on a sketch by means of numbered triangles.

References and Selected Reading

Geberth, Vernon J., *Practical Homicide Investigation: Tactics, Procedures, and Forensic Techniques*, Elsevier, New York, 1983.

Kirk, Paul L., *Crime Investigation*, Wiley, New York, 1974.

O'Hara, Charles E., *Fundamentals of Criminal Investigation*, 5th ed., Charles C. Thomas, Springfield, Ill., 1980.

Svensson, A., Wendel, O., and Fisher, B. A. J., *Techniques of Crime Scene Investigation*, 3rd ed., Elsevier, New York, 1981.

Ward, Richard H., *Introduction to Criminal Investigation*, Addison-Wesley, Reading, Mass., 1975.

Surveillance 11

Surveillance is the covert observation of persons, places, or objects with the intention to obtain information. It may be awkward or impossible to acquire this information in any other manner. At times, to seek such information through other sources might jeopardize the investigation. The timeliness of the information may also be an important factor.

Every competent investigator is a trained observer. Surveillance, like all of the other parts of an investigator's repertoire, is an acquired skill. It is learned by doing, and "the street" is the best classroom. Few facets of the investigative function are more amenable to improvement through practice than the tactics of surveillance. Surveillance is not a haphazard operation, nor should it ever be regarded as one. The planning and familiarization phases must not be viewed as secondary to the actual field exercise; they are crucial to the success of the operation. Once the field exercise has commenced, reorganization is virtually unfeasible.

Possible objectives for surveillance operations are the following:

to identify a pathologic fire setter,

to obtain evidence of a crime,

to provide protection for informants and undercover investigators,

to develop probable cause for a search warrant,

to locate suspects or wanted persons,

to identify associates and coconspirators,

to develop background information for use during subsequent interviews/interrogations, to corroborate the reliability of an informant,

to prevent an arson, or

to corroborate a suspected motive.

Planning the Surveillance Operation

All members of the surveillance team should be present during each planning session. They should be directed by one team leader, appointed on the basis of rank, position, or seniority. The team should check all available files and other information sources for data relating to:

name(s) used by the subject;

address(es) used;

known associates;

mannerisms, characteristics, and habits;

probable area of operation (type of neighborhood, character of population, types of occupancy, etc.);

vehicles used by subject and associates (year, color, make, and license number); and

type of equipment (e.g., electronic surveillance) that might be necessary.

Reconnaissance

Time permitting, the team members should survey the possible area(s) of operation to determine:

supplemental information not available in the files;

street names, traffic conditions, location of one-way and dead-end streets;

other modes of transportation available to the subject (e.g., subway or train, buses, taxicabs); and

best method of surveillance to be used and the number of investigators needed.

The reconnaissance phase may also permit each member of the team to gain a personal view of the subject. Photos of the subject may be taken at this time; later these will be carried by each member of the team.

Surveillance Methods

The methods of surveillance that are universally recognized are by foot, by automobile, and by electronic devices. When available, aerial surveillance by helicopter can be an excellent investigative tool. The choice of method is determined by the location and prevailing conditions of the area to be surveilled and by the number of investigators available.

Foot Surveillance

Of the methods available, one-man foot surveillance represents the weakest form and should be avoided. Without backup, the single tailing investigator is, of necessity, required to maintain close contact with the subject in buildings and other off-street locations. The tailing investigator should position himself on the side of the street opposite the subject and stay abreast of him.

Two-man foot surveillance affords the tailing officers much greater latitude, since they can each maintain an "eyeball" on the subject. One investigator positions himself some distance opposite and abreast of the subject. This right-angle approach is effective in having at least one investigator reach an approaching corner of intersection with the subject, thereby minimizing the possibility of losing the subject if he should suddenly turn the corner. The two tailing investigators may, instead, both choose to follow the subject on the same side of the street, maintaining the "eyeball" position.

Another variation involving three investigators would have two investigators remaining behind the subject while one positions himself in front of the subject, again all on the same side of the street.

In the field, be conscious of counter surveillance. If you believe that you are being followed, cross the street in the middle of the block and use the store window glass as a mirror. If you determine that someone is tailing you, double back and challenge him or lose him in a crowd or busy restaurant.

Automobile Surveillance

The number of vehicles to be used for an auto surveillance is determined by availability, setting (rural/urban), traffic conditions, and availability of other resources. The vehicles to be used should be nondescript, and should not be the standard, official (unmarked) fleet automobiles used exclusively by law enforcement agencies and recognizable to the criminal element. A wide variety of vehicles should be used, possibly including those seized or impounded as the result of other investigations (narcotics, untaxed cigarettes, etc.).

Auto surveillance in a congested, urban area is very difficult. Heavy traffic flow, traffic lights, and the mix of one-way and two-way streets mandate the use of several tail vehicles. Radio contact is essential. A subject who is either paranoid or aware of the tail will use the traffic conditions to advantage. He may, for example, drive through a red light and watch to see if another vehicle takes the light behind him. He may turn into a dead-end or one-way street the wrong way, again to see if anyone follows. He may turn a corner sharply and immediately park or cut a corner by driving through a gas station or parking lot, observing the reaction of other vehicles.

A moving automobile surveillance operation on a multilane freeway or expressway is called a *convoy*. Multiple tail vehicles are required. As in foot surveillance, vehicles should periodically rotate their position. The appearance (in the subject's rearview mirror) of vehicles used in nighttime moving-surveillance operation can be disguised by alternating parking lights with high and low beams.

Electronic Surveillance

Electronic surveillance involves the use of sophisticated audiovisual equipment to monitor conversations and physical movement.

Recording and/or listening to verbal communication without the consent of one of the parties involved in the conversation is unlawful and cannot be conducted without a judge's authorization. This authorization takes the form of an *ex parte* warrant. Because there is a great deal of case law regarding electronic surveillance, an investigator should consult legal counsel before conducting it in any form. Electronic eavesdropping is commonly called wiretapping or bugging. However, these terms are not synonymous.

Wiretapping is the cutting in on (tapping of) a telephone line to overhear or record the conversation that passes through the line. A direct tap is completed by connecting an additional earpiece to the telephone's electric circuit anywhere between the transmitter and receiver.

Bugging is the use of concealed microphones (bugs) or other such devices (e.g., transmitters) within a room to overhear conversations. A telephone headpiece may also be bugged (fitted with a microphone) as opposed to tapped. A *mini microphone* may be secreted on a person so that direct person-to-person conversation may be overheard (transmitted) and/or recorded.

Electronic surveillance and eavesdropping provide a qualified investigator with a wide range of technical support. Some of the most commonly used equipment in this area allows an investigator the following options:

to trace or tap telephone calls,

to record dialed telephone numbers,

to trace the movement of vehicles or packages,

to receive or transmit telephone or person-to-person conversations, and

to photograph or videotape movement or meetings occurring in almost complete darkness.

Fixed Surveillance

Fixed or stationary surveillance applies to the observation of a fixed point, premises, or object. A van or truck, equipped for surveillance (including a portable toilet), is ideally suited for this type of an operation. The van is simply maneuvered into a position offering a good vantage point of the target. Once there, the driver exits, locks the vehicle, and walks away. The surveilling investigators, secreted in the rear of the vehicle, have a full view of the target area through one-way mirrored glass. Such a seemingly unoccupied commercial vehicle, legally parked, draws little attention.

If a surveillance van is not available and another vehicle is to be used, certain precautions must be taken. If the vehicle is to be manned by one investigator, it should be driven several doors beyond the target and parked legally. The driver should shift to the passenger's seat after shutting the vehicle off. The passenger-side rear-view mirror should be adjusted to give the investigator a good view of the target. The investigator should avoid turning around in the seat and viewing the target through the rear window, which may draw attention. Female investigators are ideally suited as part of a two-person operation: a man and a woman in a parked car are less likely to draw attention than two men.

Because automobile surveillance may be prolonged and confining, investigators should plan for their own creature comforts by bringing food and drink. Empty containers are also useful, particularly if the vehicle is not equipped with a portable toilet. The lighting of cigarettes at night should be avoided, and the car's lighter, *not matches*, should be used.

If foot surveillance is to be used in the observation of a fixed point, the investigator(s) should attempt to gain a vantage point in another building on the same block. For long-term, fixed surveillance, an empty apartment several stories higher than the target is ideal. Criminals will routinely and habitually look up and down a street as they enter or exit the target building; rarely, if ever, will they look up to the roofline or windows above them. An investigator attempting to watch the target building from adjacent or opposite doorways is very obvious.

Moving Surveillance (Tailing)

If the target is likely to move, then the team surveillance must choose the type of tailing (moving surveillance) required; that is, close, loose, or progressive (leap frog).

Close

In *close* surveillance, the investigator maintains a narrow distance between himself and the subject. Various circumstances may require close surveillance:

The tailing is to take place in a highly congested urban area. Under these circumstances, the investigator is required to maintain close contact with the subject to avoid losing him in a crowd. In this circumstance the subject is not aware that he is being tailed.

The subject *is* aware of the tail and the close tail is intended to create a psychological pressure. The subject may panic and say or do something that benefits the investigation. Close tailing also forces the subject to change plans in an effort to avoid making prearranged contacts with individuals whose identities he does not want revealed to the investigating agency. At other times, the subject and the matter being investigated are of such a sensitive nature that the tailing investigator(s) dare not lose subject contact. For example, the subject may be the target of death threats or may have made known his intention to leave the country.

Loose

A *loose* tail simply allows greater distance between the subject and the tailing investigator. Circumstances that require loose surveillance include the following:

An investigator maintaining a close surveillance believes that he has been "made" (detected) by the subject. Rather than break off the tail completely, the investigator simply follows at a longer distance until a second tailing investigator could take the "eyeball" position. It is imperative that the subject not become aware that he is being tailed.

Progressive

Progressive or *leap-frog* surveillance requires that the operation be broken into several segments. For example, on day 1, the investigators tail the subject from his home to a second point, then break off the tail. On day 2, the tailing investigators go directly to point two, pick up the subject and follow him to point three, where they again break off the tail. This tactic continues until a connection is made between the subject and a particular location or person.

There are drawbacks associated with the progressive approach. In one case, several investigators had been assigned to tail a particular organized crime figure. On day 1, they followed him from his home in Brooklyn to a point just within the borough of Manhattan and broke off. On day 2, they waited for the subject at the point where they had broken off the day before. The subject, however, never appeared. The tailing investigators returned day after day to point 2. After five days, just as the investigators were about to scrap the operation, the subject finally appeared. Some time later, when the subject was finally arrested, the investigating officers questioned him about the route that he traveled between his home and a particular restaurant. The subject stated that he followed a different route each day. One of these routes required the subject to travel through New Jersey, almost 50 miles out of his way. The subject admitted that he believed he was constantly being followed (even when he was not) and that the telephones in his home were tapped (which they never were).

It is important to realize that full-time criminals may exhibit paranoid behavior. They may unreasonably believe that their every action is being recorded or photographed, and may take evasive action routinely because of this belief. Inexperienced tailing officers often misconstrue this odd behavior, believing that they have been "made," even though these criminals exhibit this behavior whether they are tailed or not.

Applying Surveillance to Arson Investigation

Identifying a Pyromaniac

When the totality of circumstances (reported fires, arson analysis, and pin maps) leads an investigator to believe that a pyromaniac is operating within a specific area or neighborhood, it is imperative that a detailed surveillance operation be mounted. The size of the area to be covered (streets/city blocks) and the times of such coverage can be determined from a careful analysis of available fire/arson data. A neighborhood that has suffered numerous losses due to a seemingly random fire/arson pattern can be narrowed down (through the use of *pin maps*) to a few streets with the highest concentration of fires. This area is known as the *saturation area*, and every block within it must be covered by a surveillance team during the hours of highest incidence.

To be most effective, these surveillance teams must be in constant radio communication with each other and should have the following types of equipment available:

binoculars,

nightscope (for night surveillance), and

camera equipment, including videotape capability.

A surveillance van or truck is ideally suited for this type of work. Specially equipped closed-circuit television (CCTV) systems, originally installed to monitor and deter violent street crimes, can also be utilized for fire/arson surveillance.

Cancellation of Insurance

Certain real estate holders and building owners have a much higher incidence of suspicious fires in their buildings than others. In some of these cases, the building's owner may be suspected of having initiated some or all of these fires. The real estate holder and his or her various properties may be targeted for special attention and immediate response by an investigative team in the event of any reported fire.

When an investigator is warned that a notice of cancellation has been sent by an insurance company to a targeted building owner for coverage on one of his or her holdings, then a fixed surveillance of that building should be commenced and maintained on a 24-hour basis until insurance coverage is actually terminated. This is to deter any attempt to cash in on the insurance before it lapses.

Confidential Informants

A registered confidential informant may provide information, either that a particular building has been targeted to burn or that an identified "torch" has been contracted to burn some unknown building.

In the first instance, fixed surveillance at the building should be started immediately in an attempt to catch the torch before the act. If probable cause is developed and it seems likely that the building's owner contracted the arson, then a court-ordered wiretap or other form of electronic surveillance should be used in an attempt to listen to and record conversations that demonstrate a conspiracy to commit the crimes of arson and/or insurance fraud.

When the torch is known, but the target building and the date and time of the planned fire are unknown, then all legal attempts should be made to monitor the torch's telephone, person-to-person conversations, and physical movements.

If the informant has access to the suspected torch and is willing to cooperate with the authorities, he can hide an electronic transmitter or body recorder on his person and attempt to engage the torch in a conversation about the planned fire. The following information should be elicited from the torch:

Who hired him?

What building is to be burned?

How much is he to be paid?

When and how does he plan to burn the building?

If it is necessary to tail the torch, then a detailed surveillance operation should be planned. This would include:

fixed surveillance of the torch's residence and

moving (automobile and foot) surveillance of the torch's movements outside his residence; and

a tracking device wired to the torch's car, if the torch owns one.

Wiring a Co-conspirator

In some cases, investigators have been able to infiltrate organized arson rings. In one case, a torch willingly cooperated with authorities after discovering that his co-conspirator had put out a contract to have him killed. More common is the situation where a torch has been indicted or convicted of a serious crime (e.g., arson, sale of narcotics) and, through his attorney, agrees to cooperate with authorities in the infiltration of ongoing arson conspiracies. This cooperation comes prior to sentencing in the torch's conviction in order for him to show good faith, influence the trial judge, or reduce his possible jail time.

If the decision is made to use this co-conspirator as an informant against the others involved in the arson conspiracy, an investigator must choose between two operations:

1. wire the cooperating co-conspirator with a wireless transmitter or body recorder and attempt to record the incriminating conversations of the other conspirators, or
2. have the co-conspirator introduce an undercover investigator to the other conspirator as a trusted friend or relative who needs and is willing to do anything for money.

The second option is preferable. It ensures that trained personnel are carrying out the operation, and eliminates the need for a warrant when actions sufficient to establish probable cause for arrest occur in the presence of the undercover investigator.

Appearance and Behavior

The appearance and behavior of surveillance personnel should follow these guidelines:

> be inconspicuous, of medium height and weight;
>
> fit the environment, dress, and demeanor of the neighborhood;
>
> do not wear conspicuous jewelry or other distinctive articles;
>
> maintain normal gait and manner;
>
> do not do anything that would attract attention (shout, wave, peek around corners, etc.);
>
> have a hat, glasses, and other accessories available in order to change appearance;
>
> do not make eye contact with the subject;
>
> have a cover story prepared, if challenged;
>
> carry loose change, tokens for local modes of transportation, contact telephone number (in case you get separated from the team), credit cards, and cover credentials;
>
> plan for every eventuality—know what you would do if the subject suddenly enters a taxi, bus, train, or elevator; and
>
> avoid drawing the attention of the public and of law enforcement officers who may not be aware of your operation.

Recording Observations

The investigator must accurately record his observations either in the form of written notes and/or still photographs, videotape, or motion pictures. A chronologic log should be maintained, describing actions taken and observations made during the duration of the operation. The following types of equipment have traditionally been used during surveillance operations:

> *photographic*—35-mm camera, video camera and recorder, appropriate lenses, adequate film and/or tape;
>
> *electronic*—portable radios, tape recorder, homing device, additional batteries and cassettes, watch, and binoculars.

Summary

Good surveillance techniques can be learned, but must be practiced. Teamwork and proper preplanning are the keys to success. Choose the method of surveillance (or combination of methods) that best suits the circumstances. Remember that there is no shame attached to losing a subject.

One-on-one surveillance, whether by foot or auto, is generally unproductive and frustrating. Several surveillance officers can bracket the subject and periodically change positions. Inexperienced surveillance officers commonly misinterpret a subject's deceptive tactics; not realizing that this behavior is routine, the officer will mistakenly think that he has been "made." Remember, you are not as conspicuous as you think.

References and Selected Readings

Kirk, Paul L., *Crime Investigation*, Wiley, New York, 1974.

O'Hara, Charles E., *Fundamentals of Criminal Investigation*, 5th ed., Charles C. Thomas, Springfield, Ill. 1980.

Scott, James D., *Investigative Methods*, Reston Publishing, Reston, Va., 1978.

Ward, Richard H., *Introduction to Criminal Investigations*, Addison-Wesley, Reading, Mass., 1975.

Interviewing and Interrogation

12

Regardless of the investigator's field of expertise (arson, homicide, robbery, etc.), the one predominant skill that cuts across all investigative endeavors is the ability to elicit information through interpersonal communication. The incriminating or contradictory statements made by a suspect, along with information gained from interviews of victims and witnesses, tie the investigation into a narrowly circumscribed, cohesive package. The overwhelming majority of the testimony presented at trial will involve information gathered from other than physical evidence.

The fact that a crime was committed may well be determined after a diligent examination of the scene. However, the development of a valid link between that crime and a suspect will probably result from the skillful application of carefully selected interviewing and interrogation styles.

Interview: the questioning of a person who is believed to possess knowledge of official interest to the investigator and who is not reluctant to furnish such information. It is interpersonal communication intended to gather information about an event, person, place, or thing; some exchange of information is understood and expected.

Interrogation: the questioning of a person who is reluctant to make a full disclosure of information; it is a goal-oriented interview without the free exchange of information.

Investigative Canvass

An investigative canvass is a door-to-door and street-to-street quest for local residents and people on the street who may have information about the incident under investigation. A thorough canvass is an integral part of any criminal investigation. Canvassing investigators should record the name and address of each person interviewed and whether or not that person could provide any information. Buildings and residences facing, adjoining, and to the rear of the fire building should be given special attention.

In larger urban areas, an investigator can almost presume that someone will have been looking out a window, regardless of the time of day or night. Bus, taxi, and truck drivers who travel through and frequent the area should also be questioned as to anything that they might have seen or heard and about any passengers that they might have discharged or picked up around the time and location of the fire.

Not every investigator is a good or even adequate interviewer. Even with extensive training, some otherwise excellent investigators exhibit such serious shortcomings in this area as to be dysfunctional to the case.

Evaluating the Subject

The subject of a forthcoming interview or interrogation must be evaluated (sized up) in relation to the circumstances of the case and with regard to the timing and environment in which the interview or interrogation will take place. Understanding the subject's background and experiences may provide insight into how best to pursue or evaluate the interview.

Anxiety

Many individuals who witness or are the victims of violent, life-threatening circumstances experience varying degrees of *psychological trauma*—emotional shock accompanied by high levels of anxiety. This adversely affects an individual's ability, not only to recall the incident, but also to cooperate with the investigating authorities. Many investigators, failing to recognize trauma for what it is, tend to label a traumatized witness as uncooperative.

Patience and tact are required to coax the witness to talk about his or her fears. A sympathetic approach is necessary to facilitate emotional unblocking and release (*catharsis*). Your willingness to hear and, to some extent, share in the witness's traumatic experience will lessen the anxiety and promote the flow of information.

Motivation

Is there any hidden agenda motivating the individual to come forward or to cooperate with the investigation? A registered informant may be seeking monetary reward. A criminal may be attempting to eliminate his competition. An injured party may be seeking revenge. An investigator must separate the "good-guy" informants from the "bad-guy" informants.

Location

What is the best location in which to conduct the interview? Would the interviewee be more at ease discussing the case in the comfort of his or her own living room? If the interview were to be conducted in the "official setting" of a police station, would it encourage cooperation? It generally helps to categorize witnesses into "street people," "good citizens," and "professional types." For example, a "street person" would probably want to avoid being seen with a police officer or being interviewed at home. For such an individual, an alley or the back of a patrol car might be the best location.

Previous Encounters with Law Enforcement

Another factor that may affect both the style of interview chosen by the investigator and the attitude displayed by the interviewee is the nature of any previous encounters between the interviewee and other law enforcement bodies. A streetwise person will react differently than will your average citizen, as will an individual who has a criminal record, is on parole, or may have had negative interactions with other official investigating units.

Possible Involvement

Every investigator must be ever mindful of the fact that a supposed witness may have been an active or passive participant, or at least an interested party, in the criminal enterprise. If self-incriminating statements are made, the interview must be stopped and the Miranda warnings given. The totality of the circumstances surrounding the interview will be closely examined and actively contested when and if the case goes to trial.

Timeliness

The longer the lapse between the incident and the follow-up interview, the greater the opportunity for other factors to cloud the witness's recollection:

1. The witness may "fill in the gaps" in his recollection of the incident

by adding inferences. The witness may subsequently find it impossible to distinguish between the facts and his fabrications.

2. The witness may not have attached much significance to the incident when it occurred. This failure to attend to the particulars or circumstances of the event may adversely affect later recollection.

3. The witness's recollection of the incident may be colored by his observations and conversations regarding the event since its occurrence.

For these reasons, the witness should be interviewed as soon as possible after the incident. However, even under ideal conditions, an investigator must utilize every verbal skill within his repertoire to determine what the witness actually observed.

Many cases have been "made" by the investigator standing in the street, mingling with the occupants of a still-smoldering apartment house. These possible victims do not need to be reminded of the experience that they just endured or be motivated in any other way. The smell of the fire is still fresh in their clothing. The level of anxiety and confusion is very high and easily perceived. Under these circumstances, the investigator need do no more than listen. If any of the occupants have any reason to believe that the fire was not an accident, it will be evident from their conversation. In one case, a female who had just lost all of her belongings in a two-alarm fire was overheard to say, "That son of a bitch went too far this time!" With one simple question—"What son of a bitch?"—the investigator had the name and apartment number of a possible suspect. In another case, a woman still clinging to her two children, stated, "I'm going to kill the mother f----- in 3B. He almost killed me and my kids!" A possible suspect in the case had been identified.

Initial Interview Procedure: An Example

A businessman who, either on his way to or from work or while on his lunch hour, sees someone throw a Molotov cocktail through the window of an occupied building, tells what he has seen to responding emergency units who, in turn, tactfully hold him until the investigator arrives. A sharp investigator, realizing that the witness will be anxious to get to work, should:

quickly explain that he only needs five minutes of the witness's time;

request that the witness accompany the investigator to the investigator's office, if nearby; and

guarantee the witness that he will be driven to wherever it was that he was going as soon as the brief interview is completed.

Once in the office:

obtain a complete pedigree of the witness;

get as accurate a description of the suspect as the witness can recall; and

if possible, have the witness draw a sketch of the block where the crime occurred.

The sketch should be drawn on blank typing paper and include as much information as possible. For example:

Where was the witness standing in relation to the building and in relation to the other buildings on the block?

If the suspect fled in a vehicle, where had the vehicle been parked? Was anyone else inside it?

Through which window was the Molotov cocktail thrown?

What other information might affect the investigation?

Intentional Loss of Memory

People, in a moment of confusion or at the height of anxiety, will make statements spontaneously. In time, however, their stories may change completely or be lost to lapses in memory. This is one of the reasons that investigators should elicit as much information as possible at the first meeting.

The intentional loss of memory, however, is a condition with which investigators must cope continuously. This problem is not apparent until the second time you meet a witness, during the follow-up interview. Although full of information at the first interview, the witness now tells you that he cannot remember anything. This strange loss of memory is usually self-induced after the witness has had an opportunity to discuss the incident with his fellow workers, family, and friends. Now, his boss wants to know whether he is going to lose any time at work. In addition, his wife, family, and friends have convinced him that if he cooperates with the authorities, the suspect will probably retaliate.

An experienced investigator will identify this far-too-frequent scenario immediately. Uncooperative and "forgetful" witnesses regularly frustrate investigative efforts. The witness must be rehabilitated through either rational argument or investigative ploy. The investigator can point out the witness's obligation to the faceless people who suffered as a result of the fire he witnessed, in an effort to touch some "sensitive nerve." Alternatively, the investigator may attempt to convince the witness that he is already deeply involved in the investigation. This ploy depends to a great extent upon the witness's level of sophistication. The documentation needed for this to work includes:

any number of serialized, official reports prepared after your first, brief meeting. These complaint reports, investigative follow-up reports, and so on will list and categorize all of the witness's prior statements in the case;

the witness's rough sketch of the crime scene, now vouchered as evidence;

all of the other forms and official crime-scene reports and requests for information that could be found in any case folder; and

the arson case folder itself, the jacket of which is now covered with case and control numbers, telephone numbers for notifications made, and other pertinent data. These official-looking and -sounding forms, reports, and materials might be enough to convince the witness that he is indeed an active participant in the investigation, causing his memory to return as well.

Be aware that "civilians" locate incidents chronologically in terms of routine events that occur during the course of their daily activities. Try to equate each incident with a specific time on the 24-hour clock:

I had just opened the store (= 0730 hours).

I had just put out the garbage (= 1745 hours).

I was watching television (= 2130 hours).

I was walking my dog (= 1930 hours).

Try to get the witness as involved as possible in the limited amount of time you have. If the witness explains that he must leave:

give him a business card and request that he call you if he recalls anything in addition to what he has told you;

advise him that you will get back to him in a few days; and

arrange to have him driven home or back to work.

Interviewing and Interrogation Strategies

The underlying presumption in every interview should be that the person being interviewed has information that is pertinent and material to the case. The investigator's task and intent should be to extract that information.

There are several strategies that may be employed in interviews. Each is situational and designed to elicit information from a respondent under interrelated and particular circumstances. No one strategy will suffice under practical conditions; an investigator, to be successful, will probably employ a combination of strategies.

Role Playing

The investigator must be able and willing to play the role that is required depending upon the circumstances in order to promote the most open response of the interviewee. Possible roles to be assumed include:

father-confessor,

concerned listener,

best friend,

protector,

benefactor,

tough cop, and

many others.

The father-confessor and concerned listener roles are quite similar. In both cases, the investigator maintains a nonjudgmental attitude and conveys a feeling of sympathetic understanding. The interviewer offers a "sympathetic ear."

In the *father-confessor* role, the investigator plays the part of an understanding minister, and the interview takes on the character of a religious confession. The subject of the interview is encouraged to:

unload his feelings;

release the tension by talking about the sources of the tension; and

discuss his feelings of guilt and pangs of conscience.

As the *concerned listener*, the interviewer plays the part of an understanding stranger. The line of communication sounds more like a conversation between two frustrated people over drinks in a neighborhood bar than it does an interview. The investigator attempts to have the subject believe that he (the investigator) not only understands and identifies with the subject's predicament, but that he grudgingly accepts the subject's choice of a criminal act to solve or deal with the problem. To be successful, the investigator must avoid threatening words such as "jail," "crime," and "punishment" in favor of words such as "incident" or "problem."

During the early stages of the interviewing process, an investigator may realize that a witness, victim, or criminal has some personal problem—defense mechanism, fear, or other more conscious reaction—that prevents him from cooperating in the investigation. It is imperative that the interviewer identify and address the interviewee's problem before attempting to conduct the interview. For example, the investigator may play the role of a *best friend* to a person who has been traumatized by his arrest. By taking the time to explain the arrest process, providing coffee, and so on, the interviewer may put the person at ease and foster further communication.

Some witnesses and victims are reluctant to cooperate with authorities because they fear for their personal safety or because they fear that their involvement will create an undue burden (time, money) on their families. In these instances, the investigator may attempt to calm the person by playing the role of a *protector* or *benefactor*. The police cannot guarantee protection but can often allay the person's fears by explaining the full range of agency resources that are available. Some larger investigative and prosecutorial agencies even provide car and babysitting services when necessary.

When interviewing the streetwise person or habitual criminal, the investigator may find it useful to play the role of *tough cop*. This role requires the investigator to control the pace of the interview and to structure selected questions in such a way as to have the interviewee believe that the questioner knows more than he actually does. The investigator must be prepared to summarize ideas quickly and to constantly redirect the flow of conversation toward the desired objective.

Common Interviewing Errors

Although there are many common interviewing errors, two seem to be the most common:

1. The interviewer does not allow the interviewee to tell his or her story.

2. The interviewer talks too much.

The first is easily understood when you realize the normal career path followed by the average public investigator. A police investigator (detective) most probably served in a uniform assignment for several years before being selected or promoted to the investigator's rank. The bulk of the uniformed officer's time was probably devoted to the preparation of complex crime reports. In time, report writing became a mechanical skill: just "fill in the boxes." This matter-of-fact, mechanical approach in dealing with crime victims, witnesses, and suspects tends to carry over, unconsciously, into the individual's approach to investigation, and manifests itself in the form of constant interruptions. These interruptions confuse the interviewee and result in a disjointed account of the incident. This is illustrated in the following exchanges during the initial interview of a cooperative witness:

WITNESS: "I had just put out the garbage, when I heard what I thought was an explosion."

INVESTIGATOR (*interrupting*): "What time was that?"

* * *

WITNESS: "I saw these two guys run from the building and get into a car."

INVESTIGATOR (*interrupting*): "Can you describe them and the car?"

* * *

WITNESS: "All of a sudden the building burst into flame."

INVESTIGATOR (*interrupting*): "What color was the flame and smoke, and where did you first see the flames?"

In these illustrations, the investigator is actually interrupting the natural thought processes of this cooperative witness by unconsciously shifting into a report-writing mode. He has obviously disregarded several basic principles of interviewing. If this type of approach continues throughout the course of the investigation, it will certainly have an adverse impact on its outcome. This investigator should have allowed the witness to talk *without interruption*, permitting the witness to "tell his story" in its entirety at least once, and perhaps several times, before asking the first question.

The second common problem is that the interviewer tends to talk too much. As stated earlier, some exchange of information is expected, but not to the extent that the investigator describes the case in detail. An interviewee should not end an interview knowing much more than when he was first approached.

Summary of Guidelines

1. The investigator must control the interview or interrogation.
2. Prior preparation is essential. Review the facts of the case and all available records and data before commencing the interview. Know what you are talking about.
3. Carefully evaluate (size up) the subject of the interview.
4. Play whatever role is required to facilitate the free flow of information.
5. Tactfully select the best combination of verbal strategies to use.
6. Do not automatically discredit information that is favorable to the suspect.
7. Remember that your job is to *gather information.*

Provocation

It is sometimes necessary to motivate or induce a response from a prospective witness. The person may or may not have information; however, the mere fact that he or she does not want to get involved does not warrant exemption from examination. The investigator, after questioning, can determine whether this witness can be of any further value.

In provoking a reaction or response, the investigator is attempting to keep the conversation alive. Statements such as "I don't know anything" or "I don't want to get involved" should not be accepted. The investigator should encourage the individual to cooperate by relating the incident to the witness's emotional frame of reference. The following examples illustrate this point:

WITNESS: "I heard about the fire, but I don't want to get involved."
INVESTIGATOR: "Listen, I'm trying to save your neighborhood, but I can't do it without your help."

* * *

INVESTIGATOR: "A couple of innocent people died in that fire, and your family could be next if we don't stop the arsonist."

This type of emotional stimulus will generally induce either a verbal or physical reaction.

Paraphrasing

The investigator might *paraphrase* a response, twisting it to his advantage. Paraphrasing, in this context, is the careful rewording of another person's response in order to test or alter its meaning. It is not the mere parroting of what the individual has said. The investigator must be prepared to test the witness's commitment when he appears to respond to provocation in a positive way. For example:

WITNESS (*provoked response*): "You have to get that guy before he hurts anyone else."
INVESTIGATOR: "Then you'll talk to me for five minutes? I can't stop this guy without your help."

* * *

WITNESS: "I'll see what I can find out."
INVESTIGATOR: "Then you'll find out what the 'word' is out on the street and get back to me?"

Empathy

Empathy is the feeling associated with an emotional identification with another person. In some cases, where the victims are children or elderly, the investigator's concern for them may be sincere and easily expressed. In other cases, it is no more than an act. When used correctly, the mutual concern (real or imagined) that results will ensure the free flow of information. In fact, when used properly, the empathetic approach is the most effective interviewing technique. The interviewer must follow these guidelines for its effective use:

Appear sincere.

Use a very understanding approach.

Have a nonjudgmental attitude.

Be careful to disguise negative feelings and lack of compassion for the respondent.

The investigator's manner of speech, choice of language, and facial expressions will serve as the focal points for the respondent.

"Let's Make a Deal"

In this strategy, the investigator may induce the cooperation of an otherwise uncooperative respondent by offering a concession in exchange for specific information. Conversely, the witness may intimate that he might have information to exchange. In either case, the agreement to act by one party requires a reciprocal agreement by the other:

WITNESS: "I may know something about the fire, but I don't want to get into trouble."

INVESTIGATOR: "Tell me what you know and I'll tell the prosecutor that you cooperated."

This approach is often used when dealing with a registered informant. It is fairly common to meet an uncooperative informant at his place of work or other area where he is well known, the idea being that the informant does not wish to be seen talking to the authorities. This type of meeting might involve the following conversation:

INFORMANT: "Are you crazy, man? I told you not to come around here! Are you trying to get me killed?"

INVESTIGATOR: "You've been trying to avoid me. I need information about the fire on 3rd Street."

INFORMANT: "O.K. man, I'll meet you tomorrow night at 11:00 P.M. at the usual spot. I'll see what I can find out."

INVESTIGATOR: "Be there, or I'll be back."

The investigator, in this example, is making a deal with the informant, securing the informant's cooperation in exchange for implied agreement not to be seen in the informant's company in the "wrong" places.

"Choice of Evils"

This approach can only be used when the investigator is dealing from a position of strength. The uncooperative respondent is offered a "choice of evils"—one alternative is more distasteful than the other, and no other options are offered. It might be used when the investigator has a good understanding of the facts in the case and knows that he is interviewing our interrogating a "weak link" in the case. For example, take the case of two partners who jointly own a failing business. One partner opted to "sell the business to the insurance company;" the other attempted to dissuade his associate but did not notify the authorities. This second partner is a family man whose son worked full-time in the business and knew nothing about the fire.

As the motive for and circumstances of the fire become clear to the investigator, he might well choose to attempt to break this "weak link." After giving the second partner his Miranda warnings, the investigator may offer him a choice between two undesirable alternatives:

1. he can discuss the case with the investigator, *or*
2. the investigator can discuss the case with his son.

Lying Witnesses

Investigators must often deal with respondents who lie during an interview. One might expect the subject under investigation to lie only when he or she has a vested interest in the outcome of the case. In fact, complainants, witnesses, and even victims lie in their conversations with the authorities.

It is important and necessary for the investigator to identify lies and confront the liar as soon as possible. The method of confrontation should be determined after a careful evaluation of the respondent.

In some cases, a direct attack is warranted. After listening to an obviously untruthful account offered by a streetwise person, the investigator may choose to call that person a liar to his face. The investigator might add that he is determined to find out what happened and that it might be in the respondent's best interests to cooperate.

In other cases, a more subtle approach works best. The investigator tactfully makes it clear to the respondent that it is somewhat difficult to accept the story. The investigator might then review the respondent's account of what happened, pointing out the various inconsistencies and illogical statements. Afterwards, the respondent should be asked once again to describe the incident to the best of his or her recollection without adding to or omitting information.

An investigator must be cautious to avoid misinterpreting a witness's inconsistent statements by inferring that the witness is lying intentionally. Ten different people can watch the same event and, when interviewed, relate ten different descriptions of the event. As previously mentioned, a traumatized witness might be unable to cooperate if questioned too soon after the incident and might, in fact, invent a story to placate an overzealous investigator. Some witnesses exhibit psychological defense mechanisms, which the investigator, in his haste, may fail to recognize. How many investigators would react favorably when the victim of a fire laughs or giggles? What about the victim who refuses to believe that the event ever took place (denial of reality)? Other witnesses are unable to relate correctly to questions due to chronologic confusion. Thus, the order in which they choose to relate the event may be difficult to comprehend, even though their facts may be accurate.

APPENDIX: SAMPLE OWNER/TENANT INTERVIEW FORM*

I am _____ of the _____
                                        (Department/Agency)
interviewing Mr./Mrs. _____concerning the

fire at _____
                              (address)
that occurred on _____ at approximately _____ AM/PM.
                    (date)   (time)

1. Your full name is _____
2. Your age is _____
3. Your date of birth is _____
4. Are you aware that this statement is being recorded? _____
a) Do we have permission to record your statement? _____
5. Mr./Mrs. _____ do we have your permission
to enter upon your property at _____,
investigate the fire, and remove any evidence that may point to the cause and
origin of the fire?
a) If necessary, do we have your permission to return to your property at a
later date to collect evidence from the fire? _____
6. Your present address is _____
7. Your present phone number is _____
8. Were you the owner or tenant of property located at _____
_____ at the time of the fire? _____
9. Are you the sole owner? _____ If a partnership, who is the other owner?
_____
10. Are you married? _____
11. Wife's/husband's name _____
12. Is he/she on the deed to the property? _____
13. Is he/she named on the insurance policy? _____

---

* Courtesy of David Redsicker, New York State Fire Academy.

14. Do you have any children? _____

15. Their names and ages: _____

_____

_____

16. Do you have pets? _____

a) Were they injured in the fire? _____

17. How long have you owned the property at _____

_____? (Weeks/months/years)_____

18. Did you and your wife/husband live in the house? _____

19. Where were you when the fire occurred? _____

20. How did you find out about the fire? _____

21. Who was the last person in the house? _____

22. Did you personally lock up the house when you left? _____

_____

23. Have you had the locks changed since you have owned the house? ____

24. Who has keys to the locks? _____

25. Have you had any burglaries/prowlers? _____

26. Were there any signs of forcible entry when the fire department arrived?

_____

27. Have you had any electrical problems recently? _____

28. Have you had any heating/furnace problems recently? _____

29. Have you had any TV problems recently? _____

30. Do you or your wife/husband smoke? _____

31. Were you smoking before you left the house? _____

32. Did you have any visitors prior to leaving the house? _____

33. Are you aware of any enemies that would want to start a fire on your property? _____

34. Do you know for sure how the fire started? _____

35. Do you have any idea how the fire started? _____

36. Do you know who started the fire? _____

37. Were there any flammable liquids stored in the building? _____

_____

38. Have you ever had a fire before on this or any other property? _____

_____

39. Have you ever had an insurance claim before? _____

If yes, what company, when, and where? _____

40. Has the house been for sale recently or were you going to sell it? _____

_____

41. Has the house been appraised recently? _____ If yes, what value and why the appraisal? _____

42. Have you done any remodeling recently? _____ If yes, exactly what? _____

43. What was the purchase price of the house? _____

44. From whom did you purchase the house? _____ _____ On what date? _____

45. Where is the house financed? _____

46. What are the monthly payments? _____ Are they current or in arrears? _____

47. Do you have any other loans or debts?

Where	Amount	Monthly Payment	Current or in Arrears

48. Do you have any other insurance besides this policy with _____ _____? _____

49. Was anything removed from the building prior to the fire? _____ _____

50. Was anything removed from the building after the fire? _____ _____

51. Did you find anything missing after the fire that would indicate a burglary? _____

52. Are you planning to rebuild the property? _____

53. Can you think of anything else that would help us with the investigation? _____

54. Were there any liens or judgments against you or the property? _____ _____

55. Do you have any health, sanitation, zoning, or building violations against the property? _____

56. Are there any county, township, or city violations against the property? _____

57. If a business place, what was the approximate amount of daily or weekly business (net)? _____

58. Are all of the statements made by you in this recorded statement true and complete to the best of your knowledge? _____

59. Please state your name again. You are aware this statement was being recorded, and we had your permission to record it? _____

60. This statement was completed at _____ AM/PM on _____

Court Qualification and Testimony 13

An investigator's responsibility is far from over with the arrest of one or more suspects. Pure theorists may argue that once the investigator has introduced the defendant to the judicial system, his job is done. However, this theoretical approach flies in the face of reality. A good investigator attentively follows a case through to its end. Preparing for and undergoing cross examination by a skilled defense attorney is hardly an experience that can be accurately described by theorists; it is the type of experience that must be endured to be appreciated. The trial is the point in an investigation when many months of rigorous digging, persuading, interviewing, and analysis are put to the test. To think that an investigator has no vested interest in its outcome is ludicrous: the sleepless nights and countless hours on the telephone and in the field, gorged with coffee, seeking leads, and double-checking information hardly represent a fleeting interest.

In most contested arson cases, the fire investigator is the prosecution's principal witness. The criminal prosecution may fail unless the investigator:

dresses appropriately and gives a professional appearance;

has been properly prepared by the prosecutor;

knows the rules of evidence; and

presents his testimony clearly, understandably, and in an outright manner.

Pretrial Testimony

In most criminal cases, an investigator will have testified at least several times about the facts of a case prior to the trial. He may have testified under oath before the grand jury that handed down the indictment in the case, or at various pretrial hearings where a defense attorney contested the legality or constitutionality of seized evidence, a confession, or lineup procedure. This prior sworn testimony may be used to impeach the credibility of that witness who tenders contradictory statements during the trial.

Over the years, an experienced arson investigator may have testified as a court-recognized expert at numerous trials. The court records of those trials, absent unusual circumstances, are a public record. A practical defense attorney, knowing that investigator Jones is the state's principal witness in an upcoming trial, could gain access Jones's prior testimony, a painstaking analysis of which could yield an interesting and informative portrait of the investigator. The defense attorney is likely to focus on certain material elements, such as:

reaction to stress under different questioning techniques;

quality of testimony, including weaknesses and strong points; and

apparent level of the investigator's expertise and training.

This type of pretrial intelligence would be a valuable tool when designing the defense strategy.

Trial Preparation

Preparing for trial is much more than simply reviewing one's notes, although the review of all notes, reports, and evidence, pertaining to the case is a necessary element. Scrutinize every piece of paper prepared during the investigation. Look for mistakes, omissions, and inconsistencies—a defense attorney certainly will! Discuss any problems or inconsistencies with the prosecutor before the trial commences; do not ignore them or write them off as inconsequential. Are there any photos, reports, statements, and so on in the case file that might be construed as beneficial to the defendant and therefore "Brady" material?* If so, discuss them with the prosecutor. To knowingly disregard this type of material constitutes malfeasance and may be grounds for a mistrial.

Ensure that witnesses, assisting investigators, laboratory personnel, and the coroner or medical examiner (if necessary) will be available at the time of the trial.

If the jury has already been selected (as in a Federal case, where the judge selects the jury), ask the prosecutor if any common thread or

---

* According to *Brady v. Maryland* (373 US 83, 83 S.Ct. 1194), suppression by the prosecution of evidence favorable to an accused (exculpatory evidence) who has requested it (discovery) violates due process where the evidence is material either to guilt or to punishment, irrespective of the good or bad faith of the prosecution.

line of questioning was obvious during the defense attorney's *voir dire* (preliminary examination regarding competency) of the potential jurors. The prosecutor may be able to identify the defense attorney's trial strategy, e.g.:

prosecution witnesses are all liars;

defendant was away or abroad at the time of the fire (or other alibi); or

prosecution expert witness is not an expert, and defense expert will present the "true" facts.

Forewarned is forearmed.

Witness Stand Behavioral Guidelines

Expect the defense attorney to stand away from the jury, on the opposite side of the courtroom. This is intentional. We have a tendency to look and talk to the individual who is questioning or talking to us. This defense tactic, although subtle, is intended to prevent the witness from making eye contact with the jury while answering questions. Remember, the judge is the trier of the law, but the jury is the trier of the facts. Look at the jury when answering questions.

The following guidelines should be followed when testifying in court:

Identify yourself to the court stenographer, by rank, name, and assignment or unit, in a clear and audible manner.

Stand erect and respond with an audible "I do" when the oath is administered.

Sit erect with both feet on the floor and hands in a natural position.

Tell the truth, remembering that it is *how* you tell the truth that makes the difference.

Presume that the defense attorney has visited the fire scene and reviewed every shred of evidence, piece of paper, and photograph concerning the case.

Consider the defense attorney as a master of the English language.

Do not become aggressive or "cute" in your responses to defense questions.

Listen carefully to questions and delay at least three seconds before answering, allowing the prosecutor sufficient time to object.

Allow the judge to rule on an objection before answering.

Do not exaggerate answers.

If you do not understand a question, wait until it is explained or rephrased before answering—chances are the jury did not understand it either.

Do not volunteer information—where appropriate, answer with a simple "yes" or "no."

Request the judge's permission before referring to your notes or memo book to refresh your memory.

If a question requires a technical answer, explain the technical language to the jury in simple, understandable terms.

Remember that, many times, the prosecutor can rehabilitate damaging testimony during the redirect.

If you cannot remember a specific fact of piece of information, simply answer, "I don't remember," *not* "I don't know."

When the prosecutor asks your opinion of the cause of the fire, the proper answer is "I could find no natural or accidental cause," not "Arson."

In testifying about patterns from accelerants, refer to them as "pour patterns" to show deliberateness, as opposed to "spill," which may imply accident.

Cross Examination

Be prepared for and expect an aggressive defensive counterattack during your *voir dire* as an expert witness. Keep available an updated résumé listing formal and specialized education and training, total number of cases investigated (separating physical examinations and automobile salvages), and all the courts where you have been previously recognized as an expert. Remember, when you qualify as an expert in an arson trial, you are qualifying as an expert in the entire field of fire investigation; as such, you are subject to a wide and diversified range of questions, some (or all) of which may have little or nothing to do with the circumstances of the case on trial.

Cross examination could proceed as follows. The defense attorney approaches the witness stand carrying a number of textbooks. The subject or topic covered in all of the books is fire and/or arson investigation. Handing the witness one book after the other, the defense attorney asks whether the witness recognizes the author as an expert in the field of arson investigation. The witness is then asked if he has read the book and whether or not he views it as the product of the author's expertise.

The prosecutor's witness is in a very difficult position, regardless of his answers at this point. If he answers that the authors are in fact recognized experts in the field of arson investigation, but he either does not recognize the book as the product of that expertise or has never read it, the defense attorney will claim that a "supposed" expert witness does not take the time to stay current in his field. If the witness states that the authors are recognized experts and that the book is, indeed, the product of their expertise, then the witness will be asked, at random, whether or not he agrees with any particular author's opinion on any given issue. Unless the witness is very well read and has a superhuman memory, he is about to be made to look foolish before the judge and jury. It is almost a no-win situation. Regardless of how the judge rules on the prosecutor's contention that his witness is an expert, the defense counsel has scored a major point. Even if the judge rules that the witness may testify as an expert, the defense attorney has succeeded in damaging that witness's credibility with the jury.

Answer what might be considered "trick" questions with special care. For example:

> "Did you discuss this case with anyone?" The answer is "Yes." You discussed the case with your partners and the prosecutor.

> For questions using the words "ever" or "never"— "Mr. Jones, do you ever make mistakes?"—an appropriate answer might be, "Yes, but not in this case."

A defense attorney, after soliciting a long litany of "I don't remembers" and "I don't knows" from a witness may add, for effect, "Well, what *do* you know?" just before stating that he has no further questions. This is intended to damage your credibility by having the jury believe that you really don't know anything. An inexperienced investigator might sink into the witness chair, feel intimidated, or sit silently waiting to be dismissed. Think! The defense attorney has asked a wide-open question. Answer by telling the jury what you *do know* about the case: "Well counselor, I do know that your client told me he started the fire, but didn't intend for anyone to get killed." To stop you from answering, the defense attorney will have somehow to object to his own question.

Defense Expert

The defense in an arson trial has the right to introduce and court-qualify its own professional fire investigator as an expert witness. This witness will have examined the same fire scene, evaluated the same evidence, and yet reached a totally different conclusion as to cause and origin. Although you have stated that the fire was not an accident, he will testify that the cause could not be determined, or that it was, in fact, accidental in origin. The language and terminology used to describe the fire scene and the various phases of its examination are very technical and, no matter how simply expressed, can confuse a lay jury. Unless there is other overriding evidence to the contrary, a jury deliberating guilt or innocence may well find for the defendant. After all, if two equally qualified experts cannot agree on the cause of the fire, how can the jury be expected to do so?

New York State Law Governing Arson

14

by Naomi Werne*

Introduction

Article 150 of the Penal Law sets forth the degrees of the offense of arson. It should be noted that arson is restricted to damaging a "building" or "motor vehicle." Other unlawful property damage by fire or explosion is governed by the criminal mischief provisions of Penal Law §§145.00–145.12. If a person commits arson and causes the death of another person who was not a participant in the crime, the felony murder statute [Penal Law §125.25(3)] applies.

Definitions

1. *Building.* As used in Article 150, "building," in addition to its ordinary meaning, includes any structure, vehicle, or watercraft used for overnight lodging of persons, or used by persons for carrying on business therein. Where a building consists of two or more units separately secured or occupied, each unit shall not be deemed a separate building (Penal Law §150.00). "Building" includes an abandoned building. *People* v. *Richberg*, 56 A.D.2d 279, 392 N.Y.S.2d 16 (1st Dept. 1977).

2. *Motor vehicle.* As used in Article 150, "motor vehicle" includes every vehicle operated or driven upon a public highway that is propelled by any power other than muscular power, except (a) electrically

* Senior Staff Attorney, Bureau of Prosecution and Defense Services, New York State Division of Criminal Justice Services.

Revised July 1984 by John L. Callaghan, BPDS Staff Attorney.

Reprinted by permission of the author and the New York State Division of Criminal Justice Services.

Note: This chapter is included as an excellent example of the types of law governing arson-related legal procedures. Such laws in states other than New York may differ decidedly.

driven invalid chairs being operated or driven by an invalid, (b) vehicles that run only upon rails or tracks, and (c) snowmobiles as defined in Article 47 of the Vehicle and Traffic Law.

This inclusion of a motor vehicle as a structure that may be the subject of an arson (L.1979, c.225) was part of a larger enactment establishing a State Office of Fire Prevention and Control to coordinate statewide efforts to combat arson-for-profit, which extends to the destruction of automobiles and trucks. (See Hechtman, Arnold D., *Supplementary Practice Commentary*, 1979 to Penal Law §150.00, Vol. 39, p. 20, *McKinney's Consolidated Laws of New York, Annotated*.) Prior to the amendment to this statute, setting fire to a vehicle could be the basis only for a conviction of criminal mischief; see *People* v. *Hollis*, 73 A.D.2d 994, 424 N.Y.S.2d 31 (3d Dept. 1980) where, despite evidence that defendant set fire to a commercial trailer, he was convicted only of criminal mischief and the arson count against him was dismissed.

Elements and Degrees of Arson

A person is guilty of arson in the *fourth degree*, a class E felony, when he recklessly damages a building or motor vehicle by intentionally starting a fire or causing an explosion (Penal Law §150.05). A person who commits arson in the fourth degree does not act intentionally in damaging the building or motor vehicle, according to the definition of intentional conduct in Penal Law §15.05(1): "A person acts intentionally with respect to a result or to conduct described by a statute defining an offense when his conscious objective is to cause such result or to engage in such conduct."

The mental culpability accompanying the act of damaging a building or motor vehicle in the commission of arson in the fourth degree is *recklessness*:

A person acts recklessly with respect to a result or to a circumstance described by a statute defining an offense when he is aware of and consciously disregards a substantial and unjustifiable risk that such result will occur or that such circumstance exists. The risk must be of such nature and degree that disregard thereof constitutes a gross deviation from the standard of conduct that a reasonable person would observe in the situation. A person who creates such a risk but is unaware thereof solely by reason of voluntary intoxication also acts recklessly with respect thereto. [Penal Law §15.05(3)]

The other element of mental culpability in fourth-degree arson that must accompany the act of starting the fire or causing the explosion that damages the building or motor vehicle exists where the defendant starts the fire or causes the explosion intentionally, according to the language of the statute, though no conscious deliberate intent to cause damage is in the mind of the defendant.

Where the evidence justified a finding by the jury that defendant threw a lit cigarette in a hayloft knowing it was lit without caring whether it started a fire, defendant was properly convicted of fourth-degree arson [see *People* v. *Keith A.U.*, 47 A.D.2d 791, 365 N.Y.S.2d 570 (3d Dept. 1975)]. The Appellate Division so held though there was no proof that the defendant intentionally started a fire. See also *People* v. *Kazmarick*, 99 Misc.2d 1012, 417 N.Y.S.2d 671 (Sullivan Co. Ct. 1979), *aff'd without opinion*, 75 A.D.2d 1026, 427 N.Y.S.2d 1021 (3d Dept. 1980), *aff'd* 52 N.Y.2d 322, 438 N.Y.S.2d 247, 420 N.E.2d 45 (1981), where the court denied defendant's motion to dismiss the indictment for murder on the ground that defendant could be convicted of one of the lesser included offenses of manslaughter or criminally negligent homicide if it were proved that he had, as charged, dropped a lighted match on a paper-strewn floor in a wood-frame building with knowledge that people were sleeping inside. But see *People* v. *Lebron*, 68 A.D.2d 836, 414 N.Y.S.2d 518 (1st Dept. 1979), where the court vacated defendant's plea of guilty to arson in the fourth degree since the pre-plea colloquy established only that defendant had thrown a cigarette on the floor of an apartment he was painting.*

Setting a fire or causing an explosion that damages a building or motor vehicle is the conduct required for fourth-degree arson. The result of "damage" is required to complete the crime, that is, an injury to the building or motor vehicle that impairs its use or lowers its value.

Affirmative defense: In any prosecution under Penal Law §150.05, it is an affirmative defense that no person other than the defendant had a possessory or proprietary interest in the building or motor vehicle [Penal Law §150.05(2)].†

---

* Proof of criminal negligence, that is, a failure to perceive a substantial and unjustifiable risk where such a failure would constitute a gross deviation from the standard of care that a reasonable person would observe in the situation [Penal Law §15.05(4)], is not the required mental culpability accompanying the act of damaging a building or motor vehicle in the crime of arson in the fourth degree. Similarly, there is no such crime as "felony arson," analogous to felony murder, that imposes criminal liability for a negligent burning of a building or motor vehicle during the commission of a felony other than arson; unless of course, it is proved beyond a reasonable doubt that the defendant acted recklessly when he damaged the building or motor vehicle. For example, if a person unlawfully entered another's barn and lit a match, intending to steal liquor, but tripped and fell, starting a fire, he has not committed fourth-degree arson. (See Hechtman, Arnold D., *Practice Commentaries* to Penal Law §150.05, Vol. 39, p. 86, *McKinney's Consolidated Laws of New York, Annotated*.)

† The defendant has the burden of proving by a preponderance of the evidence that he alone had a possessory or proprietary interest in the building or motor vehicle. This defense does not deny due process by placing on a defendant the burden of proving his innocence since the statute does not shift to the defendant the burden to disprove any fact essential to the crime of fourth-degree arson [see *Patterson* v. *New York*, 432 U.S. 197, 97 S.Ct. 2319, 53 L.Ed.2d 281 (1977)].

A person is guilty of arson in the *third degree,* a class C felony, when he intentionally damages a building or motor vehicle by starting a fire or causing an explosion (Penal Law §150.10). The element of mental culpability in the crime of third-degree arson is present where the defendant intends to damage a building or motor vehicle by starting a fire or causing an explosion. Damage must be his conscious objective; otherwise he does not have the required mental culpability for a conviction of third-degree arson. The required result in the crime of third-degree arson is the same as that element in fourth-degree arson: damage to a building or motor vehicle.*

Affirmative defense: In any prosecution under Penal Law §150.10, it is an affirmative defense under subdivision 2 that:

a. no person other than the defendant had a possessory or proprietary interest in the building or motor vehicle, or if other persons had such interests, all of them consented to the defendant's conduct;

b. the defendant's sole intent was to destroy or damage the building or motor vehicle for a lawful and proper purpose; and

c. the defendant had no reasonable ground to believe that his conduct might endanger the life or safety of another person or damage another building or motor vehicle.

A person is guilty of the class B felony of *second-degree* arson when he intentionally damages a building or motor vehicle by starting a fire, and

a. another person who is not a participant in the crime is present in such building or motor vehicle at the time; and

b. the defendant knows that fact or the circumstances are such as to render the presence of such a person therein a reasonable possibility (Penal Law, §150.15).

There are actually two elements of mental culpability in the crime of second-degree arson:

1. *Intent* (a conscious objective) to damage a building or motor vehicle by starting a fire. This is the same element of mental culpability that must be proved to convict a person of third-degree arson.

2. *Knowledge* that a person who is not a participant in the crime is present in the building or motor vehicle at the time, or the existence

---

* As of July 1, 1982, arson in the third degree carries a mandatory term of imprisonment [Penal Law §60.05(4)].

of circumstances that render the presence of such a person a reasonable possibility.*

The element of conduct in the crime of second-degree arson is damaging a building or motor vehicle by starting a fire when another person, not a participant in the crime, is present therein at that time or in an adjoining building to which the fire spreads [see *People* v. *Davis*, 89 Misc.2d 535, 392 N.Y.S.2d 195 (Sup. Ct. Kings Co. 1977)]. The conduct proscribed does not include damaging the occupied building or motor vehicle by causing an explosion; such an act, if committed with the required mental culpability, is proscribed under Penal Law §150.20 as first-degree arson.

A person is guilty of *first-degree* arson (a class A-I felony) under Penal Law §150.20 when he intentionally damages a building or motor vehicle by causing an explosion or a fire where:

a. such explosion or fire is caused by an incendiary device, propelled, thrown, or placed inside such building or motor vehicle, or when such explosion or fire is caused by an explosive;

b. another person who is not a participant in the crime is present in such building or motor vehicle at the time; and

c. the defendant knows that fact or the circumstances are such as to render the presence of such person therein a reasonable possibility.

Penal Law §150.20 further provides:

2. As used in this section, "incendiary device" means a breakable container designed to explode or produce uncontained combustion upon impact, containing flammable liquid and having a wick or a similar device capable of being ignited.

This statute was amended to include in the definition of first-degree arson the setting of a fire by an incendiary device, as well as by causing

---

* *Knowledge* (acting "knowingly") is defined in Penal Law §15.05(2) as awareness by an actor that his conduct is of the nature described by a statute defining an offense, or awareness that a specific circumstance, described by a statute defining an offense, exists. However, a person who did not have actual knowledge of the presence in a building or motor vehicle of another person who was not a participant in the crime is still criminally liable for second-degree arson if he intentionally damages that building or motor vehicle by starting a fire if he reasonably should have known that another person was present. For example, the defendant owns a run-down hotel in a town in the mountains; the hotel is not occupied by guests during winter, but transient tramps passing through the town often spend the night there, and defendant knows this fact. A tramp is sleeping in the building on a winter night when the defendant sets fire to the building, trying to make it look like an accident so that he can collect the insurance money. Defendant has committed second-degree arson and, if the tramp were to die, the defendant would be guilty of felony murder. However, if nobody ever trespassed into the hotel and the defendant reasonably believed that the hotel was unoccupied, since no guests or workers were there and the surrounding area was deserted, but the night of the arson a burglar had entered, defendant would not be guilty of second-degree arson. He would, however, be guilty of arson in the third degree because, although he owned the building and had no reason to believe he was endangering the life or property of another, he was damaging the building to commit an insurance fraud, an unlawful purpose.

an explosion. The purpose was apparently to punish arson committed with a Molotov cocktail or similar device as arson in the first, rather than the second, degree, overruling *People* v. *McCrawford*, 47 A.D.2d 318, 366 N.Y.S.2d 424 (1st Dept. 1975), where the court held that a Molotov cocktail was not an explosive device, relying on the definitions in the Labor Law, General Business Law, and the Vehicle and Traffic Law.*

Problems of Proof in Arson Prosecutions

Search and Seizure in Premises Where Fire Occurred

Evidence acquired without a search warrant while fire fighters are lawfully on the premises putting out the fire or within a reasonable time thereafter is admissible under the "plain view" doctrine [see *People* v. *Calhoun*, 90 Misc.2d 88, 393 N.Y.S.2d 529 (Sup. Ct. Kings Co. 1977), *aff'd without opinion*, 67 A.D.2d 1110, 413 N.Y.S.2d 535 (2d Dept. 1979), *aff'd* 49 N.Y.2d 398, 426 N.Y.S.2d 243, 402 N.E.2d 1145 (1980)]. But once the fire has been extinguished, is a warrant required before a fire marshal may search the burned premises and make observations or seize evidence for use in an arson investigation?

The trial court in *Calhoun* rejected defendant's contention that such a search violated the Fourth Amendment. Defendant, a tenant, was charged, *inter alia*, with second-degree arson in his New York City apartment, which he was occupying at the time of the fire although an unexecuted dispossess order had been issued by the Civil Court. Two fire marshals arrived at defendant's apartment approximately four hours after the fire had been extinguished and the fire fighters had left the premises to investigate the origin of the fire pursuant to New York City Administrative Code §488(2)-1.0, which authorizes fire marshals to investigate "[t]he origin, detail, and management of fires in the city, particularly of supposed cases of arson, incendiarism, or fires due to criminal carelessness." [Other subdivisions of Administrative Code §488(2)-1.0 authorize fire marshals to inspect for violations of the Fire Commissioner's regulations or orders, or violations of Administrative Code safety provisions.] The defendant's apartment was open when they entered since the door had been destroyed in the fire. At defendant's trial for arson, he objected to the proposed introduction of testimony by one of the marshals and photographs of the apartment, citing *People* v. *Tyler*, 399 Mich. 564, 250 N.E.2d 467 (Sup. Ct. Mich. 1977), in which the Supreme Court of Michigan had held that such evidence

---

* The mental culpability in the crime of first-degree arson is the same as that which must be proved to convict a defendant of second-degree arson.

seized without a warrant violates the Fourth Amendment. An appeal in *Tyler* was decided by the United States Supreme Court in *Michigan v. Tyler*, 436 U.S. 499, 98 S.Ct. 1942, 56 L.Ed.2d 486 (1978), and will be discussed *infra*.

The trial court in *Calhoun* first distinguished the case from *Tyler*, finding that since defendant's apartment was destroyed by the fire and was no longer habitable, the premises were in effect abandoned and defendant had no reasonable expectation of privacy in the premises, a prerequisite to a Fourth Amendment right, citing *Katz* v. *United States*, 389 U.S. 347, 88 S.Ct. 507, 19 L.Ed.2d 576 (1967). The court further found that since a fire is an emergency and the prompt warrantless investigation of a fire is authorized by the Administrative Code, it is an administrative search in an emergency situation and, therefore, is permissible under *Camara* v. *Municipal Court*, 387 U.S. 523, 87 S.Ct. 1727, 18 L.Ed.2d 930 (1967). The trial court analogized the case to *People* v. *Neulist*, 43 A.D.2d 150, 350 N.Y.S.2d 178 (2d Dept. 1973), which held that a police warrantless search of premises where a death occurred, subsequent to a finding by the medical examiner that the death was homicide, was valid since the police entered originally to answer an emergency call and a specific local law (Nassau County Government Law §2101) gave the medical examiner power to investigate the circumstances of a death.

The New York Court of Appeals affirmed Calhoun's conviction and upheld the reasonableness of the search, although on a different ground than that upon which the trial court based its decision. The Court specifically rejected the trial court's finding that the occurrence of a fire renders a premises abandoned:

> The classic statement that even a "ruined tenement" may be secure against the sovereign (see *Miller* v. *United States*, 357 U.S. 301, 307, 78 L.Ed.2d 1332) is literally applicable. For, people often continue to live and work in buildings that have sustained fire damage and, even when the ensuing destruction has made that impossible, remaining personal effects may very well invoke continued and respected expectations of privacy. To reinforce this protection, a warrantless intrusion by a government official is presumptively unreasonable, the burden of justifying it devolving upon the *People* (*Vale* v. *Louisiana*, 399 U.S. 30, 34, 90 S.Ct. 1969, 1971, 26 L.Ed.2d 409; *People* v. *Hodge, supra*, 44 N.Y.2d, p. 557, 406 N.Y.S.2d, p. 737, 378 N.E.2d, p. 101). (*Calhoun*, 426 N.Y.S.2d at 245)

The Court, citing *Michigan* v. *Tyler*, then affirmed the trial court's holding that the occurrence of a fire, whatever its cause, falls within the scope of the so-called emergency exception to the search warrant requirement. This doctrine sanctions warrantless searches and seizures in circumstances presenting immediate danger to life or property, or, on the same general principle, threat of destruction or removal of contraband or other evidence of criminality. The Court then reviewed the role of the fire marshal in New York City. It noted that although the marshals do not respond to every fire as a matter of routine, there was proof that their task was to investigate all fires of undetermined origin, rather than to conduct a search for evidence of arson. In this case, the fire marshals had no actual knowledge until hours after their arrival that arson was a possibility, for it was only then that they learned that defendant had made arson threats to his landlord. While arson was a possible cause of the fire, other causes, natural and accidental, were theories to be tested by the marshals at the time of their arrival. The Court stressed that if there had been a finding by the trial court that the fire marshal's visit to the premises was motivated primarily by an intent to gather evidence for an arson prosecution, the warrantless intrusion might well have exceeded the bounds of the emergency exception and trespassed on the constitutional guarantee of the Fourth Amendment.

The New York Court of Appeals in *Calhoun* relied in part in its decision on the recent opinion of the United States Supreme Court in *Michigan* v. *Tyler*, 436 U.S. 499, 94 S.Ct. 1942, 56 L.Ed.2d 486 (1978), decided after the decision of the trial court in *Calhoun*. In *Michigan* v. *Tyler*, the United States Supreme Court reviewed the decision of the Michigan Supreme Court in *People* v. *Tyler, supra*, to consider the applicability of the Fourth Amendment to official entries onto fire-damaged premises. Defendants in *Tyler* were lessees of a furniture store that had burned down on January 21, 1970. Fire fighters called in the police after they had just about quenched the fire, because of the discovery of two containers of flammable liquid. The police came and took several pictures, but had to leave because of the smoke and steam. Four hours after the blaze was extinguished, a fire inspector came, left, and returned an hour later with a detective. They discovered suspicious burn marks in the carpet and pieces of tape with burn marks on the stairs. On February 16, the police returned, investigated, took pictures, and seized a piece of fuse.

At defendant's trial, a police officer testified that his investigation had determined that the fire was not accidental. Defendants did not challenge the admission of photographs taken while the fire was smoldering, but challenged the admission of the evidence seized five hours later and the evidence seized during, and testimony relating to, the search on February 16, on the ground that a search warrant was required by the Fourth and Fourteenth Amendments. The Michigan Supreme Court had held that "[once] the blaze [has been] extinguished and the fire fighters have left the premises, a warrant is required to reenter and search the premises, unless there is consent or the premises have been abandoned" (*People* v. *Tyler*, 399 Mich. at 583, 250 N.W.2d at 477).

The Michigan court accordingly reversed defendant's convictions and ordered a new trial, having found neither consent nor abandonment. The United States Supreme Court, in reviewing the holding of the Michigan Supreme Court, first reiterated the principle that the protection of the Fourth and Fourteenth Amendments applies to any search by a government official, even if it is an inspecting "administrative search" (a search to enforce a nonpenal statute or regulation), unless the premises searched involved a heavily regulated industry, such as alcohol or firearms, citing its recent decision in *Marshall* v. *Barlow's Inc.* 436 U.S. 307, 98 S.Ct. 1816, 56 L.Ed.2d 305 (1978).* The United States Supreme Court rejected the prosecution's argument that burned-out premises are "abandoned"; that is, that the occupants and/ or owners have no reasonable expectation of privacy because (a) if they set the blaze, they have abandoned the premises and (b) even if they did not set it, their privacy interest is rendered negligible by the damage. The Court stated:

[E]ven if the petitioner's contention that arson establishes abandonment be accepted, its second proposition—that innocent fire victims inevitably have no protectable expectations of privacy in whatever remains of their property—is contrary to common experience. People may go on living in their homes or working in their offices after a fire. Even when that is impossible, private effects often remain on the fire-damaged premises. The petitioner may be correct in the view that most innocent fire victims are treated courteously and welcome inspections of their property to ascertain the origin of the blaze, but "even if true, [this contention] is irrelevant to the question whether the . . . inspection is reasonable within the meaning of the Fourth Amendment." [Citation omitted.] Once it is recognized that innocent fire victims retain the protection of the Fourth Amendment, the rest of the petitioner's argument unravels. For it is of course impossible to justify a warrantless search on the ground of abandonment by arson when that arson has not yet been proved, and a conviction cannot be used *ex post facto* to validate the introduction of evidence used to secure that same conviction.

Thus, there is no diminution in a person's reasonable expectation of privacy nor in the protection of the Fourth Amendment simply because the official conducting the search wears the uniform of a firefighter rather than a policeman, or because his purpose is to ascertain the cause of a fire rather than look for evidence of a crime, or because the fire might have been started deliberately. Searches for administrative purposes, like searches for evidence of crime, are encompassed by the Fourth Amendment.

---

* After both *Marshall* and *Michigan* v. *Tyler* were decided, the United States Supreme Court in *Donovan* v. *Dewey, 452 U.S. 594,* 101 S.Ct. 2534, 69 L.Ed.2d 262 (1981) ruled that in a regulated industry such as mining, where workplace safety is crucial, a warrantless inspection in compliance with specific authorized statutory procedures or regulations (the Mine Safety Act) does not violate the Fourth Amendment.

And under that Amendment, "one governing principle, justified by history and by current experience, has consistently been followed: except in certain carefully defined classes of cases, a search of private property without proper consent is 'unreasonable' unless it has been authorized by a valid search warrant." [Citation omitted.] The showing of probable cause necessary to secure a warrant may vary with the object and intrusiveness of the search, but the necessity for the warrant persists. (*Michigan v. Tyler*, 436 U.S. at 505–7, 98 S.Ct. at 1947–8)

The Court added:

To secure a warrant to investigate the cause of a fire, an official must show more than the bare fact that a fire has occurred. The magistrate's duty is to assure that the proposed search will be reasonable, a determination that requires inquiry into the need for the intrusion on the one hand, and the threat of disruption to the occupant on the other. For routine building inspections, a reasonable balance between these competing concerns is usually achieved by broad legislative and administrative guidelines specifying the purpose, frequency, scope, and manner of conducting the inspections. In the context of investigatory fire searches, which are not programmatic but are responsive to individual events, a more particularized inquiry may be necessary. The number of prior entries, the scope of the search, the time of day when it is proposed to be made, the lapse of time since the fire, the continued use of the building, and the owner's efforts to secure it against intruders might all be relevant factors. Even though a fire victim's privacy must normally yield to the vital social objective of ascertaining the cause of the fire, the magistrate can perform the important function of preventing harassment by keeping that invasion to a minimum. See *See v. City of Seattle, supra*, at 544–545, 87 S.Ct., at 1739–1740; *United States v. Chadwick*, 433 U.S. 1, 9, 97 S.Ct. 2476, 2482, 53 L.Ed.2d 538; *Marshall v. Barlow's Inc.*, 436 U.S., 323, 98 S.Ct., at 1826. (*Michigan v. Tyler*, 436 U.S. at 507–8, 98 S.Ct. at 1949)

The Court noted that another purpose of the warrant is to provide the property owner with information to reassure him of the legality of the entry.

The Court further held that where the investigators find evidence of wrongdoing in a search under an administrative warrant, it would be admissible in an arson prosecution and could be used to establish probable cause for a search warrant to gather additional evidence. The Court also ruled that where the officers are seeking evidence of arson, the court in which they apply for the search warrant must determine the existence of probable cause to believe a crime was committed before it issues the search warrant. The standard is more stringent than the standard of reasonable cause sufficient to justify the issuance of an administrative search warrant. Reasonable cause for an administrative search warrant exists when conditions are present that reasonably justify a search under the statute or regulations sought to be enforced. The reasonableness of the administrative criteria for the search is determined in light of the specific purpose of the particular statute or regulation.

However, the Court further ruled that there is an exception to the warrant requirement where a fire has occurred. The existence of "exigent circumstances" creates a recognized exception and

> [a] burning building clearly presents an exigency of sufficient proportions to render a warrantless entry "reasonable." Indeed, it would defy reason to suppose that firemen must secure a warrant or consent before entering a burning structure to put out the blaze. And once in a building for this purpose, fire fighters may seize evidence of arson that is in plain view. *Coolidge* v. *New Hampshire*, 403 U.S. 443, 465–466, 91 S.Ct. 2022, 2037–38, 29 L.Ed.2d 564. Thus, the Fourth and Fourteenth Amendments were not violated by the entry of the firemen to extinguish the fire at Tyler's Auction, nor by Chief See's removal of two plastic containers of flammable liquid on the floor of one of the showrooms. (*Michigan* v. *Tyler*, 436 U.S. at 509, 98 S.Ct. at 1950)

The Court added that the Michigan Supreme Court had recognized a right to make a warrantless entry in an emergency such as fire, but then had held that the need for a warrant arises when the last flame is extinguished. The United States Supreme Court ruled that the Michigan Court's holding was too narrow, declaring that officials may remain on the premises for a reasonable time thereafter where the condition of the building, as in *Tyler*, prevented them from making an effective inspection. The Court found that a warrant was not necessary for the early-morning reentries on January 22, since these entries were an actual continuation of the first valid entry. However, the Court agreed with the Michigan Supreme Court that the subsequent warrantless entries on February 16 were unconstitutional and, accordingly, affirmed that court's decision ordering defendant's new trial, stating:

> In summation, we hold that an entry to fight a fire requires no warrant, and that once in the building, officials may remain there for a reasonable time to investigate the cause of the blaze. Thereafter, additional entries to investigate the cause of the fire must be made pursuant to the warrant procedures governing administrative searches. See *Camara*, 387 U.S., at 534–539, 87 S.Ct. at 1733–1736; *See* v. *City of Seattle*, 387 U.S., at 544–545, 87 S.Ct. at 1739–1740; *Marshall* v. *Barlow's Inc.*, 436 U.S. at 320–321, 98 S.Ct., at 1824–1825. Evidence of arson discovered in the course of such investigations is admissible at trial, but if the investigating officials find probable cause to believe that arson has occurred and require further access to gather evidence for a possible prosecution, they may obtain a warrant only upon a traditional showing of probable cause applicable to searches for evidence of crime. *United States* v. *Ventresca*, 380 U.S. 102. (*Michigan* v. *Tyler*, 436 U.S. at 511–12, 98 S.Ct. at 1951)

In a recent U.S. Supreme Court case, the Court dealt again with administrative warrants. In *Michigan* v. *Clifford*, 104 S.Ct. 641 (1984), the Supreme Court held that a warrantless search at the residence of a couple who were out of town, five hours after fire fighters extinguished a fire of suspicious origin and left the premises, violated the Fourth Amendment. The 5–4 decision refused to exempt from the warrant requirement all administrative investigations into the cause and origin of a fire.

The majority concluded that where reasonable expectations of privacy remain in fire-damaged premises, either consent or exigent circumstances must be present to justify a warrantless search. Here, the occupants of the private home were not told of the search and took steps to secure their remaining privacy interests in the damaged home against further intrusion. Moreover, several hours separated the initial exigent intrusion to extinguish the fire from the search in question. When a warrant is required, an administrative warrant is sufficient if the primary purpose of the search is to determine the origin and cause of the fire, but a criminal search warrant based upon probable cause is required when authorities seek evidence of criminal activity.

In this instance, a basement search revealed the cause of the fire, so that the search of the rest of the house would have required a criminal search warrant even if the search of the basement was valid.

Administrative Warrant Not Provided for in New York Law

The New York Court of Appeals specifically stated in footnote 3 to its opinion in *Calhoun* that it did not reach any question involving the use of the administrative warrant and its application to fire inspections that are not incidental to a recent fire. It should be noted that nowhere in New York's Criminal Procedure Law is there a specific provision for an administrative warrant. Article 690 governs the issuance of search warrants, which authorizes *only* police officers or peace officers appointed by a state university, to search a designated person, place, or vehicle, CPL §690.05. Note that the New York Court of Appeals in *Sokolov* v. *Village of Freeport*, 52 N.Y.2d 341, 438 N.Y.S.2d 257,420 N.E.2d 55 (1981), in holding that the Fourth Amendment was violated by an ordinance that forced landlords to consent to warrantless inspections of their property as a condition precedent to obtaining a rental permit, noted that there is a requirement of a warrant for an administrative inspection, without stating whether such a warrant could be obtained under Article 690. [*Accord, People* v. *James Northrup, Inc.*, 106 Misc.2d 440, 432 N.Y.S.2d 45 (Sup. Ct. App. T. 9th and 10th Jud. Dist. 1980), *aff'd* as *mdf'd*, 53 N.Y.2d 689, 439 N.Y.S.2d 108, 421 N.E.2d 503 (1981).]

It is not clear that a legislative action creating an administrative warrant is necessary. Judiciary Law §2-b(3) gives courts of record the power to "devise and make new process and forms of proceedings, necessary to carry into effect the powers and jurisdiction possessed by it." In addition, District Attorney's offices of the various counties might be advised to draft a written consent form to enter burned premises for presentment to owners in cases where the time lapse is such that exigent circumstances are no longer clearly present. Certainly an owner of burned premises, who is either a victim or posing as a victim, is unlikely to withhold his consent. [But note that in a motion to suppress, where the legality of the search and seizure is predicated on consent, the People have a heavy burden of proving consent [*Bumper v. North Carolina*, 391 U.S. 543, 88 S.Ct. 1788, 20 L.Ed.2d 797 (1964)]. Consent is void if it was obtained as submission to overbearing authority (ibid.).

Proof of Corpus Delicti

The corpus delicti in arson is damage to a building or motor vehicle from a fire or explosion caused by a criminal human agency, not by accident [*People* v. *Reade*, 13 N.Y.2d 42, 241 N.Y.S.2d 829, 191 N.E.2d 891 (1963); *People* v. *Guernsey*, 46 A.D.2d 698, 360 N.Y.S.2d 101 (3d Dept. 1974)]. For example, the fact that a torch was found was evidence that the fire was of incendiary origin [*People* v. *Cannizzaro*, 285 App. Div. 747, 141 N.Y.S.2d 169 (3d Dept. 1955), *rev'd on other grounds*, 1 N.Y.2d 167, 151 N.Y.S.2d 379, 13 N.E.2d 206 (1956)]. In *People* v. *Moore*, 18 A.D.2d 417, 239 N.Y.S.2d 967 (1st Dept. 1963), *aff'd without opinion*, 13 N.Y.2d 1070, 246 N.Y.S.2d 216, 195 N.E.2d 894 (1963), the corpus delicti of attempted arson of a bar and grill was established by a police officer's testimony to the following facts:

> In the basement of the bar and grill was an incendiary apparatus controlled by an operating radio clock set for 7:45 A.M. The extension cord of a three-burner electric hot plate was plugged into the radio clock. The dials of the hot plate were turned to the hot plate position. Over the hot plate was toweling saturated with gasoline. The toweling stretched through the basement, up the basement stairs, through the kitchen and along the rear of the bar. In front of and below the hot plate were pyramided records, check books and carpeting soaked with gasoline through which was passed the saturated toweling. [*People* v. *Moore*, 239 N.Y.S.2d at 968–79].

"In arson cases, proof of criminal agency is, of necessity more often than not solely circumstantial because, in the very nature of things, the fire generally consumes and destroys all evidence of its incendiary origin" (*People* v. *Reade*, 241 N.Y.S.2d at 832).* If the only evidence is circumstantial, it is hornbook law that the defense is entitled to a charge that all the evidence must be inconsistent with innocence and exclude, to a moral certainty, every other reasonable hypothesis but that of guilt. But see concurring opinion of Fuchsberg, J. in *People* v. *Gonzalez*, 54 N.Y.2d 729, 442 N.Y.S.2d 980, 426 N.E.2d 474 (1981), a murder prosecution, where the Court held that failure to give the requested circumstantial evidence charge, including the words "to a moral certainty," was not error as the jury was adequately informed of the burden of proof. Judge Fuchsberg stated that he was in agreement with the district attorney, who contended that there is no difference in the burden of proof in a circumstantial case as opposed to a case where direct evidence was presented, noting that the charge employing the phrase "to a moral certainty" is increasingly disapproved.

In one arson case involving circumstantial evidence, a fire marshal who investigated the fire that partially burned and damaged a rooming house in which defendant was a tenant, determined on the basis of his expertise that the fire had originated in a closet in defendant's room because of the extensive damage in that area. There were no electrical wires or heating fixtures near the closet, and defendant testified that he did not smoke and was the sole occupant of the room, which he left shortly before the fire was discovered. In addition, there was evidence of defendant's consciousness of guilt; there was proof that he had absented himself from his usual haunts and his job, though wages were owing to him, and that he changed his appearance since the fire by dyeing his hair. This circumstantial evidence excluded to a moral certainty every hypothesis except that the fire was willfully set by human agency (see *People* v. *Reade, supra*).†

The testimony of the fire chief that the fire in question was not caused by electricity, natural gas, or spontaneous combustion, thus negating the possibility of accident, and that there was heavy charring

---

* Note that sophisticated laboratory techniques employed today to detect evidence of arson cast doubt upon the applicability of this statement to current prosecutions.

† In *Reade*, the Court declared that although the circumstantial evidence described in the above example sufficiently proved to a moral certainty that the fire was not caused by accident but by a willful human agency, the circumstantial evidence alone did not exclude to a moral certainty every hypothesis except the guilt of the defendant. However, in *Reade*, the defendant had made a full confession, repudiated at the trial; this confession was sufficiently corroborated by the circumstantial evidence to prove the defendant's guilt beyond a reasonable doubt.

Witnesses testified that at a particular time, defendant left her home in her father's automobile. Shortly thereafter, they saw her father's automobile parked by his barn and they saw a person who resembled defendant in height and hair length standing in the middle door of the barn throwing straw or hay onto a small fire. The local fire coordinator, who had investigated the fire, stated that in his opinion the fire was not the result of spontaneous combustion. The fire had damaged the barn. The evidence was sufficient to prove that the crime of arson had been committed. [See *People* v. *Guernsey*, 46 A.D.2d 698, 360 N.Y.S.2d 101 (3d Dept. 1974), where the defendant's full voluntary confession was held to be sufficiently corroborated to justify a verdict of guilty.]

in the closet, indicating that the fire originated in the closet, was evidence from which the jury could conclude that the fire was of incendiary origin [*see People* v. *Pettis*, 62 A.D.2d 1110, 404 N.Y.S.2d 428 (3d Dept. 1978)].

Expert Testimony

Since the fact of arson is one that can ordinarily be easily understood by a jury, professional fire investigators may testify concerning the facts found during the course of their investigation into the origin of the fire, but it is reversible error in the usual case for the court to permit such an expert to state that the fire was caused by a guilty human agency. The conclusion that the fire was accidental or that it was willful is to be drawn by the trier of fact [*People* v. *Tyler*, 14 A.D.2d 609, 221 N.Y.S.2d 804 (3d Dept. 1961); *People* v. *Grutz*, 212 N.Y. 72, 105 N.E. 843 (1914); *People* v. *Brown*, 110 App. Div. 490, 96 N.Y. Supp. 957 (4th Dept. 1906), *aff'd without opinion*, 188 N.Y. 554, 80 N.E. 1115 (1907)].

A chief special investigator of the National Board of Fire Underwriters testified at defendant's trial for second-degree arson. He testified that an accelerant, possibly gasoline or kerosene, had been poured on the walls of the building and then stated, "I felt the fire was of an incendiary nature." Defense counsel objected to this last statement. The court overruled the objection, and counsel excepted. Reversible error was committed. The expert's testimony that kerosene or gasoline had been poured on the walls was admissible, but his conclusory statement that the fire was of "incendiary nature," that is, that it had been willfully started by someone, was inadmissible opinion evidence (see *People* v. *Tyler, supra*). A city assistant fire marshal testified at defendants' joint trial for second-degree arson. He stated "[i]n my opinion the fire was set." The court's admission of this statement was reversible error (see *People* v. *Grutz, supra*).

At defendant's trial for arson, the chief of the fire department was permitted to testify that, after the fire that defendant was accused of causing, he had his men watching the premises at night. The admission of such testimony constituted reversible error. In effect, the chief was giving his opinion that the fire was caused by a criminal human agency, since the jury would conclude that he took these security measures because he thought that the initial fire was caused by arson and wanted to prevent a repetition of the crime [see *People* v. *Brown*, 110 App. Div. 490, 96 N.Y.Supp. 957 (4th Dept. 1906)].

At defendant's trial for committing arson by burning her father's barn, the local fire coordinator testified that in his opinion the fire was not caused by spontaneous combustion. His statement was admissible since he did not state the conclusion that the fire was deliberately set; he merely excluded the possibility that the fire was caused by spontaneous combustion (see *People* v. *Guernsey, supra*).

Proof of Defendant's Guilt of Arson by Circumstantial Evidence

Often the only evidence connecting a defendant with the crime of arson is circumstantial. Proof of a defendant's guilt of arson may be established by circumstantial evidence [*People* v. *Moore,* 18 A.D.2d 417, 239 N.Y.S.2d 967 (1st Dept. 1963)]. Of course, the rule governing proof of guilt of a crime by circumstantial evidence applies; the proof must exclude to a moral certainty every other reasonable hypothesis except the defendant's guilt. For example, at defendant's trial for arson, the People's witnesses testified that:

1. Apartment No. 3 at 435 East 5th Street was not burned or charred, nor was there any rubbish in front of that apartment at 1:00 A.M. when the occupant came home.
2. The occupant did not know defendant and had never seen him before in his life.
3. At 3:00 A.M., defendant entered 435 East 5th Street although he did not live there.
4. Defendant leaned in a crouched position against the door of Apartment No. 3 shortly after he entered the building.
5. Defendant left the building quickly, shortly after he was seen crouching against the door of Apartment No. 3.
6. No one else entered or left the building between the time defendant entered and left it.
7. The door of Apartment No. 3 was discovered to be on fire five or ten minutes after defendant left the building.
8. The remains of burned garbage were found outside the door of Apartment No. 3 after the fire was extinguished.
9. The garbage found outside the door of Apartment No. 3 belonged to a tenant of another apartment in the building, who had earlier in the day disposed of it in the lobby of the apartment house.

Proof of the above facts was sufficient to convict defendant of arson [*People* v. *Morganne,* 142 N.Y.S.2d 859 (Ct. Gen. Sess. N.Y. Co. 1955), *appeal dism'd,* 1 A.D.2d 878, 152 N.Y.S.2d 405 (1st Dept. 1956)]. "It is not essential that the evidence exclude to an absolute certainty the mere possibility that someone else might have set the fire" (*People* v. *Cannizzaro,* 141 N.Y.S.2d at 171).

In *People* v. *Sibblies,* 63 A.D.2d 934, 406 N.Y.S.2d 84 (1st Dept. 1978), the court reversed the defendant's conviction for arson and dismissed the indictment on the ground that the circumstantial evidence was insufficient to exclude every reasonable hypothesis except defendant's guilt. The record established that on August 13, 1975,

> at about 5 p.m. there was a fire in a building owned by the defendant. From about 1 p.m. to 4:50 p.m. defendant and his nephew were observed by 6 or 8 of their neighbors removing personal property from the building. Defendant was seen carrying several paint cans and three one-gallon milk containers with their tops cut off into the building. Approximately 10 minutes after defendant and his nephew left, the neighbors noted that there was a fire in progress in the building. Several fire department engine companies extinguished the blaze and on the second floor found some plastic containers containing what appeared to be a residue of gasoline and having cloth stuffed into their tops. There was a strong gasoline odor on the first floor. In the area where the fire started, the cockloft of the building, there were several plastic containers filled with a liquid. Eight containers were taken to the precinct and vouchered at the police laboratory. Upon analysis, they proved negative as to the presence of gasoline.
>
> Defendant claims that when he arrived at the house, he found the cellar door smashed and a window open. During the course of transferring his belongings from the house, he had occasion to talk to several of the neighbors. He returned to his home at about 3:55 p.m. and left at 4:15 p.m. for a camp 90 miles from New York City, to visit his daughter and his estranged wife, who was a cook there. Further testimony places him at the camp at about 6:15 p.m. A phone call from a relative advised him of the fire on the following day, and he left camp three days later. As to the building itself, the last rent-paying tenant left in June, 1975; the last mortgage payment had been made at the time, and no electric bills had been paid since that time. Defendant did not file an insurance claim and says that he intended to abandon the building. (*Sibblies*, 406 N.Y.S.2d at 85)

The court noted that:

> [t]he People argue that presence at the scene, proof of motive, evidence of flight, and other conduct indicating consciousness of guilt are factors relevant to the question of guilt (citing *People* v. *Reade*, 13 N.Y.2d 42, 46, 241 N.Y.S.2d 829, 831, 191 N.E.2d 891, 892). It is undisputed that defendant was in and out of the building over a period of several hours, during which he engaged in conversation with at least three people. It does not appear that he attempted to avoid conversation or that he skulked or otherwise behaved furtively. His presence then was not that of one who was about to commit a crime and feared identification, but was rather more consistent with his avowed purpose to move books and other items from the abandoned building. (*Sibblies*, 406 N.Y.S.2d at 86)

The court further found that the alleged evidence of motive was inconclusive, noting that "evidence indicates that the mortgagee settled its claim for $500 *less* than the mortgage balance. The property had been income-producing and apparently heavily encumbered. The defendant would have been in better financial condition if he had re-furbished and re-let the premises" (ibid). The court added that the People's argument that defendant failed to file an insurance claim to avoid suspicion of arson was "unsupported conjecture" and that the defendant's visit to his family was not conclusive evidence of flight (ibid).

Similarly, in *People* v. *Piazza (William)*, 48 N.Y.2d 151, 422 N.Y.S.2d 9, 397 N.E.2d 700 (1979), a case arising out of a prosecution of a father and son for felony murder resulting from an arson, the Court of Appeals reversed the son's conviction for third-degree arson on the ground that the evidence, all circumstantial against the son, was equivocal. The Court found the following:

1. The coconspirator's admissions did not directly implicate the son.
2. The son's presence at his building, shortly before it burned down, could be attributed to legitimate business, as his tenants had just been served with violation orders from the building department.
3. The son's bulldozing of the building site after the arson could conceivably be attributed to the fact that he had received an official order to demolish the hazardous leaning wall left standing after the fire.

In another case, *People* v. *Feuerstein*, 74 A.D.2d 853, 425 N.Y.S.2d 379 (2d Dept. 1980), *petition for writ of habeas corpus denied in Feuerstein* v. *New York*, 515 F. Supp. 573 (E.D.N.Y. 1981) the following circumstantial evidence was found to exclude innocence to a moral certainty:

1. On the day of the fire, defendant remained in his shoe store after closing time, contrary to his usual practice.
2. Defendant was then observed in the back of the store throwing cartons.
3. Expert testimony indicated that the origin of the fire was inside the store and that an accelerant had been used.
4. At the time of the fire, defendant owed $1,403.35 for back rent and taxes.
5. Defendant had stated that business was bad.
6. The store was insured for a total of $87,000 and, after the fire, defendant presented an insurance claim for the full amount.
7. The defense acknowledged that, prior to the fire, the defendant wanted to sell the store.

Motive

One type of circumstantial evidence is evidence that the defendant had a motive to commit the crime of arson. *Motive* has been defined as "an inducement, or that which leads or tempts the mind to indulge the criminal act" [*People* v. *Fitzgerald*, 156 N.Y. 253, 258, 50 N.E. 846 (1898)]. A defendant could be motivated to commit arson as a means of collecting fire insurance or from a desire to injure an enemy.

Motive to Injure Another. The prosecutor introduced evidence that defendant, charged with setting fire to the house that his estranged wife and child were occupying, had treated his wife cruelly during their marriage, and had threatened to kill her. This is admissible evidence of motive [see *People* v. *Bates*, 271 App. Div. 550, 67 N.Y.S.2d 1 (4th Dept. 1947)].*

Motive to Collect Fire Insurance. Evidence that a defendant was overinsured and that his business was failing is admissible to prove motive for arson (*People* v. *Cannizzaro, supra*). Similarly, where the People proved that there were housing violations pending against thirty-two burned properties, which were the subject of the alleged arsons with which the defendant was charged, evidence that defendant collected insurance on twenty-five of these thirty-two properties was admissible [*People* v. *Goldfeld*, 60 A.D.2d 1, 400 N.Y.S.2d 229 (4th Dept. 1977)]. See also *People* v. *Feuerstein*, 74 A.D.2d 853, 425 N.Y.S.2d 379 (2d Dept. 1980), *petition for writ of habeas corpus denied in Feuerstein* v. *New York*, 515 F. Supp. 573 (E.D.N.Y. 1981), where evidence was admitted that, before the fire, defendant had stated that business was bad and that he owed $1,403.35 for rent and taxes, and after the fire, defendant, who had been insured for $87,000, presented a claim for the full amount of insurance.

However, evidence of insurance was insufficient as a matter of law to constitute the required corroborative evidence of an accomplice's testimony where the burned restaurant was a profitable business and was not overinsured [*People* v. *Ice*, 265 App. Div. 46, 38 N.Y.S.2d 32 (3d Dept. 1942)]. Similarly, where the defendant was the mortgagee of the burned property that an accomplice testified that he [the accomplice] has been paid to "torch," this evidence did not sufficiently corroborate the accomplice testimony as a matter of law where it was proved that the property destroyed was worth more than the mortgage and the mortgagor was a solvent corporation [*People* v. *Lashkowitz*, 257 App. Div. 518, 13 N.Y.S.2d 663 (3d Dept. 1939)].

Evidence that defendant's uncle owned insurance policies on the burned premises was inadmissible in the absence of any claim by the

---

* Motive can only be inferred from proven facts [*People* v. *Lewis*, 275 N.Y. 33, 9 N.E.2d 765 (1937); *People* v. *Sowma*, 252 App. Div. 413, 299 N.Y. Supp. 523 (4th Dept. 1937)].

People that the uncle was implicated in the crime [*People* v. *Nicolia*, 287 N.Y. 398, 89 N.E.2d 929 (1942)].

Evidence of Other Fires. Evidence that only establishes that the defendant had other fires on property that he owned, where there is no evidence that he was criminally implicated in those fires, is inadmissible on the People's direct case [*People* v. *Grutz*, 212 N.Y. 72, 105 N.E. 843 (1914); *People* v. *Brown*, 110 App. Div. 490, 96 N.Y.S. 957 (4th Dept. 1906); *People* v. *Vincek*, 75 A.D.2d 412, 429 N.Y.S.2d 928 (4th Dept. 1980)]. In addition, if the evidence of prior arsons cannot be classified within the *Molineux* doctrine exceptions (that is, that they are relevant to show motive, intent, common scheme or plan, or to negate mistake or accident), then such evidence is not admissible on the People's direct case. See, for example, *People* v. *Chaffee*, 42 A.D.2d 172, 346 N.Y.S.2d 30 (3d Dept. 1973), where the People committed reversible error because they did not redact from defendant's confession references to prior arsons, which crimes were not relevant to prove motive, or intent, or common scheme or plan or to negating mistake or accident.

If the defendant testifies, defendant may be asked upon cross examination about other fires that he has had since such a question relates to his credibility; *People* v. *Brown, supra* [citing *People* v. *Jones*, 181 N.Y. 516 (1905), *aff'g without opinion* 100 App. Div. 511 (4th Dept. 1905)]. But if defendant has previously been implicated in prior arsons, the rule in *People* v. *Sandoval* [34 N.Y.2d 371, 357 N.Y.S.2d 849, 314 N.E.2d 413 (1974)] applies; the defendant is entitled to a hearing before the court decides whether the prosecutor will be permitted to cross examine him about these prior crimes, the applicable criteria being whether the probative value of these crimes on the issue of defendant's credibility will be outweighed by their prejudicial impact. See, for example, *People* v. *Park*, 62 A.D.2d 1176, 404 N.Y.S.2d 198 (4th Dept. 1978), where conviction was reversed because trial court after *Sandoval* hearing erroneously ruled that prosecutor could cross examine defendant about prior arsons and defendant did not testify. See also *People* v. *Anderson*, 75 A.D.2d 988, 429 N.Y.S.2d 117 (4th Dept. 1980), *conviction rev'd after remand*, 80 A.D.2d 33, 437 N.Y.S.2d 985 (4th Dept. 1981), an arson prosecution, where the case was remanded for a hearing to make a record on the *Sandoval* issue. The Court held that although the prior crime was arson and, thus, there was a possibility of prejudice, cross examination about the prior crime was not necessarily precluded. After remand, the Fourth Department reviewed the case again and concluded that the trial court erred when it refused to preclude the People from cross examining about the prior arson since defendant had been charged with the arson of a social club, apparently motivated by a desire for revenge against his girlfriend, and the prior arson, for which defendant had never been arrested, was allegedly committed six years earlier when defendant was angry with a previous girlfriend when she severed their relationship. The court found that the prior arson was not a crime so substantially relevant to credibility as to render the proposed cross examination of sufficient probative value to outweigh the prejudice that would inure to defendant if the jury heard that defendant allegedly committed a prior arson with a similar motive.

Evidence of Other Acts Evincing Motive. Evidence of commission of another crime is admissible to prove motive for the crime charged "only if it has a logical relationship to the commission of the crime 'according to known rules and principles of human conduct' [citation omitted] . . ." [*People v. Napoletano*, 58 A.D.2d 83, 395 N.Y.S.2d 469, 475 (2d Dept. 1977)]. In *Napoletano*, two defendants were charged with attempted arson of a restaurant. The prosecution called the former assistant manager of the restaurant as a witness who testified over objection that, on a prior occasion, one of the defendants had stolen a piece of pizza from the restaurant and that he (the assistant manager) had told the defendant not to come back. This testimony should have been excluded. It was evidence of a prior uncharged crime and an immoral act adduced at a time when the defendant had not put his character or credibility in issue, and it bore "'no logical relationship to commission of the criminal act with which the defendant was charged' [citation omitted]" (ibid.).*

Consciousness of Guilt

Evidence establishing a consciousness of guilt, such as flight, is another type of circumstantial evidence tending to prove defendant's guilt (*People v. Reade, supra*).

Testimony of Accomplices and Coconspirators

Testimony of an accomplice must be corroborated by evidence tending to connect the defendant with the crime [CPL §60.22(1)]. It is insufficient if it merely connects the defendant with the accomplice (*People v. Ice, supra*). For example, evidence that the defendant had paid the fine to get his alleged accomplice, who was his employee, out of jail

---

* When the only evidence that the People have is circumstantial, a complete absence of motive is strong exculpatory evidence (*People v. Lewis, supra*).

on an unrelated charge was insufficient to corroborate the accomplice's testimony (*People* v. *Ice, supra*). Similarly, an accomplice's testimony was not corroborated by the testimony of a witness that:

1. He saw the defendant give the accomplice a key.
2. The witness accompanied the accomplice to defendant's business premises, which the accomplice opened with a key.
3. The accomplice told the witness that it was the key provided by defendant (*People* v. *Lashkowitz, supra*).

There was no evidence, other than the statement of the accomplice, that the key was the same and, hence, no corroborative evidence connecting the defendant with the crimes.

An accomplice's testimony in an arson prosecution was held to be sufficiently corroborated by proof of:

1. defendant's ownership of the burned properties;
2. the incendiary nature of the thirty-two fires with which defendant was charged;
3. defendant's collection of insurance proceeds from twenty-five of the thirty-two fires;
4. the pendency of housing code violations against many of the burned premises and the fact that some of the fires occurred shortly after defendant received notice of these violations; and
5. defendant's access to keys to the uninhabited apartments where the fires occurred, coupled with the fact that tenants testified that previously locked doors were found unlocked (*People* v. *Goldfeld, supra*).

In addition, this same court held that taped incriminating conversations to which the defendant was a party corroborated the testimony of the accomplice-informant who made the tapes[*] since the evidence necessary to corroborate an accomplice may be supplied by the defendant himself.

Sufficient corroboration of accomplice testimony was also found in *People* v. *Canale*, 76 A.D.2d 1032, 429 N.Y.S.2d 495 (3d Dept. 1980), where another witness testified that he was present at a meeting in a nightclub between defendant and two men to whom he was in debt, and he heard them order defendant to burn his restaurant so that he

---

[*] A foundation must be laid for consent recordings; it may be established by the testimony of a participant or a third party who heard a simultaneous transmission that the conversation has been fairly and accurately reproduced (*Goldfeld, supra*); see also *People* v. *Rodriquez*, 78 A.D.2d 659, 433 N.Y.S.2d 650 (4th Dept. 1980), where defendant's conviction for arson was reversed and a new trial ordered because there was no testimony that defendant's taped conversations with the "torch" were a fair and accurate representation.

could pay the debt with the insurance proceeds. In addition, other witnesses testified to the presence of the accomplice in defendant's restaurant on the night of the fire and to defendant's financial distress.

A court held that an insurance agent's testimony for the defense that defendant had said to him as a joke, "Do you know anyone who could burn my property?" could not be considered as corroboration of the accomplice's testimony [*People* v. *Ice, supra*].

If there is *prima facie* proof of a conspiracy—a question of law—the declarations of coconspirators made in furtherance of the conspiracy are admissible against the defendant [*People* v. *David*, 56 N.Y. 95, 103 (1874); *Ormsby* v. *People*, 53 N.Y. 472, 473 (1873); see also 46 A.L.R.3d 1148, 1156: "Necessity and Sufficiency of Independent Evidence of Conspiracy to Allow Admission of Extrajudicial Statements of Coconspirators."] Therefore, a witness's testimony that the alleged accomplice told him that the key that the witness saw the defendant give the accomplice was the one that the accomplice used to open defendant's premises to commit arson was inadmissible against the defendant in the absence of any other proof of the conspiracy apart from the accomplice's testimony [*People* v. *Lashkowitz, supra*]. In addition, the statements must be made in furtherance of the conspiracy; if they were made after its termination they are not admissible [*People* v. *Lashkowitz, supra*]. Thus, the testimony of an accomplice's chauffeur that five years after the crime, he heard the accomplice ask defendant for payment for the arson, was inadmissible [*People* v. *Lashkowitz, supra*].

Admissions to Private Parties

At least one court has held that the constitutional right to privacy renders confidential admissions of a child to his parents concerning a crime a confidential privileged communication [*Matter of A. and M.*, 61 A.D.2d 426, 403 N.Y.S.2d 375 (4th Dept. 1978); see also *People* v. *Fitzgerald*, 101 Misc.2d 712, 422 N.Y.S.2d 309 (Westchester Co. Ct. 1979)].* Therefore, parents subpoenaed to appear before a grand jury to answer questions concerning their son's alleged involvement in an arson could invoke this privilege when questioned about his confidential statements to them [*People* v. *Doe, supra*]. If necessary, the court could hold an evidentiary hearing on the factual context of the communication to determine if the privilege is applicable.

However, a privilege based on a confidential relationship no longer exists when the relationship is destroyed. See *People* v. *D'Amato*, 105

---

* The Fifth Circuit has expressly refused to recognize New York's interpretation of the constitutional right to privacy, at least as applied to a child claiming the privilege during a grand jury investigation of her parents [*in re Grand Jury Proceedings*, 647 F.2d 511 (5th Cir. 1981)].

Misc.2d 1048, 430 N.Y.S.2d 521 (Sup. Ct. Bronx Co. 1980), an arson prosecution, where the court ruled that the statutory marital privilege, which prevents either spouse from testifying to confidential communications made by the other, was inapplicable under the facts of that case. In *D'Amato*, the court permitted an estranged wife to testify to an admission to the arson made by her husband, the defendant, as the admission was made in the context of his threat to burn her home. The court noted that the purpose of the marital privilege was to preserve the integrity and confidentiality of the marital relationship, and since, in the case before it, the marriage was in fact destroyed by the time defendant made the admission, the privilege did not apply. Similarly, if the communications are not confidential but are made in the presence of third parties, there is no marital privilege and the spouse may testify to these communications [*People* v. *Scalise*, 70 A.D.2d 346, 421 N.Y.S.2d 637 (3d Dept. 1979)]. In *Scalise*, the wife was also permitted to testify that her husband gave her an envelope with money to give to a third person, which the prosecution contended was payment to the "torch," because the husband had never told her what the money was for.

Character Witness Testimony

Testimony of a character witness, if believed, is enough to raise a reasonable doubt [*People* v. *McDowell*, 9 N.Y.2d 12, 210 N.Y.S.2d 514, 172 N.E.2d 279 (1961); see also *Richardson on Evidence* §150]. One court in an arson prosecution, after reversing defendant's conviction on the ground of insufficient corroboration of the accomplice testimony, noted that "[b]oth [accomplices] are desperate and depraved characters . . . [One accomplice] served a prison sentence for arson . . ." By contrast, "[p]roof of defendant's good character was furnished by his neighbors who had known him many years" [*People* v. *Lashkowitz, supra*, 13 N.Y.S.2d at 667, 673]. In another arson prosecution where defendant's conviction was reversed for lack of sufficient corroboration of accomplice testimony, the court stated:

> This appellant, who had been a practicing dentist, member of the Wyoming State Board of Dental Examiners, a Captain in the First World War, the father of a young man who had been appointed and was a student at West Point, is not the type which ordinarily in adult years would commit a crime of this kind. The record should be subjected to close scrutiny. (*People* v. *Ice*, 38 N.Y.S.2d at 36–7)

Imposition of a Fine in an Arson Case

If the defendant gained property, i.e., insurance proceeds, as a result of the arson, the court, upon conviction, may impose a fine not exceeding $5,000 or double the amount of the defendant's gain from the crime [Penal Law §80.00(1)]. "Gain" means the amount of money or the value of property derived from the commission of the crime, less the amount of money or the value of property returned to the victim of the crime or seized by or surrendered to lawful authority prior to the time sentence is imposed [Penal Law §80.00(2)]. When the court imposes a fine for a felony, it must make a finding as to the amount of the defendant's gain from the crime. If the record does not contain sufficient evidence to support such a finding, the court may conduct a hearing upon the issue [Penal Law §80.00(3)].

The Appellate Division in *People* v. *Goldfeld*, 60 A.D.2d 1, 400 N.Y.S.2d 229 (4th Dept. 1977), rejected the contention of the defendant, convicted of arson, that the fact that his insurance company was suing him and that the insurance proceeds which he had collected were placed in an escrow account precluded the sentencing court from fining him an amount equal to the insurance he had received because:

1. the sentencing court could not determine his gain, and
2. he was making restitution.

The Appellate Division upheld the imposition of the fine, holding that "[t]he fact that the defendant may be required to refund the insurance proceeds as a result of the pending civil action is irrelevant to the imposition of the fine because the statute refers to a refund of money to the victim 'prior to time sentence is imposed' [Penal Law §80.00(3)]"*; (*People* v. *Goldfeld, supra*, 400 N.Y.S.2d at 236).

Use of Reckless Endangerment Charge in Arson Prosecution

Prosecutors might consider charging the alleged arsonist with reckless endangerment under Penal Law §120.25, based on proof that the fire created a grave risk of death to the occupants and/or fire fighters. A person is guilty of this crime "when, under circumstances evincing a depraved indifference to human life, he recklessly engaged in conduct which creates a grave risk of death to another person."

In *People* v. *Rodriguez*, 110 Misc.2d 828, 442 N.Y.S.2d 948 (Sup. Ct. Kings Co. 1981), Justice Gloria Goldstein refused to dismiss a charge of reckless endangerment in an indictment that charged, among other crimes, arson in the third degree, based on allegations that defendants conspired to have an unoccupied supermarket burned and endangered the lives of fire fighters. The court found that since the fires set were sufficiently serious to pose a grave risk of death to the fire fighters, it was irrelevant that the fire fighters were not present when the fire

---

* The cited section is now §80.00(2).

actually started, because their eventual arrival was not only foreseeable, but inevitable. This decision declined to follow *People* v. *Buckman*, 110 Misc.2d 753 (Sup. Ct. Kings Co. 1981), where another court dismissed a charge of reckless endangerment based on allegations that the fire endangered the fire fighters, reasoning that, because the fire fighters were not present when the fire was started, the endangerment was not directed at them, and, therefore, the charge was deficient on its face. However, the *Buckman* opinion, as Justice Goldstein notes, ignores the 1978 decision of Judge Milonas in *People* v. *Arzon*, 92 Misc.2d 739, 401 N.Y.S.2d 156 (Sup. Ct. N.Y. Co. 1978), where the court refused to dismiss a charge of "depraved mind" murder under Penal Law §125.25(2), which has the same element of intent as reckless endangerment. That charge in *Arzon* was based on allegations that defendant had deliberately ignited the fifth floor of an abandoned apartment house, and that a fire fighter died of injuries sustained when he evacuated the building after a second fire apparently spontaneously broke out on the second floor. The court, in so holding, noted that the casual connection between the homicide and defendant's criminal behavior was not negated by the presence of other contributing factors. See also *People* v. *Lozano*, 107 Misc.2d 345, 434 N.Y.S.2d 588 (Sup. Ct. N.Y. Co. 1980), where defendant could be charged with felony murder based on allegations that he caused the death of a fire fighter who died of a heart attack triggered by smoke he inhaled while fighting the fire that defendant allegedly set.

Use of Insurance Law to Aid Prevention and Investigation of Arson

Insurance Law §336 requires insurance companies to cooperate with law enforcement in furnishing all relevant information, and protects them from incurring any liability for releasing such information. In addition, any law enforcement agency receiving such information may give it to another agency [Insurance Law §336(4-a)]. By contrast, law enforcement may, in its discretion, make its records available to the insurer within 30 days of a written request to do so by the insurer [Insurance Law §336(4)].

The Superintendent of Insurance, pursuant to regulations that he may promulgate, must establish a central organization to register property loss to which the insured must report all property losses in excess of $500 [Insurance Law §336(a)]. This information is available to law enforcement (ibid.).

New §168j of the Insurance Law requires the adoption of an antiarson application by insurance companies in cities of over 400,000 persons*

---

* ¹⁻ ⁿ̣ are based on the 1970 census.

in issuing fire policies and explosion insurance to cover all buildings except primarily residential owner-occupied real property consisting of four or fewer dwelling units. The information that must be furnished in this application shall include, but not be limited to:

a. the name and address of the applicant, any mortgages, and any other parties who have an ownership in the property or a real interest in the property or the proceeds of the claim;

b. the amount of insurance requested and the method of valuation used to establish the amount of insurance;

c. the dates and selling prices in all real estate transactions involving such property during the last three years;

d. the applicant's loss history over at least the last five years with regard to any property in which he held an equity interest or a mortgage and where any such loss exceeded $1000 in damages;

e. all taxes unpaid or overdue for one or more years, and any mortgage payments overdue by 3 months or more;

f. all current violations of Fire, Safety, Health, Building, or Construction Codes on the property to be insured; and

g. the present occupancy of the structure. [Insurance Law §168-j(3)(a–g)*

Prior to paying on a policy, all insurers, whether authorized or unauthorized, must notify the tax districts in which the damaged property is located and demand an officer's certificate indicating all outstanding liens, including interest and penalties [Insurance Law §33-a(4)]. Further, General Municipal Law §22, which provides that local laws may enable tax districts to claim liens against property from the proceeds of paid fire insurance claims, now provides in subdivision 4 that such claims may only be made where the tax district adopts a local law providing for release or return to the insured of any amounts that it would otherwise be entitled to claim, provided that the insured contracts in writing to restore the premises, subject to such conditions locally legislated to guarantee performance, including but not limited to the deposit of such proceeds in an escrow account or the obtainment by the insured of a performance bond.

In addition, Insurance Law §40-d (unfair settlement claims practices) excuses the insurer from the prompt settlement requirement where there is a reasonable basis for suspecting arson, provided that the insurer notifies the insured of acceptance or denial of the claim within thirty working days from receiving a properly executed proof of loss.

---

* A material misrepresentation on the antiarson application is grounds for rescission of the policy [Insurance Law §168-j(5)]. Further, the insured must give written notice to the insurer of any changes in the information contained in the antiarson application, either annually or upon renewal, whichever is sooner [Insurance Law §168-j(6)]. A material misrepresentation in such written notice is grounds for rescission of the policy (ibid.).

Examination Under Oath; Prosecution's Use of Statements

A useful tool for the prosecutor is the insurer's examination under oath. The insured who wishes to collect is required by the cooperation clause in his policy to submit to such an examination. If an insured individual or a corporate insured's agent pleads the Fifth Amendment or demands that the examination under oath be postponed until after any criminal proceedings are concluded, the insurer has a defense to refusal to pay [*Dyno-Bite, Inc.* v. *Travelers Companies*, 80 A.D.2d 471, 439 N.Y.S.2d 558 (4th Dept. 1981)].

Caveat: All insurance investigators and prosecutors should work together, but the prosecutor who gives explicit directions to insurance company representatives about questions that should be asked at the examination under oath may make the representatives his agents. Consequently, if the insured is represented by counsel, even if counsel is not present during the examination, a Sixth Amendment issue may arise if the prosecutor attempts to use any statements made by the insured at the examination. See *People* v. *Skinner*, 52 N.Y.2d 24, 436 N.Y.S.2d 207, 417 N.E.2d 501 (1980), where the New York Court of Appeals held that a represented defendant, even if he is not in custody, may not be interrogated by police unless he waives counsel in the presence of counsel.

Insurance Frauds Bureau Agents May Be Designated Peace Officers

CPL §2.10 has new subdivision 47, which provides that employees of the newly created Insurance Frauds Bureau may be designated by the Superintendent of Insurance as peace officers.

Prosecution for Insurance Fraud

Losses by arsonists are commonly inflated. This is grounds for a prosecution for larceny by false pretenses under Penal Law Article 155. In addition, Penal Law Article 176 proscribing insurance fraud was enacted, effective November 1, 1981. This statute is set forth below.

> §176.00 *Insurance fraud; definition of terms.* The following definitions are applicable to this article:
>
> 1. "Insurance policy" has the meaning assigned to insurance contract by section 41 of the insurance law except it shall include reinsurance contracts, purported insurance policies, and purported reinsurance contracts.
>
> 2. "Statement" includes, but is not limited to, any notice, proof of loss, bill of lading, invoice, account, estimate of property damages, bill for services, diagnosis, prescription, hospital or doctor records, x-ray, test result, and other evidence of loss, injury, or expense.

3. "Person" includes any individual, firm, association, or corporation.

4. "Personal insurance" means a policy of insurance insuring a natural person against any of the following contingencies:

(a) loss of or damage to real property used predominantly for residential purposes and which consists of not more than four dwelling units, other than hotels, motels and rooming houses;

(b) loss of or damage to personal property which is not used in the conduct of a business;

(c) losses or liabilities arising out of the ownership, operation, or use of a motor vehicle, predominantly used for nonbusiness purposes;

(d) other liabilities for loss of, damage to, or injury to persons or property, not arising from the conduct of a business;

(e) death, including death by personal injury, or the continuation of life, or personal injury by accident, or sickness, disease or ailment, excluding insurance providing disability benefits pursuant to article 9 of the workers' compensation law.

A policy of insurance which insures any of the contingencies listed in paragraphs (a) through (e) of this subdivision as well as other contingencies shall be personal insurance if that portion of the annual premium attributable to the listed contingencies exceeds that portion attributable to other contingencies.

5. "Commercial insurance" means insurance other than personal insurance.

§176.05 *Insurance fraud; defined.* A fraudulent insurance act is committed by any person who, knowingly and with intent to defraud presents, causes to be presented, or prepares with knowledge or belief that it will be presented to or by an insurer or purported insurer, or any agent thereof, any written statement as part of, or in support of, an application for the issuance of, or the rating of an insurance policy for commercial insurance, or a claim for payment or other benefit pursuant to an insurance policy for commercial or personal insurance which he knows to: (i) contain materially false information concerning any fact material thereto; or (ii) conceal, for the purpose of misleading, information concerning any fact material thereto.

§176.10 *Insurance fraud in the third degree.* A person is guilty of insurance fraud in the third degree when he commits a fraudulent insurance act.

Insurance fraud in the third degree is a class A misdemeanor.

§176.15 *Insurance fraud in the second degree.* A person is guilty of insurance fraud in the second degree when he commits a fraudulent insurance act and thereby wrongfully takes, obtains or withholds, or attempts to wrongfully take, obtain or withhold property with a value in excess of two hundred fifty dollars.

Insurance fraud in the second degree is a class E felony.

§176.20 *Insurance fraud in the first degree.* A person is guilty of insurance fraud in the first degree when he commits a fraudulent insurance act and thereby wrongfully takes, obtains, or withholds, or attempts to wrongfully take, obtain, or withhold property with a value in excess of one thousand five hundred dollars.

Insurance fraud in the first degree is a class D felony.

Index